Competing for Capital—A Financial Relations [obscured]
Bruce W. Marcus

How to Improve Profitability through More Effective Planning
Thomas S. Dudick

Financial Analysis and Business Decisions on the Pocket Calculator
Jon M. Smith

Managing Innovation
Edwin A. Gee and Chaplin Tyler

The Management System: Systems Are for People
Leslie H. Matthies

Financial Accounting Estimates through Statistical Sampling by Computer
Maurice S. Newman

Forecasting Methods for Management, Second Edition
Steven C. Wheelwright and Spyros Makridakis

Decision Making and Planning for the Corporate Treasurer
Harold Bierman, Jr.

Corporate Financial Planning Models
Henry I. Meyer

Strategies in Business
Shea Smith, III, and John E. Walsh, Jr.

Program-Management Control Systems
Joseph A. Maciariello

Contemporary Cash Management: Principles, Practices, Perspective
Paul J. Beehler

Contemporary Cash Management

Contemporary Cash Management

- Principles
  - Practices
    - Perspective

PAUL J. BEEHLER

A Wiley-Interscience Publication
JOHN WILEY & SONS
New York • Chichester • Brisbane • Toronto • Singapore

Copyright © 1978 by John Wiley & Sons, Inc.

All rights reserved. Published simultaneously in Canada.

Reproduction or translation of any part of this work beyond that permitted by Sections 107 or 108 of the 1976 United States Copyright Act without the permission of the copyright owner is unlawful. Requests for permission or further information should be addressed to the Permissions Department, John Wiley & Sons, Inc.

Library of Congress Cataloging in Publication Data

Beehler, Paul J
  Contemporary cash management.

  (Wiley series on systems and controls for financial management)
  "A Wiley-Interscience publication."
  Includes bibliographies.

  1. Corporations—Cash position. 2. Electronic funds transfers. I. Title.

HG4028.C45B43   658.1'5244   77-18998
ISBN 0-471-06172-7

Printed in the United States of America

10 9 8 7

To

My wife—Irene
My son—Paul
My daughter—Stacy

> *For their sacrifices,
> encouragement, and dedication . . .*

My parents

> *For the conditioning
> I needed*

My Friends—Alex and Mila

> *For inspiration*

SERIES PREFACE

No one needs to tell the reader that the world is changing. He sees it all too clearly. The immutable, the constant, the unchanging of a decade or two ago no longer represent the latest thinking—on *any* subject, whether morals, medicine, politics, economics, or religion. Change has always been with us, but the pace has been accelerating, especially in the postwar years.

Business, particularly with the advent of the electronic computer some 20 years ago, has also undergone change. new disciplines have sprung up. New professions are born. New skills are in demand. And the need is ever greater to blend the new skills with those of the older professions to meet the demands of modern business.

The accounting and financial functions certainly are no exception. The constancy of change is as pervasive in these fields as it is in any other. Industry is moving toward an integration of many of the information gathering, processing, and analyzing functions under the impetus of the so-called systems approach. Such corporate territory has been, traditionally, the responsibility of the accountant and the financial man. It still is, to a large extent—but times are changing.

Does this, then, spell the early demise of the accountant as we know him today? Does it augur a lessening of influence for the financial specialists in today's corporate hierarchy? We think not. We maintain, however, that it is incumbent upon today's accountant and today's financial man to learn *today's* thinking and to *use today's* skills. It is for this reason the Wiley Series on Systems and Controls for Financial Management is being developed.

Recognizing the broad spectrum of interests and activities that the series title encompasses, we plan a number of volumes, each representing the latest thinking, written by a recognized authority, on a particular facet of the financial man's responsibilities. The subjects contemplated for discussion within the series range from production accounting systems to planning, to corporate records, to control of cash. Each book is an in-depth study of one subject within this group. Each is intended to be a practical, working tool for the businessman in general and the financial man and accountant in particular.

ROBERT L. SHULTIS
FRANK M. MASTROMANO

PREFACE

During the maturation process of business knowledge, various disciplines have developed and evolved. The evolution of a body of knowledge from separate but loosely related information cells into an embryonic microcosm takes place with the recognition of the need to identify and relate a systematic approach to problem-solving knowledge. Accounting, as a business discipline, emerged as a body of knowledge born from the more general areas of financial and commercial transactions requiring accurate and detailed record keeping. This evolutionary process culminated only after a significant number of business community members recognized the need to separate a group of functions, relate them to a common objective, and form the framework of an autonomous but functionally related body of knowledge. This is the evolutionary stage of cash management. Over the last ten years increasing focus has been placed on the development of cash management techniques and discussion of the primary goal of increasing the return on assets. As techniques and their application have been increased by both companies and banks, so have the sophistication and professionalism of the contemporary cash manager. The traditionally subverted role of cash management has just recently evolved to a level of overt recognition in terms of demonstrated contribution to corporate profitability. Testifying to the emerging professional status of cash management is the recently formed Cash Management Institute, which complements developed cash management groups in cities from New York to Los Angeles.

Documentation-describing techniques and application of cash management exist in many different functional business areas, from financial analysis to mathematical programming. However, unlike other areas of professional knowledge, a compendium of information describing cash management as a business discipline has been lacking. The purpose of this book is to unite the separate but related cells of cash management information into a cohesive body of knowledge. This is accomplished by discussing the framework and application of contemporary cash management techniques to satisfy cash management operational requirements. However, this contemporary application is supplemented with a view toward the evolution of cash management in such areas as automated remittance processing and automated cash information services.

Beyond the daily operation of a cash management program is the application of cash flow forecasting. Evolution in this area has primarily been empirical in nature, with profession-wide perspective lacking. A framework is presented in this book to view forecasting and relate it to cash management that stresses separation of form and technique. Specific application of both form and technique is illustrated to relate theory to practice.

The expanding international nature of cash management is discussed to highlight significant factors that merit special consideration in the international sphere. Specific strategies are not formulated, because indigenous economic differences among nations would require several volumes to be effective.

Contemporary cash management is viewed myopically if the elements of electronic funds transfer services (EFTS) are not evaluated for their emerging impact. A detailed evaluation of the elements of EFTS is reviewed in the book and related specifically to its effect on the application of cash management techniques. Not only are the effects of EFTS on the application of cash management identified but specific guideposts are defined to indicate the appropriate timing of evolutionary changes.

Growth and change are indigenous to all life forms. Consequently, the body of knowledge assembled in this book will change over time. However, the fundamental structure of cash management is drawn together here as a building block of conceptual and practical knowledge for the novice, the professional, and the student.

PAUL J. BEEHLER

Orinda, California
February 1978

ACKNOWLEDGMENTS

This book is based on knowledge accumulated from many personal and professional relationships. I wish to acknowledge the contributions made by:

John Benzie, *Financial Vice President, Transamerica Mortgage Company*
J. H. Dethero, *Senior Vice President, Crocker National Bank*
Don Erbel, *Senior Analyst, Bank of America*
Bruce Erickson, *Vice President, Crocker National Bank*
Bernerd Ford, *Treasurer, Transamerica Mortgage Company*
Lynn Kuckuck, *Vice President, Crocker National Bank*
Edward Lozowicki, *Senior Counsel, Owens-Corning Fiberglas Corporation*
Al Mammini, *Product Manager, Bank of America*
Lyn Merkle, *Vice President, Bank of America*
Edwin Protiva, *Vice President, Union Bank*
Ken Parkinson, *Director, Cash Management, RCA Corporation*
Ralph Rasmussen, *Senior Vice President, Crocker National Bank*
James Reiner, *Financial Manager, Levi Strauss & Company*
Warren Solt, *Partner, Haskins & Sells*
Arnold Testa, *Consultant*
George C. White, Jr., *Vice President, Chase Manhattan Bank*
David Yancey, *Vice President, Bank of America*

                                                             P. J. B.

CONTENTS

	List of Exhibits	xv
PART I	INTRODUCTION	1
1	Corporate Banking Relations: Essential Considerations for Cash Management	3
2	Corporate Criteria for Bank Selection	18
	Bibliography	36
PART II	CONTEMPORARY CASH MANAGEMENT TECHNIQUES	37
3	Cash Management Techniques	39
4	Lockbox Banking—Definition, Methods, and Trends	63
5	Specialized Bank-based Corporate Services	100
	Bibliography	112
PART III	FORECASTING CASH FLOWS	115
6	Cash Forecasting: The Environment	117
7	Accounting Approaches to Cash Flow Forecasting	140
8	Quantitative Forecasting Techniques	169
9	Cash Forecasting Models	190
	Bibliography	213
PART IV	INTERNATIONAL CASH MANAGEMENT	215
10	The Characteristics of International Cash Management	217
11	International Funds Flow Control	238
	Bibliography	261

xiv　Contents

PART V	EFTS AND CASH MANAGEMENT	263
12	EFTS—Aspects and Elements	265
13	EFTS—The Impact on Cash Management	296
	Bibliography	318

INDEX 319

EXHIBITS

1-1	Short-term interest rates	5
1-2	Sample distributions for large corporations	9
1-3	Input–output relationship of corporate subsystems	10
1-4	System flow of cash management system	12
1-5	The check clearing process	16
2-1	Table of real versus stated interest rates	28
2-2	Account Analysis Form	29
3-1	Overview of lockbox processing system	41
3-2	Pre-authorized check system	43
3-3	Automated cash management control system	47
3-4	A Pro Forma Guide in Authorizing the Use and Acceptance of Depository Transfer Checks	48
3-5	Depository transfer check example	48
3-6	Typical concentration network processing using depository transfer checks	50
3-7	Concentration system design architecture	54
3-8	Techniques used to increase corporate float funds	58
3-9	Zero balance disbursement flow, Alpha Corporation	60
4-1	Matrix of mail times between 12 Federal Reserve cities—1970	65
4-2	Matrix of mail times between 12 Federal Reserve cities—1975	66
4-3	Uniform lockbox service	69
4-4	Lockbox simulation analysis: annual savings on $100,000	73
4-5	Output example of lockbox optimization location	77
4-6	Lockbox envelope system	81
4-7	Basic flow of the Lockbox Photocopy system	82

xvi   Exhibits

4-8	Magnetic tape transmission lockbox system	83
4-9	Standard optically scannable input document	85
4-10	Lockbox system: hardware components	91
4-11	Automated processing system	93
5-1	Developing bank-offered cash management services	103
5-2	Automated payroll system flow	106
5-3	Automated payables processing system	108
5-4	Accounts receivable bank service	109
5-5	Automated inventory management system	111
6-1	Basic flow of daily cash forecasting	127
7-1	Comparative balance sheet	145
7-2	Income statement	146
7-3	Funds flow statement	148
7-4	Forecasting format, structural development analysis	150
7-5	Cash flow statement	151
7-6	Cash receipts and disbursements forecasts	158
7-7	Float Report	162
7-8	General cash receipts and disbursement format	165
8-1	Moving average forecast for the Nova Corporation	172
8-2	Moving average forecasting errors	174
8-3	Exponential smoothing forecast	176
8-4	Straight line projection of accounts receivable	178
8-5	Development of 5-day moving average for daily cash receipts for 10-week period	183
8-6	Seasonal index factors for daily cash receipts	185
8-7	Matrix of time horizon and applicable cash management forecasts	187
8-8	The cash flow forecasting family tree	188
9-1	Historical cash balances	200
9-2	Daily cash forecasting worksheet	201
9-3	Daily forecast management summary	208
10-1	Overview structure of international cash management	219
10-2	Government financial support matrix	228
11-1	Example of single country pool account	246

12-1	Contemporary EFTS considerations	266
12-2	Elements of EFTS	267
12-3	The infrastructure	270
12-4	Local EFTS network	271
12-5	Operation of automated clearing house system	273
12-6	ACH computer-operating cost summary	274
12-7	Item check-processing costs experienced by a bank	275
12-8	Point of sale terminal system	284
12-9	Pre-authorized debit	285
13-1	Current business payment costs	304

Contemporary Cash Management

PART I

INTRODUCTION

CHAPTER 1

CORPORATE BANKING RELATIONS: ESSENTIAL CONSIDERATIONS FOR CASH MANAGEMENT

INTRODUCTION

Cash management in its simplest form has existed in business since the initial use of money as a medium of exchange. Merchants have long recognized the need to have sufficient funds on hand to pay debts as they come due, meet emergencies, and have a store of speculative cash available. Although these concepts are not new, the importance of effective management of company cash has accelerated over time. As a result of economic changes brought about after World War II, business enterprises have significantly altered their approach to conducting business. The surge in global demand for goods and services after World War II provided the impetus for significant business expansion from containable domestic operations to multidivisional and multinational corporate structures. This rapid expansion of corporate structures has also spawned the "profit center" concept, which often duplicates and complicates the controlling and funding of world-wide corporate business transactions.

The expansion of domestic corporations, which provides the impetus for their now historic growth patterns, was most profoundly affected by the Employment Act of 1946. The goals of the Employment Act were to reduce the then high unemployment rate while encouraging an increased standard of living. As a result of this stimulus, a strong consumer demand was created for capital goods producing commensurate corporate expansions and a demand for "social goods." The social demand reflected itself in goods and services that the government has undertaken to satisfy. Typical of any supply and demand situation, the cost of available resources rose in response to the increased demand. Cash and its associated borrowing expense also responded to demand pressures over the past 25 years as Exhibit 1-1 demonstrates. Even though history might support the postulate that demand for an item declines as price increases, this has not been affirmed through recent experience. As resources, including cash, became less available, increased prices did not act as an effective control over demand. Consequently, corporate managers must become accustomed to more expensive funds in the long-term situation until a new equilibrium is reached. Interest rates, once thought usurious, have become prime rates. Significantly, monetary policies are also used more frequently as an economic tool to stiffle or stimulate the productive forces of industry by government. Historically, rising interest rates, coupled with the more recent use of monetary policy to affect the short-term economic environment, have stimulated avid interest in more sophisticated cash management techniques in the past 10 years. Evidence of this increase in interest can be found in corporations such as General Electric, which operates with essentially the same cash balances it had in 1946 even though sales have grown sixfold. Other multinational corporations such as Samsonite Corporation and Standard Oil of California have maintained relatively level cash balances, even though their businesses have expanded significantly.

Stimulated by the rising cost of funds, cash today is being evaluated as an asset and a scarce resource, which must be conserved and earn a reasonable return for the company. Such is the emerging view of modern corporate cash management.

Cash management as it exists today can be defined as the planning, organizing, and controlling of corporate funds to satisfy:

- Transaction-related corporate requirements
- Precautionary corporate requirements
- Speculative opportunities

Transaction-related needs can be defined as current outstanding corporate obligations. This includes the payments of payrolls and accounts payables to vendors, as well as the payment of longer-term liabilities such as dividends and stock payments.

Precautionary uses of funds have traditionally provided basic protection to a corporation from unplanned business reversals. Although this is still a motivating factor for maintaining available cash by some corporations, its

Exhibit 1.1 Short-Term Interest Rates

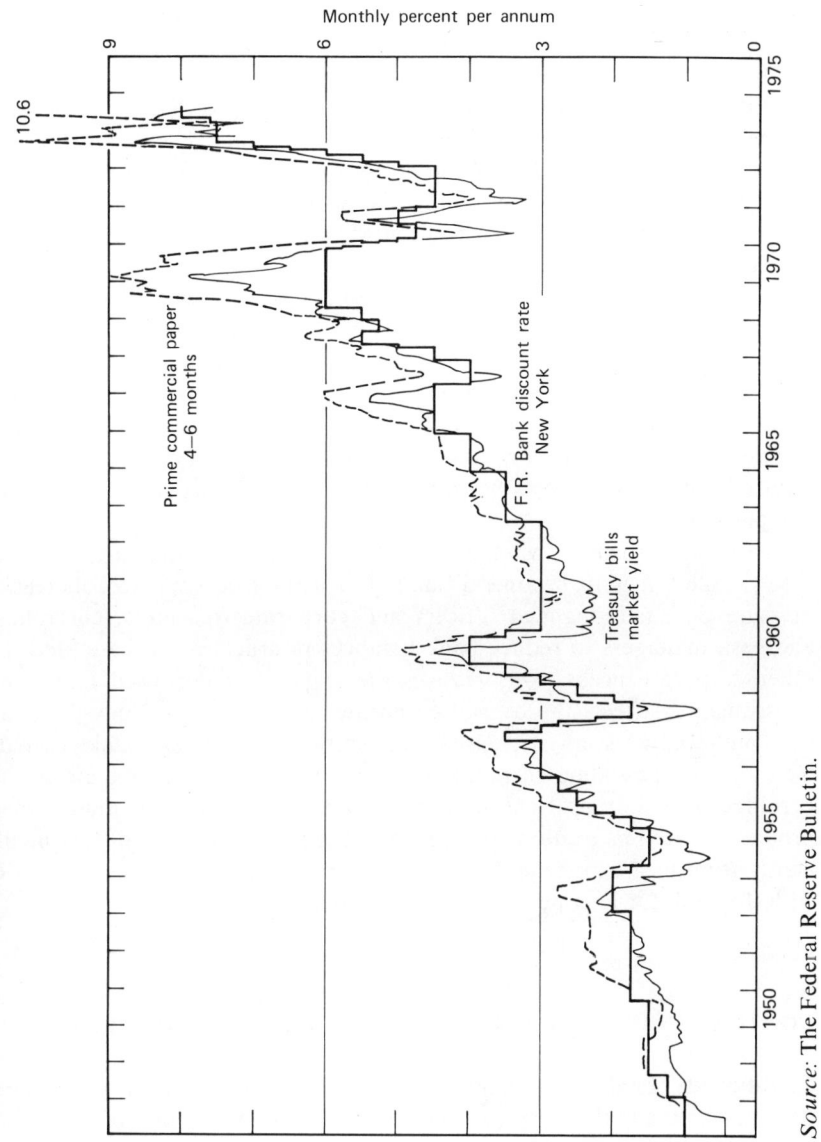

Source: The Federal Reserve Bulletin.

significance has been reduced in recent years in light of "risk management" within corporations. An example of the use of precautionary funds was demonstrated by a large west coast food processor. When the firm found itself the target of a takeover bid by a multinational conglomerate, it was able to marshal its reserve funds to purchase a business that the acquisitive-minded corporation was legally blocked from owning. The acquisition was executed quietly with existing funds thus circumventing disclosures that could have endangered the purchase. Consequently, the firm maintained its autonomy through the wise allocation of cash to meet unforeseen contingencies.

In times of economic expansion and rapid growth, cash is often allocated for speculative business opportunities. For many conglomerates, this was a prime use of cash during the 1960s. In times of economic contraction and tight money policies, the use of cash as a reserve for speculative opportunities is suboptimal for most corporations. Periods of stringent monetary policies dictate that corporations use funds for inventory financing and to meet current obligations rather than to maintain cash balances for speculative purposes.

There is a growing awareness that cash is an asset that must be used wisely, unless it is to become a liability. This philosophy places increasing pressure on chief financial officers and corporate treasurers, controllers, and cash managers to reduce bank balances in order to extricate funds for other corporate needs. This reduces the expense of borrowed funds and, consequently, affects the overall corporate financial costs. Emerging from this philosophy is an increased competitiveness among banks seeking balances and providing corporate services. Banks must become aware that earnings from corporations now need to be based on cash management products as well as traditional credit services. This awareness differs significantly from past experiences where large excess cash balances might reside with the bank for long periods producing additional bank income.

CONTEMPORARY BANKING VIEW OF CASH MANAGEMENT

Traditionally, banks have considered idle funds left on deposit by corporations as compensation for services and an economic fact of life. Consequently, any attempt to reduce available funds is considered adversely by the bank. To some extent, banks have historically valued customer relationships by the size of balances left on deposit. Although this is still encouraged by most banks, it generally is recognized as a diminishing trend. Major banks today recognize the economic factors that are pressuring corporations to optimize cash resources. Banks realize that future income will be based on a combination of competitive corporate services and future credit relationships. During the years since 1970, banks have gradually reversed their view of corporate cash management functions. Instead of discouraging this practice, major banks now offer a multitude of cash management services to its customers. These services are broken into the two basic categories of:

- Cash management consulting
- Cash management system design and implementation

Offering cash management services underscores the developing trend in banking to provide competitive corporate services. This trend is further evidenced by an increase in direct competition between banks in the pursuit of new business.

The cash management consulting offered by major banks is one of the new services offered. Bank representatives work closely with corporate treasurers and cash managers to define receivables and payables patterns. The level of detailed involvement varies depending on the product diversification of the firm and the extent of physical dispersion. Bank cash management consultants then propose alternative methods of operations to accelerate receivables and increase control over disbursements. Generally, the systems proposed use the bank's facilities for lockbox collection and account concentration. The corporation is responsible for implementation within the company.

The cash management system design and implementation team concept is another, but less common, approach. Essentially, a team of bank specialists define the detail input and outputs of the corporation. The purpose is to isolate each specific procedure for handling receipts and disbursements. Upon completion of the detail study, the team recommends a system-wide cash management program. Emphasis is usually placed on use of bank-supplied services. Detailed proposals include:

- Redefining receipts and disbursements procedures
- Defining optimal use of daily wire transfers from remote banks
- Using full concentration banking facilities
- Exploiting bank corporate services, for example, lockbox processing
- Evaluating bank investment services

After approval, the team is ready to implement the proposal in conjunction with the company. Although team approaches are not widely used today, pivotal cash management banks are evolving toward professional consulting teams.

BANK SERVICES—PHILOSOPHY AND TREND

Historically, banks have offered a number of services to corporations. Charges have traditionally been based on compensating balances as opposed to fee payment. Consequently, if sufficient funds were deposited with the bank, services were granted without further charges. Within this operating philosophy of "bundled" services and fees, it was difficult at best to identify separate service expenses. Identification of service expenses has traditionally been difficult for banks because of inadequate cost-accounting techniques. As a result of the increased emphasis on cash management and the consequent reduction in balances, banks are evolving toward a philosophy of service "unbundling." Through unbundling, each service offered by the bank (e.g., lockbox, account reconcilement) is priced separately based on volume considerations. Consequently, competition among banks will become more pronounced as corporate treasurers evaluate similar services based on price and quality. While unbundling may work to the economic benefit of corporations, it may also prove detrimental to the corporation.

A "conflict of interest" arises where minimizing service expenses results in diverse and multifarious bank relations because credit requirements of the corporation may be jeopardized. The bank/customer relationship takes on special dimensions in times of economic contraction when money supplies are used as an economic control tool. In times of stringent monetary control, banks' loan priorities are geared to the needs of proved customers. Consequently, corporations minimizing service charges through bank diversification may suboptimize in terms of meeting credit requirements.

From a bank's perspective, participating with a corporation to establish and maintain a viable cash management program is beneficial because it serves the corporation's borrowing needs while being fairly compensated for services performed. Banks must be compensated for services either through direct fees or compensating balances. The selection of lead corporate banks is an important consideration because multiple bank relationships are essential for a combination of credit and service needs. Large corporations typically conduct business with a range of banks between 20 and 100 depending upon service and credit needs. Exhibit 1-2 illustrates the results of a survey of large American corporations and the number of banks they used. Reasons for increased use of multiple banks include market expansion and national acquisition programs that require credit availability. Corporations should limit the number of banking relations when feasible to facilitate control of both receipts and disbursements. Often firms would like to reduce the number of bank relations but are constrained because local depository banks may be inadvertently penalized, which could lead to a dis-

Exhibit 1.2 Sample Distributions for Large Corporations—Major Bank Relations

Number of Banks Used	Number of Corporations	Percent of Total Corporations
5–9	8*	4.97
10–19	22	13.66
20–49	40	24.84
50–99	32	19.88
100–499	44	27.33
500–999	4	2.48
1000–1999	5	3.11
over 2000	6	3.73

* Includes two companies with less than five banks. This survey was based on 161 corporations that responded to the Conference Board Survey.
Source: Cash Management, The Conference Board, p. 39.

ruption in local working relations. Consequently, firms may be placed in the awkward position of maintaining multiple banking relations in order to assure good working relations in remote areas.

CASH MANAGEMENT PERSPECTIVE

Reduced to its simplest terms, cash management attempts to track and control the flow of funds through the corporation. The primary objective is to influence the availability of receipts while delaying the outflow of funds, thus minimizing working capital. Although this perspective is easily stated, firms too often lose overall perspective of the objective through concentrated involvement in one specific area of cash management. Consequently, the overall program is suboptimized. Cash management can be viewed as a subsystem of the entire family of business functions. Contained within each subsystem are processes indigenous to the functions performed by each area.

Exhibit 1-3 is an illustration of subsystem definitions as related to cash management.

CASH MANAGEMENT INPUTS

The system inputs are essentially of three types: revenues received by the corporation, current liabilities as generated, and information concerning

Exhibit 1.3 Input-Output Relationships of Corporate Subsystems

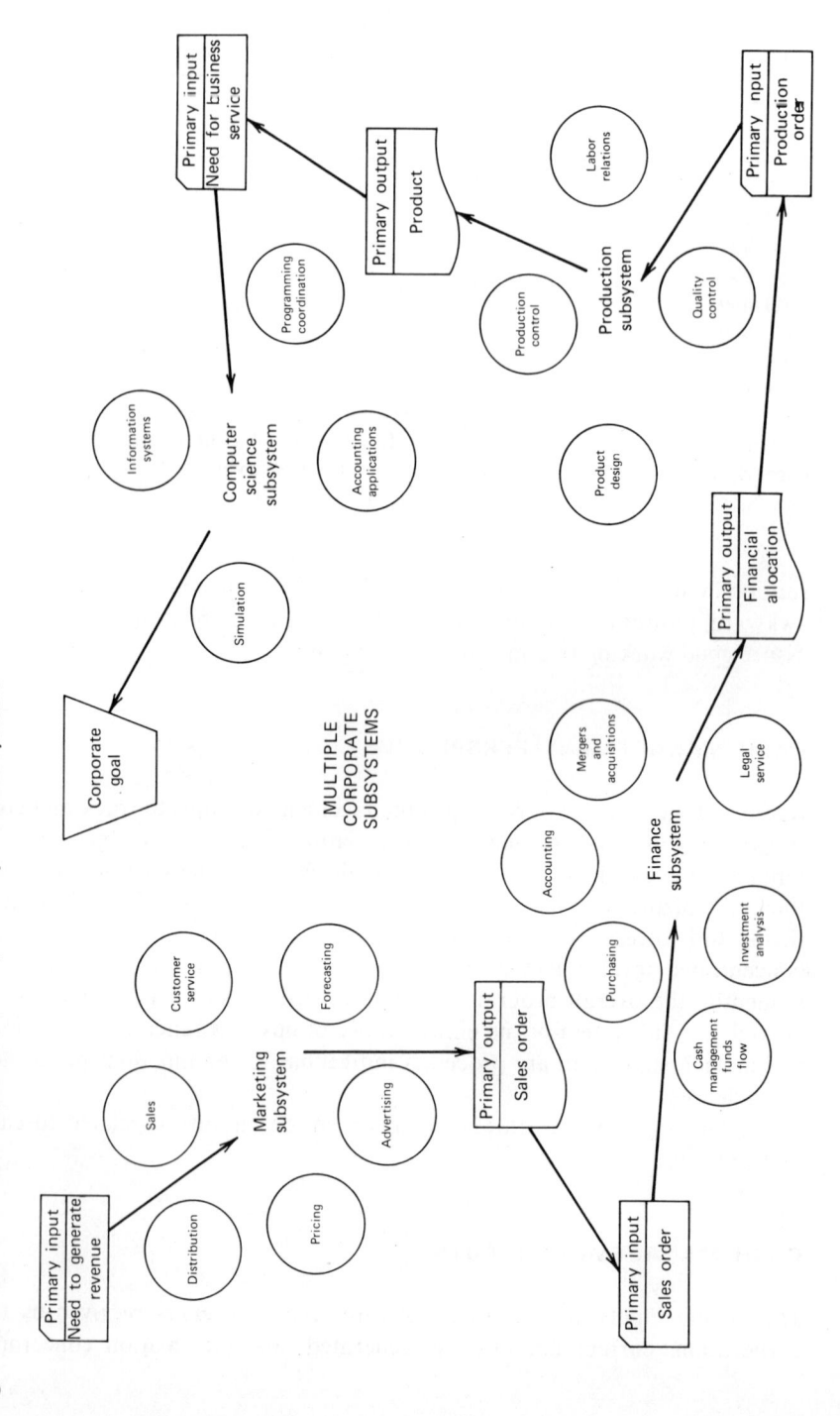

future liabilities and required business contingencies. Revenues received by corporations include cash payment for services performed, checks received (another form of cash), and outstanding receivables. Whereas cash is an immediate source of liquid funds for corporate use, checks must complete a clearing process before becoming available. Receivables are also an input to the cash management subsystem because factoring of accounts receivables can produce short-term working capital. Additionally, receivables may be pledged to a bank, thus generating working capital through secured short-term financing. Current liabilities are another input to the cash management system because they supply current information on contracted and recorded liabilities. Consequently, vendors and other creditor claims influence the distribution of funds input to the system.

Future known requirements and contingency requests also act as inputs. Long-term liabilities such as maturing sinking fund payments, dividend distributions, planned capital purchases, and contingency requirements also represent input data to the cash management system. Contingency requirements take the form of required compensating bank balances or corporate required reserves.

CORPORATE CASH MANAGEMENT PROCESSES

The processes that take place against the cash management inputs include a series of management policy decisions regarding the disbursement of funds, the use of bank services (and related bank compensation), and corporate overdraft policies. Exhibit 1-4 illustrates the cash management decision flow. Corporate philosophy regarding disbursements has the most significant impact on cash management programs. The area of policy formulation includes resolution of central versus decentralized handling of payables. Corporate policy also defines the degree of profit center autonomy each operating unit possesses. Central disbursement policies are significant because of the impact on scale economics involved in investment and management of pooled funds. Defining policies related to the size and frequency of overdrafts is another consideration defined by corporate management in conjunction with the cash-forecasting program implemented. Chief financial management establishes the tone of cash management aggressiveness.

Cash forecasting is essentially divided into microforecasting and macromathematical forecasting. Both of the general approaches are discussed later. Suffice it to say that the aggressiveness of a cash management program, and its optimization under either method, is directly affected by

12   Corporate Banking Relations: Considerations for Cash Management

Exhibit 1.4   System Flow of Cash Management System

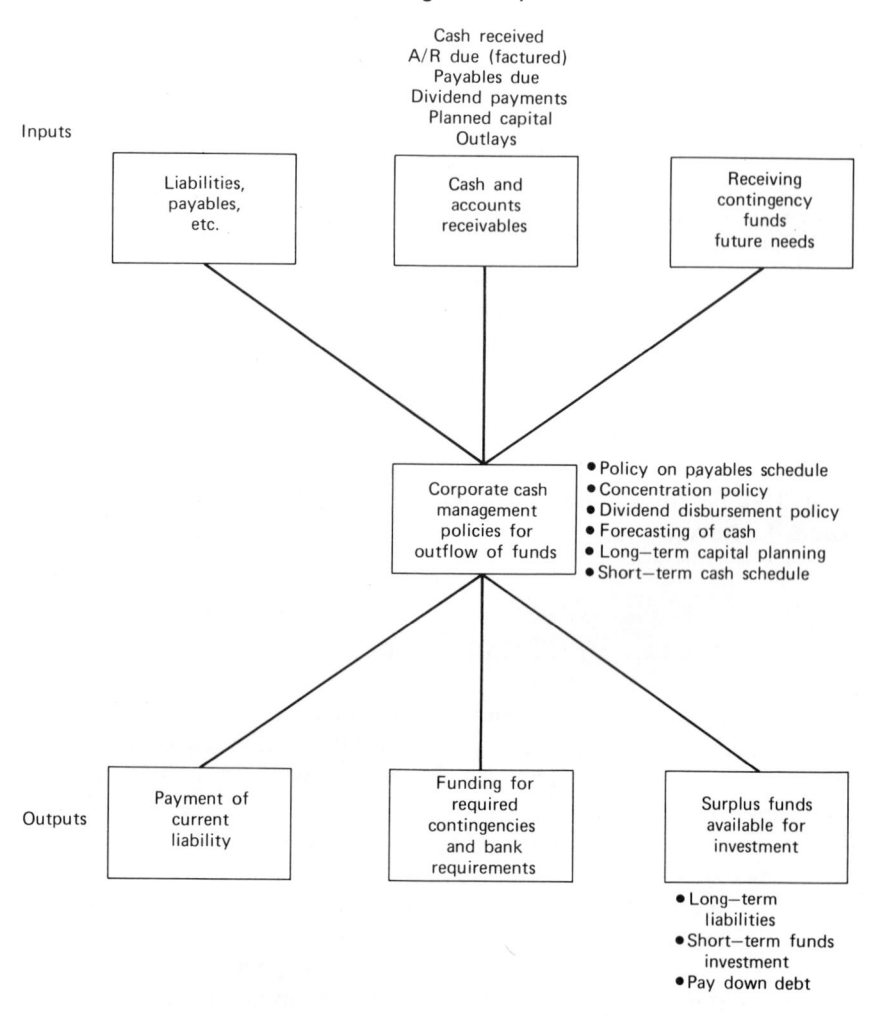

Inputs

Cash received
A/R due (factured)
Payables due
Dividend payments
Planned capital
Outlays

- Liabilities, payables, etc.
- Cash and accounts receivables
- Receiving contingency funds future needs

Corporate cash management policies for outflow of funds

- Policy on payables schedule
- Concentration policy
- Dividend disbursement policy
- Forecasting of cash
- Long—term capital planning
- Short—term cash schedule

Outputs

- Payment of current liability
- Funding for required contingencies and bank requirements
- Surplus funds available for investment

- Long—term liabilities
- Short—term funds investment
- Pay down debt

overdraft policies established in the cash management policy formulation process.

Capital requirements planning is the final major corporate process. For intermediate and long-term requirements, these are reflected on a funds flow statement, which is discussed later. It is important to isolate large capital requirements since they have a "noncyclical" effect on a cash management program. The impact of a nonrepetitive major cash requirement can adversely affect a daily cash forecast or distort averages used for subsequent forecasting. To avoid undesirable distortions, corporate management must decide on a philosophy for handling required capital expenditures in the system.

CASH MANAGEMENT OUTPUTS

The result of distilling and analyzing the elements of the cash management subsystem can be conceived as system outputs. Basic to the outputs is vendor payment for services performed. Taking timely cash discounts (or retaining funds for investment or other purposes) is resolved in the "process" section of policy formulation.

Providing required compensating balances and funds for contingencies is another use of corporate cash. Compensating balances are required by banks to support and pay for credit and noncredit services. Compensating balances often represent an additional method of charging for borrowed funds in excess of stated interest rates. If a firm is using its credit limits with a bank, compensating balances must be considered an obligation requiring reconciliation in the accounting of available cash. In effect, it reduces the total amount of cash available to the corporation. Any other required corporate contingency would also have the same effect on a cash management program. For example, if a corporate cash manager decided upon a policy of low-frequency overdrafting, it is feasible that a significant cash reserve would be required to accomodate that policy. Whereas some of the reserve would count toward any required compensating balances, the remainder would be considered idle funds to the corporation resulting in a related opportunity cost. The return on assets achieved by the cash manager is influenced by the aggressive versus conservative policies established by corporate management. Earnings from the cash management investment function is directly related to the length of time funds are available. Generally, the longer the investment time, the better the yield. Determination of long- versus short-term funds is performed in this process of cash forecasting through the analysis of past corporate bank balances and patterns of "base" cash reserves. Investment of funds as described can contribute to the corporate objective of contingency reserves with long-term investment funds while providing short-term funding to meet current liabilities.

THE CONCEPT OF FLOAT

Float, a term frequently heard in cash management circles, is strictly defined as the length of time funds are uncollected by the Federal Reserve*

---

* This is referred to as Federal Reserve float to differentiate it from mail or processing float.

Bank but credited to the sending bank. This situation occurs because of the clearing system that has evolved in the banking industry. Float occurs because the Federal Reserve has established time frames for *collection* of funds presented by member banks. The length of time varies from 1 to 2 days. Float results because the Federal Reserve Bank credits a bank (hence a customer) with collected funds based on a published availability schedule, although it may actually take the Fed longer to actually collect the funds. During the additional time the funds are available to the issuing corporation as collected for use in cash management programs. For example, a check drawn on a bank in Seattle, deposited in Washington, D.C. on Monday, would be credited as collected the following Wednesday. However, the collection of funds from Seattle may not be concluded (and the Seattle bank debited) until Friday. Consequently, funds are available in Seattle to the issuing company and in Washington, D.C. to the receiving company for investment at the same time. The Federal Reserve in essence has given a noninterest-bearing loan to the sending bank. This situation occurs because the time allowed by the availability schedule as established by the Federal Reserve Bank is less than the actual collection period. Because of physical limitations (e.g., high numbers of checks entering the system or heavy mail traffic at holiday seasons), float time increases. More frequently, however, data communications techniques are being used to facilitate the transfer of funds. The monetary supply is an economic consequence of float because funds are increased as sophisticated corporate treasurers use float for short-term investments. Through short-term investment, income is earned on funds that are already committed for payment elsewhere in the economy. The result of Fed float is to stimulate the need for expansion of funds in the monetary system to support business transactions. Fed float affects the behavior of the individual corporation in its quest to maximize profits through cash management investment while adversely impacting the monetary balance of the economy.

The Federal Reserve is constantly working toward reconciling the scheduled clearance times with actual clearance times. This is being effected through telecommunications networks and the use of computer facilities for faster check clearance and processing. Mail and processing float will be discussed later as controllable elements in cash management systems.

THE CHECK-CLEARING PROCESS

Increasingly, banks are competing today not only in traditional bank services but also in the speed with which they can collect checks for their corporate customers. The collection process is important because it determines how soon funds are available to corporate cash managers. There are essentially three methods of check clearance today. Exhibit 1-5 demonstrates the basic process of checks entering the clearing process.

As checks are presented to banks for collection, they are sorted into three categories that funnel into appropriate processing streams. The important distinction is that Fed float is only available to checks that pass through the Federal Reserve System previously described.

The collection process is based on the location of the "due from" bank. If the "due from" bank is located in a remote area where direct-send bank collection facilities are not available, the Federal Reserve Bank is used for collection. The Federal Reserve Banks constitute a simple and economical collection agency for its members. A significant portion of the checks drawn on out of town banks are processed by the Federal Reserve Banks, which debit and credit the appropriate deposit accounts of member banks. This process results in fluctuation of the cash reserve by member banks. Although Federal Reserve Banks handle only member banks, nonmembers may use them through a correspondent bank or by entering a special clearing arrangement with the appropriate Federal Reserve District Bank. It is to the cash manager's advantage to issue checks on remote banks that require Federal Reserve processing. The "collected" balance at the depository bank reflects available funds within a 2-day period. However, if the collection process takes longer, those same funds are available at the disbursing bank for an additional time for investment by the cash manager.

The second major check-clearing process is sending checks directly to correspondent banks for collection. This method was developed by banks as an alternative to the Federal Reserve Bank check collection system in order to accelerate fund availability. Checks for collection from a distant area would be batched and sent to a local correspondent bank that would collect the funds from the drawee banks. For example, if a California bank had a correspondent relationship with a New York bank, it would send all New York area checks to be collected through the New York clearing house operation, thus eliminating the Federal Reserve.

In each major metropolitan area, bank clearing houses service local members. The purpose of the local clearing house is to facilitate the collection of funds between banks in the same city and thus offer an alternative to the more lengthy Federal Reserve Bank process.

Clearing houses remain a major collection vehicle by providing 1-day processing of checks issued on banks in the local clearing house city. Checks presented at 7:30 A.M. in the San Francisco clearing house are processed in both the sending and receiving banks that night. Hence the collected funds are available that day to cash managers.

In this chapter, we have identified the basic purpose of corporate cash

Exhibit 1.5   The Check Clearing Process

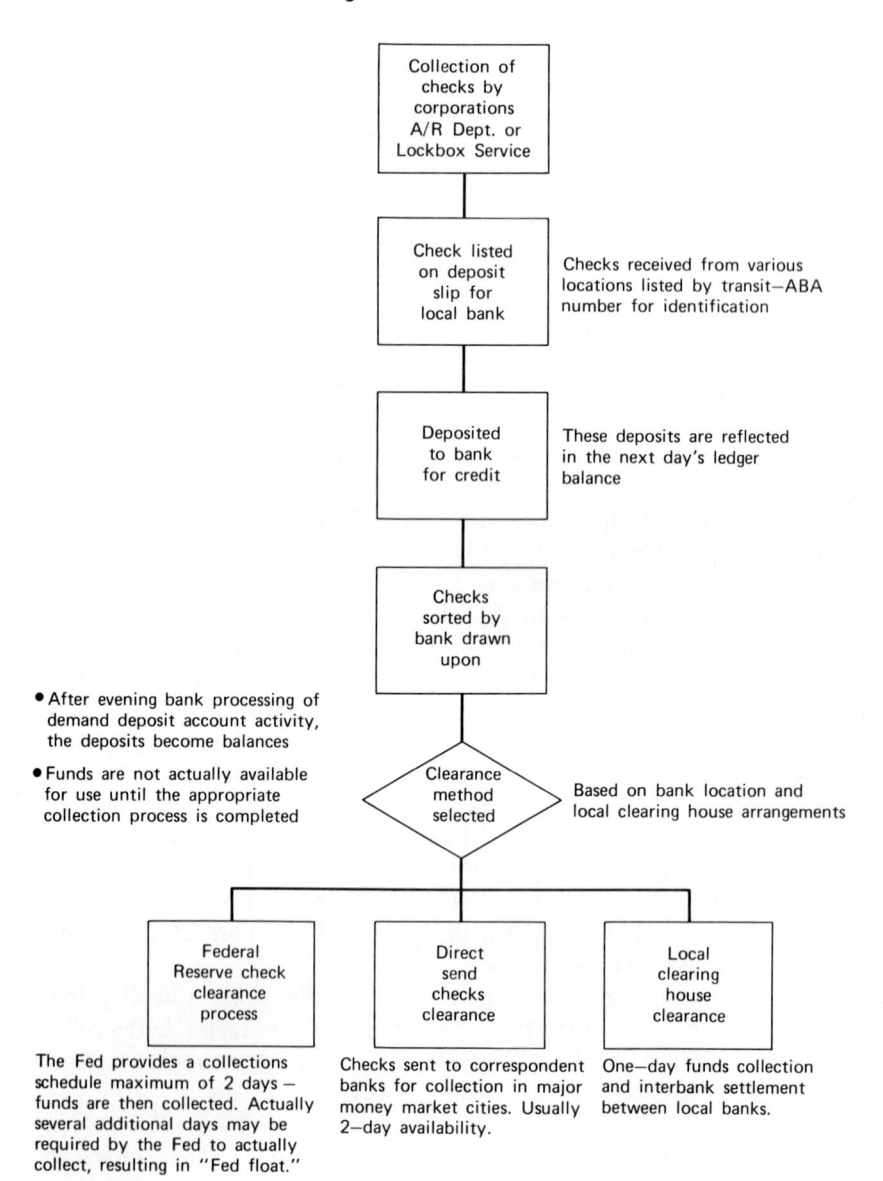

```
                    ┌─────────────────┐
                    │  Collection of  │
                    │    checks by    │
                    │   corporations  │
                    │  A/R Dept. or   │
                    │ Lockbox Service │
                    └────────┬────────┘
                             │
                    ┌────────┴────────┐
                    │  Check listed   │   Checks received from various
                    │    on deposit   │   locations listed by transit—ABA
                    │    slip for     │   number for identification
                    │    local bank   │
                    └────────┬────────┘
                             │
                    ┌────────┴────────┐
                    │    Deposited    │   These deposits are reflected
                    │     to bank     │   in the next day's ledger
                    │    for credit   │   balance
                    └────────┬────────┘
                             │
                    ┌────────┴────────┐
                    │     Checks      │
                    │    sorted by    │
                    │   bank drawn    │
                    │      upon       │
                    └────────┬────────┘
                             │
• After evening bank processing of
  demand deposit account activity,
  the deposits become balances
                          ╱─────╲
• Funds are not actually available    ╱Clearance╲
  for use until the appropriate       ╲ method  ╱   Based on bank location and
  collection process is completed      ╲selected╱    local clearing house arrangements
                                        ╲─────╱
                             │
          ┌──────────────────┼──────────────────┐
          │                  │                  │
   ┌──────┴──────┐    ┌──────┴──────┐    ┌──────┴──────┐
   │   Federal   │    │   Direct    │    │    Local    │
   │Reserve check│    │    send     │    │  clearing   │
   │  clearance  │    │   checks    │    │    house    │
   │   process   │    │  clearance  │    │  clearance  │
   └─────────────┘    └─────────────┘    └─────────────┘
```

The Fed provides a collections schedule maximum of 2 days — funds are then collected. Actually several additional days may be required by the Fed to actually collect, resulting in "Fed float."

Checks sent to correspondent banks for collection in major money market cities. Usually 2–day availability.

One–day funds collection and interbank settlement between local banks.

16

management. Additionally, various elements of economic consideration have been discussed, as has the effect of Federal Reserve deficiencies on the monetary supply. The major inputs and outputs of cash management have also been defined, as has the importance of maintaining good bank relationships. This is especially critical since some cash management techniques are viewed with a jaundiced eye by banks.

CHAPTER 2

CORPORATE CRITERIA FOR BANK SELECTION

THE BANK SELECTION PROCESS

The careful selection of bank relationships deserves special attention. Access to adequate lines of credit and other financial support is a critical consideration in an ongoing corporate/bank relationship. Corporations generally use varying criteria in the bank-evaluation process based on the type of relationship desired. The banking-related requests for a large bank relationship with international corporate requirements are significantly different from those of a local bank where operational office support is required. For most large corporations, the number of banks used vary depending upon the nature of business and the degree of financial centralization versus decentralization. Regardless of the number of banks used, only a few bank relationships are regarded as pivotal by the corporation. Cash managers use smaller banks for receipt and disbursement points and generally move funds to large concentration banks. If lines of credit are maintained at local banks, they tend to be small (in the aggregate 20% or less) and not extensively used. The money center banks that enjoy 80% or more of the corporate borrowing activity are evaluated on a host of corporate-required services. Often corporations spend months selecting their concentration banks. As a supplier of financial services, the selection process must be based on the same criteria as any other service supplier.

Prior to formal bank selection, a corporation must evaluate its business environment to determine basic financial requirements. This process includes determining the current corporation loan requirements and projecting future credit needs. If international business exposure is part of the corporate operating environment, the cash manager must also define special services required such as currency trading and international wire transmission. Internal evaluation and definition of needs by the corporation is essential if the selection process is to result in a fruitful and lasting bank relationship.

The factors most often examined by corporations in the selection process include:

- Financial stability of potential banks
- Ability to provide adequate financing
- Evaluation of pricing structure
- Accessability of bank branches and correspondent networks—domestically and internationally
- Adequate bank sophistication to meet changing needs of corporation
- Evaluation of bank services in relation to corporate operations and cash management objectives
- Personal contacts and prior experiences with banks under consideration

The financial stability of the banks under consideration is an important factor in bank selection. To some extent, a corporation's reliable reputation can be damaged if its supporting banks are in a historically weak financial condition. Additionally, corporate financial flexibility may be endangered or opportunities lost if supporting banks are unable to meet changing financial requirements. Financial stability is a growing concern among corporations as banks become more aggressive and financially vulnerable in the market place. In some cases, corporate growth rate requirements exceed the bank's capacity to adjust to changing market conditions. Consequently, the flexibility and control required for reasonable growth is limited.

Determining the borrowing requirements of the corporation is one of the central bank-selection criterion. Size is the key factor in evaluating the bank's lending ability, because lending limits are limited by law and based on total deposits. While many large corporations spread their borrowing over many banks, it is desirable to build the strongest relationship with banks who can provide the largest percentage of required corporate funds. This approach minimizes the cash manager's account control and auditing problems related to compensating balances. Although establishing strong ties with major lead banks is essential, both for credit and operational services, secondary bank relationships also need to be cultivated. In times of tight financial conditions, a corporation may find that several lines of credit are needed to satisfy financing requirements. Often secondary banks are a better source of funds because they are eager to develop expanded corporate banking relations.

Bank accessability is another area of concern to most corporations in the bank-selection process. The factors of primary consideration are physical bank locations and availability of bank officers for consulting. A corporation with a large international business base requires a bank with extensive knowledge of international business regulations and requirements. Additionally, the number of banking outlets in countries where business is concentrated is important from a control viewpoint for multinational corporations. Domestically, the correspondent bank networks of concentration banks are an important consideration for corporate cash management since this determines the total facilities available to execute business in the principle commercial centers in the United States. Historically, firms are also interested in the bank's reputation for consistant customer contact. This is important to a corporation because maintaining communication regarding the status of financial markets often has an important external informational input to the cash manager. Additionally, through consistant contact, some financial inconvenience during periods of tight credit can be avoided through cooperative planning between the corporation and bank officers.

Depending upon the aggressiveness of the corporation, the degree of bank sophistication can significantly affect the bank-selection process. For firms with moderate or slow growth rates, this may not be a major factor. For firms in highly technological fields where obsolesence develops at an accelerated pace, the flexibility and sophistication of the bank can be of prime importance. Corporate changes in procedures or the development of new cash management techniques often require approval and implementation by banks. To this extent, banks need to have a level of competence as well as an understanding both of the customer's business and of new problem solutions. The bank's willingness to develop and implement innovative approaches to corporate problems is essential to aggressive corporations.

Personal contacts are also a consideration in the selection process. Understanding corporate philosophy and goals at the level of the Board of Directors provides business insights that would not otherwise be available. Through this level of involvement, ties can be developed to meet corporate financial requirements. Consequently, personal contact, at a senior level, is often a major consideration in the selection process.

ANALYSIS OF COMMERCIAL REQUIREMENTS

A careful analysis of commercial banking requirements is necessary before the bank-selection process commenses. The major internal corporate considerations include:

- Establishing the size of the line of credit
- Establishing the need for multiple credit lines

- Establishing special service needs
- Determining the physical location requirements for the bank
- Defining desired accounting services
- Defining desired investment requirements
- Determining the availability of trust services
- Evaluating the corporate/bank level of business sophistication

Determining and Establishing the Line of Credit

For many corporations credit is an umbilical cord to short-term survival. Consequently, adequate credit must continually be available to the corporation. A large west coast mortgage banking corporation defines its credit line requirements based on forecasts of new building activity. The treasurer periodically evaluates the building industry trend nationally, considering trends in short-term interest rates. Subsequently, various banks are contacted to obtain a market reading for new short-term construction funds. Based on these market inputs, an estimate is developed of required short-term credit. Since construction funds are required nationally, the treasurer has determined that credit lines are best satisfied through a network of participating banks in key cities rather than one money center bank. Often a corporation's capital requirements may be so large that one bank might be reluctant or unable to meet the credit requirement. For example, recently a multinational corporation required a $100 million line of credit. Although the larger national banks could support this loan request, they chose to divide or "spread" the loan requirement over several participating banks. In this example, the corporation approached its west coast concentration bank to act as a "consolidation agent" in securing participation for the required loan amount. The agent bank contacted other banks (usually those with correspondent relationships) and invited them to participate in the loan program. Banks wishing to participate pledged support of a fixed percent of the total loan. Participation often ranges from 1 to 90%. As payments are made on the principal of the loan over time, they are distributed on a percent of participation basis. In this manner, each participating bank maintains a constant share of the loan balance for the duration of the loan. The bank acting as consolidation agent is responsible for the accounting and disposition of the loan. Commonly, the agent bank maintains the largest share of the loan. The terms specified for this loan are defined in a legal contract and signed by the corporation borrowing the funds and each participating bank. The terms in the document include:

- Amount of loan supported by each bank
- Annual interest rate (e.g., 120% of prime rate of a specified bank)

- Basis of interest rate by 360 or 365 days
- Dates interest due and to whom payable
- Date on which corporate reports must be filed and to whom
- Required compensating balance agreement (e.g., 10% of unused lines and 15% of used credit)
- Specification of special charges (e.g., commitment fees, loan availability fees) required in addition to compensating balances
- Conditions of default and defined actions by the lending banks

Banks are often reluctant to concentrate funding extensively in any one firm. Banks usually are careful to spread their lending risks, no matter how small, over many participating Banks. Consequently, firms often find it advantageous to maintain good working relations with many large banks. In this way, when multiple bank participation is needed, the corporation finds itself in an advantageous bargaining position. Often a corporation with good bank relations chooses to establish its multiple credit lines with banks strategically located to its business needs. When the corporation controls the securing of credit, it can better control negotiable areas involved in the loan agreement. Through central control of credit with various banks, corporations strengthen and build permanent banking relationships. Initiation of future corporate loans becomes less cumbersome because of favorable past experiences.

A method often used by cash managers to estimate credit needs is the funds flow statement. Essentially, the funds flow method (sometimes called the adjusted net income method) is based on projection of incomes and expenses of various profit centers of the corporations. The profit projections for each profit center are adjusted for known changes in noncash items such as depreciation expenses. Capital expenditures and other changes in working capital items affecting cash such as an inventory investment are reflected in the modified statement. Forecasting methods are discussed in detail in Part III.

Cash managers using the funds flow method need to maintain close working relations with all profit center managers in order to accurately determine required credit lines at various time intervals. Failure to accurately determine credit requirements can result in significant corporate charges for loan commitment fees. Loan commitment fees are sometimes charged by banks in addition to compensating balances as a "premium" paid to the bank for keeping funds currently available.

Sometimes the funds flow statement is considered a cash-forecasting requirements technique. In this regard, one of its primary functions is to determine when short-term (6 to 12 months) financing is required. This approach can aid a corporation in anticipating its borrowing needs and scheduling repayments. Corporations accurately estimating the size and timing of credit requirements not only reduce their overall borrowing expenses by minimizing borrowing but also find themselves in stronger negotiating positions with their banks. Additionally, corporations gain credibility with banks when a demonstrated schedule of requirements and sources of funds for paybacks can be presented.

Establishing Special Service Needs

An array of special service needs can exist for multinational corporations. These special requirements include:

- Handling of domestic and international drafts
- International currency exchange
- International branch locations
- Wire transfer facilities for both domestic and international funds transfer
- Facilities for corporate required trusts

Essential to a successful corporate/bank relation is the ability of the bank to provide special services required by the corporation. Often a corporation inadequately defines its special requirements prior to establishing relations with a bank. Subsequently, special processing requirements are identified that often cause operational problems and in some cases make adequate servicing impossible. Although most banks handle drafts through special arrangements with corporations, drafts can cause severe operational problems for the bank. Firms with international business requirements need to define these requirements as clearly as possible before entering a bank relationship. It is no easy task for a bank to acquire the knowledge necessary to successfully deal in the international market. Maintaining currency exchanges, processing international drafts, and providing banking services in foreign countries all require specialized bank knowledge and facilities.

Commonly, wire transfers are a service used extensively by corporations to move funds from one bank to another. Often a cash management firm transfers by wire excess funds from one bank to another to "pay down" its outstanding debt in order to reduce its interest expenses. A wire transfer is required in order to use funds on the same day. The wire transfer makes funds immediately available in the receiving bank. There are two basic wire transfer services: bank wire transfers and Federal Reserve wire transfers. Wire transfers are discussed in more detail in Chapter 3.

An area not extensively considered in the selection process is the capability of the banks trust department. This is an area the corporate cash manager should define early in the selection process. If adequate expertise is not available in a local bank, it is possible to reallocate their responsibility to another larger bank without significant detriment to the banking relationship.

Matching Corporate and Bank Requirements

Careful matching of corporate objectives and bank sophistication in the implementation of cash management techniques is necessary. Often a corporation discovers too late that its progressive posture in cash management is met with less than enthusiastic support by supporting lead banks. Recently, a billion dollar west coast corporation requested proposals from several of its major banks to develop an on-line cash management information system. To the corporation's frustration, several banks replied that they lacked the technical strength to develop such a system even though the bank was the custodian of the required cash management information. A corporation that does not match banking capabilities with its cash management objectives prior to establishing a relationship soon realizes the limitations it has unnecessarily encumbered upon itself.

Account reconcilement services is another area often considered in the bank-selection process. An automated account reconcilement service maintains records of all checks issued by a corporation and matches payments as received for the corporation. As checks are processed against corporate accounts, the program checks the lists of outstanding checks noting unpaid checks. At month's end, the account reconcilement service creates a bank statement for the corporation and lists checks outstanding. Banks receive information from the corporation on checks drawn in the form of magnetic tape, punched cards, or lists, which are converted to machine-readable form. Account reconcilement services are one of the most frequently used bank services and save significant corporate time and resources.

Bank policy regarding "double counting" of balances is a final area that is sometimes considered by cash managers in the bank selection process. Double counting is defined as the use of compensating balances required to support loans as a base for earning credit, which can subsequently be applied to service charges. Double counting is common with many banks if not by policy then by neglect. Many banks lack the systems support required to maintain an accurate accounting of each corporation's net monthly position. Double counting is advantageous for the corporate cash manager since it provides both support for loans and an earning credit to buy services such as account reconcilement. As with any financial evaluation, the corporate cash manager must evaluate all aspects of bank compensation.

BANK COMPENSATION—CORPORATE CONSIDERATIONS

In any corporate/banking relationship, it is essential that the corporation realize that the bank is in business to make money. When it comes to bank compensation, some cash managers are inclined to reduce bank earnings to unprofitable levels. The bank, like other business enterprises, is entitled to earn a fair profit. Bank compensation has long been a controversial corporate topic. The method of payment as well as charges has been the foundation of many disagreements between the bank and the corporate customer.

METHODS OF BANK COMPENSATION—OVERVIEW

No other single area has caused so much controversy as direct fee payment versus compensating balances for bank-provided services. Compensating balances are funds that corporations intentionally leave on deposit with a bank to pay for the credit and noncredit services it uses. This enables the bank to earn a profit from services such as providing checking accounts, maintaining a line of credit, and providing other related services. Historically, compensating balances have been preferred by banks for payment of financial services, whereas other related activities such as data processing, investment services, and trust services have been charged on a fee basis. However, there is a developing trend affecting both areas of fees and compensating balances.

Firms maintaining balances in excess of requirements are sometimes offered the option of applying those amounts against services that have traditionally been paid by fees. This offers the corporation the advantage of using earnings credits and providing the bank with the potential of additional income from corporations. Often excess earnings develop for large corporations when earnings computed on deposits exceed the service charge made by the bank. Under current operations, the excess earnings are absorbed back into the bank if they are not used by the corporation, since it is illegal to pay explicit interest on demand deposits. The long-range effect of this policy is that banks must provide more services for companies to use or corporations will reduce their average outstanding balances and request terms for a fee basis of payment. For this reason, banks must take a flexible approach toward compensation payment.

There is a developing trend toward fee payment for services provided by banks. To some extent this can be justified if the corporation views bank services as merely replacements for internally performed functions. Often this is not the case since overall bank relations affect the borrowing power of the corporation. During the past 5 years, banks have altered their posture on fee payment for services. As cash management expertise developed in corporations, the demand for fee services increased so that banks today are willing to negotiate for fees in many service areas that previously would have been tied exclusively to balances. The trend toward fees for service payment has produced significant problems for banks because often allocation of expenses, both fixed and variable, to specific functions is very complex and involved. Once banks can clearly identify expenses in the service areas, then the form of compensation will have less significance.

One method gaining acceptance for service payment is noninterest-bearing certificates of deposit. An amount approximating the earnings accruing from the certificate at the market rate (if it were interest bearing) is applied against deposit activity charges. Banks favor use of this noninterest-bearing time deposit because the reserve requirement is 6% compared to 17.5% for regular demand deposits. Consequently, for each $100,000 the bank holds in these certificates, it gains the use of $11,500 for its investment base. Generally, corporate money managers prefer the conventional demand deposit account since it allows access to funds as required. If balances are drawn too low one day, they can be adjusted with some succeeding deposit to maintain the required average daily balance.

Generally, banks prefer compensating balances to fee payments because deposits are an important measure of the bank's growth and prosperity. Deposit growth is the more frequently used criteria by management, investors, and analysts and is used extensively in banking progress reports. Although it does not necessarily reflect the real profitability of a bank, it cannot be denied as an important factor in the banking world. Corporate cash managers, conversely, often prefer fee payment for services primarily because any fees directly paid are a tax deductible expense. Paradoxically, in small and medium-sized firms, cash managers prefer compensating balance payment because it reduces the total expense base of their operations. Consequently, return on assets is higher than if out-of-the-pocket fees were paid for bank services. With the current system of compensating balances, for both services and lines of credit, the expenses are hidden from the accountants' ledger cards. The cost of compensating balances is clearly an expense and just as clearly not tax deductible under the current system. Cash managers are increasingly placing pressures on banks to charge fees for services performed because of the rising interest rates and subsequent higher cost of maintaining balances. This places many banks on notice to develop realistically fully burdened service costs and to establish a reasonable profit margin so that fee structures can support banking functions. In other words, in the near future, banks will need to operate more like corporations in income and expense allocations.

Compensating Balances

Despite current trends, compensating balances are still the most widely used payment method. Compensating balances are used for payment of both bank services provided and as partial payment for lines of credit established by the corporation. Application of compensating balances as partial payment for lines of credit is a controversial point between bankers and corporations. Usually a line of credit is partially paid for by maintaining a percent of the total line of credit dollar amount as an account balance in the bank. An additional amount of funds are required for amounts used out of the line of credit. A rule of thumb used by some banks is that a 10% compensating balance is required for an unused line of credit and 20% for funds used under the credit arrangement. Often these guidelines are merely a starting point for negotiations between the corporation and the bank. Personal chemistry between the negotiating parties is important because mutual understanding is the basis for equitable loan agreements. Negotiated compensating balances depend on the basic financial strength of the company and its importance and overall relationship to the banks.

Although bank philosophy regarding compensating balances often affects a company's bank selection, a primary consideration relates to the fact that use of compensating balances distorts the actual cost of money to the corporation. For example, if a firm borrows money at 8.5% per annum but is required to maintain a 20% compensating balance for funds used, the actual interest rate is 10.625%. Because of the nature of compensating balances, only 8.5% is tax deductible. (See Exhibit 2-1.) In reality, the application of compensating balances is negotiable between the corporation and the bank.

Earnings Allowances—Account Analysis

For years, banks have been allowing corporation earnings allowances on deposit funds. Until recently, however, the method of calculating the earnings credit rate has not been widely available. Traditionally, the bank periodically estimates charges based on its expenses, applies an earnings rate to funds on deposit, and notifies a company if additional funds are required to cover services performed. The trend in this area has been altered significantly in the past 5 years. Ever increasingly, banks are publishing formal analyses of accounts. Similarly, corporations often generate internal summaries of estimated earnings and credit allowances by banks.

Exhibit 2-2 is an example of the information contained on a typical account analysis form that might be used by either a corporation or a bank.

Exhibit 2.1 Table of Real versus Stated Interest Rates

	Compensating Balance Required	
Stated Interest Rate (%)	*10% + 10% (real interest rate)*	*20% + 20% (real interest rate)*
6.00	6.667	7.500
6.50	7.222	8.125
7.00	7.778	8.750
7.50	8.333	9.375
8.00	8.889	10.000
8.50	9.444	10.625
9.00	10.000	11.250
9.50	10.556	11.875
10.00	11.111	12.500
10.50	11.667	13.125

Banks use this form to determine basic account profitability, whereas corporations use it as a gauge of costs incurred for bank-performed services.

The bank earnings allowance (sometimes called earnings on funds or earnings credit) represents an income allowance to the corporation based on balances maintained in checking accounts. Since banks cannot by law (Glass–Steigal Act—1933) pay explicit interest on demand deposit accounts, earnings allowances provide to a corporation credits that apply against bank services. If an account generates more charges than credits, either additional balances or a fee payment is required. However, if earnings are not exhausted by services, they are absorbed by the bank. The evaluation period for service analysis often extends over an annual time frame. If the corporation is not "whole" on compensating its bank, it is often required to make a one time fee payment to reconcile the relationship. Traditionally, this has been beneficial to banks because of the limited number of corporate services offered. Increasingly, however, as corporations calculate their earnings allowances and monitor the charges expended on bank services, the average daily balances in banks are being significantly reduced. Resulting from the more aggressive approach to cash management, banks are finding that expanded services must be provided to corporations. This trend will expand in the future, generating greater competitive pressure on banks in relation to cost/performance criteria.

There are several viewpoints regarding how banks establish earnings allowance rates. In theory, the allowance should equal that which the cor-

Exhibit 2.2   Account Analysis Form, Bank of Newtown

Account Title   For Month Ending—_____
Account Number—_____

Earnings Allowance

Average Daily Ledger Balance	_____
Less: Average Daily Float	_____
Average Daily Collected Balance	_____
Less: Reserve Requirement @ 17.5%	_____
Gross funds for service support	_____
Less: Required Compensating Balances to support outstanding loans	_____
Net Balance (for earnings allowance)	_____
Net Monthly earnings @ 6%	_____

Monthly Service Charges

                              Cost   Volume   Amount

Account Services:

Deposits
Checks Paid
Maintenance Charge
Coin Supplied
Wire Transfers
Returned Items
    Total Account Services   _____

Special Services:

Deposit Reporting Service
Balance Reporting Services
Forecasting Services
Investment Expenses
    Total Special Services   _____

Business Services:

Payroll Service Charges
Payables Service Charges
Inventory Control Charges
Accounts Receivable Charges
Lockbox Service Charges
    Total Business Services   _____

Net Free Account Monthly Earnings   _____

poration could achieve through its investment program. However, because of varying balances on a daily basis, this would be difficult, at best, to administer. More commonly the average daily ledger balance, adjusted for float and Federal Reserve requirements, is used as a base to determine funds against which earnings credit applies. This is the base upon which an earnings rate is applied. One method of rate determination uses the 90-day treasury bill rate as quoted on a specific day of the month. The rate used reflects a high degree of liquidity and low risk. If a rate other than the 90-day treasury bill rate is used, it is explicitly stated by the bank, and the source is readily accessable to the corporate cash manager. Although general agreement on the basis of earnings calculation is not finalized across bank lines, adoption of consistant market rate policy by banks lead to better overall corporate/bank relationships.

Earnings Allowance and Compensating Balances

The bank's willingness to apply earnings allowances to compensating balances can be a significant factor in bank selection. Double counting states that a corporation's compensating balance should receive an earnings allowance that can be used to pay for bank services. This approach reduces the overall cost of the loan and is a strategy used by some banks to attract new corporate customers. The current trend is away from double counting, for banks feel compensating balances are a form of loan payment and should not be used as a basis for rebates. Although many banks currently state a policy denying double counting in practice, the final decision remains with the account officer. Consequently, stated policies are irregularly administered. Traditionally, reporting on corporate accounts by banks made the effective elimination of double counting almost impossible. However, with automated reporting systems, banks now possess the means to effectively monitor overall corporate relationships. Depending on the philosophy and needs of a corporate cash management program, double counting can be a significant consideration in bank selection.

Federal Reserve Requirements

As indicated on the account analysis summary, Federal Reserve requirements are excluded from the corporation's collected balance to develop the amount on which the earnings rate is applied. Reserves are nonearning assets required to satisfy legal requirements. Although cash managers accept the exclusion of float in account analysis, there is some disagreement regarding the exclusion of required reserve funds. Many corporations contend that reserve balances are a bank's indigenous operating expense and should not be excluded from the corporation's earning base. Building this reserve expense into the pricing structure would result in a reduction in the earnings rate to allow for the reserve expense. Regardless of the approach, the expense of reserves are reflected in charges to the corporations.

Float—Applied to Account Analysis

Float deducted from the ledger balance in the account analysis statement represents checks in the process of collection. Float in this sense is the number of days it takes for funds to be available to the bank. This does not relate to the actual number of days it takes to become collected. The two most widely used methods of float calculations are actual days and average days. Understanding the method a bank uses is important to a cash manager in order to understand short-term funds availability.

The dynamic float capture method determines funds availability by examining each check deposited. This is accomplished by using computer programs to process checks and relate the bank location (transit ABA numbers) to a table of clearance times. Through automated demand deposit systems, the location of the "due from" bank magnetically encoded on the check is matched against a collection table. This schedule of clearance times is based on the Federal Reserve clearance times and modified by improvements made by individual banks. (See check clearing process—Chapter 1.) Funds become available to the corporation after the stated number of days regardless of actual collection.

The static float capture method or average days float method is based on manual calculations reflecting the average number of days it takes a bank to collect funds in general without regard to the specific banks location. For example, if a $100,000 check were deposited and a factor of 2-days average clearance was used, the bank would allow zero available funds the first day and $100,000 on the second day.

In theory, there should be little if any difference in the method used, otherwise an advantage is gained by the bank or the corporation from one method as opposed to another. Of the two methods, the dynamic float capture method is preferred. The static float capture method requires closer scrutiny on the part of both bank and corporation. From the bank's viewpoint, changes in deposit mix could significantly alter an account's profitability. For example, if several large checks were deposited on remote locations requiring collection times longer than the average factor, then the corporation gains by use of the funds before collection. Consequently, the bank experiences reduced funds with which to work. From the corporation's viewpoint, the static float capture method may work adversely if heavy deposits of 1-day collection items are typically experienced. Instead of obtaining full credit on the day after deposit, the allocation of funds is spread over 2 days. For cash managers who use concentration accounts where the static float capture method is used, the collection factors should be based on the corporation's deposit mix and not on the bank's past general experience. In this way, the cash manager can obtain a closer approximation of clearance times related to the corporation's experience.

Tax Payments

Tax payment processing is another area that can affect the bank-selection process. A corporation can pay taxes to any bank or make payment directly to the Treasury. Tax payments made to banks are withdrawn by the Treasury on a time-delayed basis and hence represent a desirable deposit source to banks. As cash managers become more aware of banks' desires to receive tax deposits, increased pressure is being exerted to provide some earnings allowance against tax deposits. This trend is being strongly opposed by banks for two basic reasons. First, corporations must pay taxes on specified dates, and once payment is made the corporation loses funds control. The fact that banks benefit from use of funds should be incidental to the corporation. Second, funds left in bank accounts by the government represent a form of compensation to pay the bank for services performed. While these are valid reasons for corporations not to receive credit on tax balances, there still remains a developing trend of corporate requests to receive some credit for deposit of tax funds. If credit is provided, it should be remembered that loan accounts must be viewed as demand deposits since the Treasury can call on funds at any time. Consequently, full reserve requirements are necessary. The amounts of tax monies on deposit must be kept in very liquid securities such as government bonds. Consequently, the amount of interest payable by banks is based on minimal rates. An additional expense to be considered is the investment expense incurred by the bank for buying and selling approved short-term securities.

The increasing awareness and aggressiveness of sophisticated cash managers is exerting an ever-increasing pressure on banks to assure that fee-based and balance-based services are stand-alone profitable.

The emerging trend of fee charges for services as opposed to traditional balance requirements is creating significant problems for the banking community in determining service costs and establishing target profit rates.

Cost Evaluation

Historically, banks have exhibited problems in determining processing expenses for services. Partially this arises from indigenous bank-processing

Methods of Bank Compensation—Overview

requirements. Banks must process their financial data on a current basis. Consequently, the work flow for bank processing cannot usually be shifted to smooth out peaks and valley volume situations, and for legal consideration banks find that they must staff for their peak monthly requirements. Similarily, banks also must invest in data processing equipment far in excess of their *average* need to accomodate heavy volume periods. Because of stringent processing requirements, banks traditionally experience significant slack periods where overstaffing and underutilization of equipment is experienced. Since most bank personnel are salaried, layoffs are not common during slack periods. This excess capacity has often affected the manner in which banks have approached service pricing. In fact many banks base service offerings on their desire to use their known excess capacity. The problem with this philosophy is that banks often fail to consider the "full absorbtion" cost of the service but only consider "incremental" expenses. These two costing methods both take into consideration the fixed and variable costs but handle the application of indirectly fixed expenses differently. Incremental costing counts only the additional direct cost of providing a new service as chargeable expenses. Theoretically, if the service were removed, all expenses would also be removed. The philosophy behind this costing method states that any monies received over and above the bank's expense based on excess capacity serves to reduce fixed expenses. Incremental costing should be limited to specific services with known low volumes since it does not recover bank overhead expenses allocated to the department (e.g., president's salary, advertising expenses). Consequently, the total expense is not considered, and if volume expands, the gap between real expense and "stated" profit margins diminishes rapidly as fixed expenses increase in steplike fashion over varying volume levels.

Full-absorbtion pricing is the allocation of total bank expense by department to services performed. The allocation of direct expenses such as salary and indirect expenses such as administrative overhead assures the bank that a total expense estimate is allocated to services performed. Objections to full-absorbtion pricing state that it overallocates indirect expenses since these exist regardless of excess capacity.

The method of service costing by banks is an important consideration to banks and corporations. The full absorbtion method of costing is preferred to the incremental costing technique. Unfortunately, the lack of agreement between banks in the costing method has caused significant pricing problems. For example, a corporation shopping for services may find significant differences in stated costs at an estimated volume level because of the costing philosophy employed. However, a bid approach can turn to a disadvantage to both bank and corporation as service volume increases. At some point, the bank must notify the corporation of sizable price increases if disproportionate losses are to be avoided by the bank. At low volumes, indirect expenses can be absorbed, but at higher volumes significant losses are encountered. A strategy of loss leader services are employed traditionally by some banks in order to secure large account relationships. While the loss leader approach may have been applicable in the past, the growing trend toward cash management indicates that balances for which banks have traditionally contended are diminishing in size and corporations are seeking services that can be provided more effectively by banks. Charges for services performed by banks must increasingly be on a stand alone profit-oriented basis and become less entwined with the promise of hefty balances.

Profit Determination

Banks, like corporations, must make a profit on the services they provide. Providing profit-based services becomes more important as the level of cash management increases. Consequently, the degree of profit a bank establishes is clearly tied to its business goals, market plans, and philosophy. If a bank establishes a profit goal of 20% return on invested capital, the pricing for the services provided should reflect this profit objective. This can be estimated by the bank with the following equation[*]:

$$\text{Profit Rate} = \frac{\text{Returns on Invested Capital}}{\text{Total Revenue/Invested Capital}}$$

For example a bank with $100 million in invested capital desires a pretax return of 20%. What margin of profit must be realized on $80 million in revenue?

$$X = \frac{20\%}{80 \text{ million}/100 \text{ million}}$$

$$= \frac{20\%}{0.8}$$

$$= 25\%$$

A 25% profit rate is required to achieve the goal of a pre-tax-return of 20% on invested capital. It is essential, of course, that rates developed by banks consider competition. This is further affected by the bank's internal operating efficiency. For example, a bank using full-absorbtion costing with lower indirect administrative expenses requires lower prices to meet its profit goals thus out competing other banks. For banks to price services exclusively with competition is, of course, disastrous. In the final analysis,

[*] Symonds, Curtis, *Basic Financial Management,* AMA, New York, 1969, p. 125.

the bank following this philosophy experiences significant losses as volumes increase for underpriced services.

Regardless of the method chosen for establishing profit margins, the bank should always implement goals in relation to budget projections (income and expense) and short/long range bank goals. As the trend toward fees accelerates, cash management corporations have to adjust their thinking regarding inexpensive bank services and realize that the use of bank facilities requires the same "make or buy" decision analysis as any other portion of their business.

Bank Flexibility—Selection Considerations

The trend for pricing arrangements between bank and corporations is toward increased flexibility in both calculation of earnings allowances to corporations and in bank prices. The method of payment for services is negotiable to a large extent to account for use of earnings credits currently lost to the corporation and the need of banks to collect fees for services to cover total expenses. The combined fee/balance payment options also provide cash managers with the alternative to pay cash for services and to use excess deposits or to take advantage of the "automatic" earnings allowance of the bank. The willingness of a bank to enter flexible payment agreements can affect bank selection. However, this is not currently a major concern. Willingness of the bank to understand the needs and problems of the corporate cash manager and to work in the cooperative formulation of solutions is an essential selection consideration.

Account analysis is more universally used by corporations, and costs for bank-supplied services become easily comparable thus encouraging a trend of corporate service shopping. Although it may be considered reasonable to shop the market for the best financial accomodations, it can work to the detriment of both bank and corporation.

Banks, when making loan commitments, consider not only the specific loan request but also other factors such as past credibility and the total banking relationship. Consequently, firms that shop for services may find that service expense is minimized at the risk of losing valuable bank support. The chemistry of understanding and cooperation that exists between banker and corporate customer is often much more valuable than optimizing the service/expense mix. If a corporation spreads its business over too large a banking base, an undesirable reputation may result. Consequently, a corporation in need of bank support may find cool receptions waiting at many banks because of undesirable reptutations. In many cases, corporations require special handling of items or special financial services (e.g., lockbox collection for limited promotional activity), which a bank might efficiently handle. Lacking good working relationships, the bank is often reluctant to accommodate specific corporate requests. Special requests often involve customized service processing requirements to fully satisfy the corporations.

BIBLIOGRAPHY

Guthmann, Harry G., and Dougall, Herbert E., *Corporate Financial Policy,* fourth ed., Prentice-Hall, Englewood Cliffs, N.J., 1964.

Whittlesey, Charles R., Freedman, Arthur M., and Herman, Edward S., *Money and Banking: Analysis and Policy,* Macmillan, New York, 1964.

Plum, Tester V., Humphrey, Joseph M., and Bowyer, John W., *Instrument Analysis and Management,* Irwin, Homewood, Ill., 1961.

PART II

CONTEMPORARY CASH MANAGEMENT TECHNIQUES

CHAPTER 3

CASH MANAGEMENT TECHNIQUES

INTRODUCTION

As cash management has evolved as a business discipline, various approaches to increasing control of the cash receipts and disbursements flow have been developed and subsequently refined. Initially, these techniques were considered proprietary information of the corporation. However, as interest in cash management has grown so has the exchange of information regarding developed techniques not only among companies but also among banking institutions. The purpose of this chapter is to review the primary cash management techniques currently used.

Most techniques are implemented as a cooperative effort by the corporation and bank. Frequently, however, the corporation is responsible for configuring the cash management system it feels best suited for its operations. It is a customized system structuring where the artful use of techniques is used.* The corporation does have direct responsibility in establishing corporate policy that affects cash management techniques. For example, a policy decision on the centralized versus decentralized disbursement of funds significantly affects the accuracy of available funds daily. If decentralized locations issue payments to vendors directly, the corporate cash manager has many disbursements banks to control. Consequently, because of location dispursion, the number of disbursement float days will vary. Through centralization of payables funding (a corporate decision), concentration accounts can be better used to control receipts and disbursements of corporate funds. Cash management techniques and services fall into two functional areas: acceleration of receipts and disbursement control.

---

* Specific cash management system design alternatives are outlined later in this chapter.

Accelerating Receipts

Since the initiation of credit transactions, businessmen have searched for faster ways to collect outstanding receivables. Although remittance of funds from customers is the corporate responsibility, the speed with which they are cleared resides at least partially with the banking system. During the past 10 years, banks have conscientiously developed techniques to aid the corporation in receivables processing in order to make collected funds available to corporations in shorter time frames. The techniques used to accelerate receipts include:

- Lockbox services
- Pre-authorized checks
- Pre-authorized debits
- Concentration banking
- Depository transfer checks
- Deposit reporting
- Wire transfers

Lockbox Services

The Lockbox services is the oldest of the cash management techniques. It occupies such a central role that Chapter 4 is devoted to its full explanation. Lockbox services, by definition, are centrally located collection post office boxes for the purpose of intercepting corporate receivables. Although initiated by RCA Corporation, this approach became accepted as a cash management technique, and banks began to offer and refine lock box processing systems. Exhibit 3-1 is a graphic overview of a typical lockbox-processing system. The flow is initiated by corporate customers mailing their remittances to a post office box number rather than remitting to the corporation.

The location of the post office box is very important since it affects the mail time required for in-mail payments to reach the post office. Several times a day, the bank collects the lockbox receipts from the post office. The bank opens the receipts by company and performs the required company processing. Checks are then deposited directly to the company's account. Details of the transactions handled are either recorded on a hard copy "recap sheet" or in a machine-useable form such as paper or magnetic tape. The company receives detailed information, such as customer name, account number, amount paid, of the funds processed by the bank and up-dates the corporate accounts receivable file.

Exhibit 3.1 Overview of Lockbox System Processing

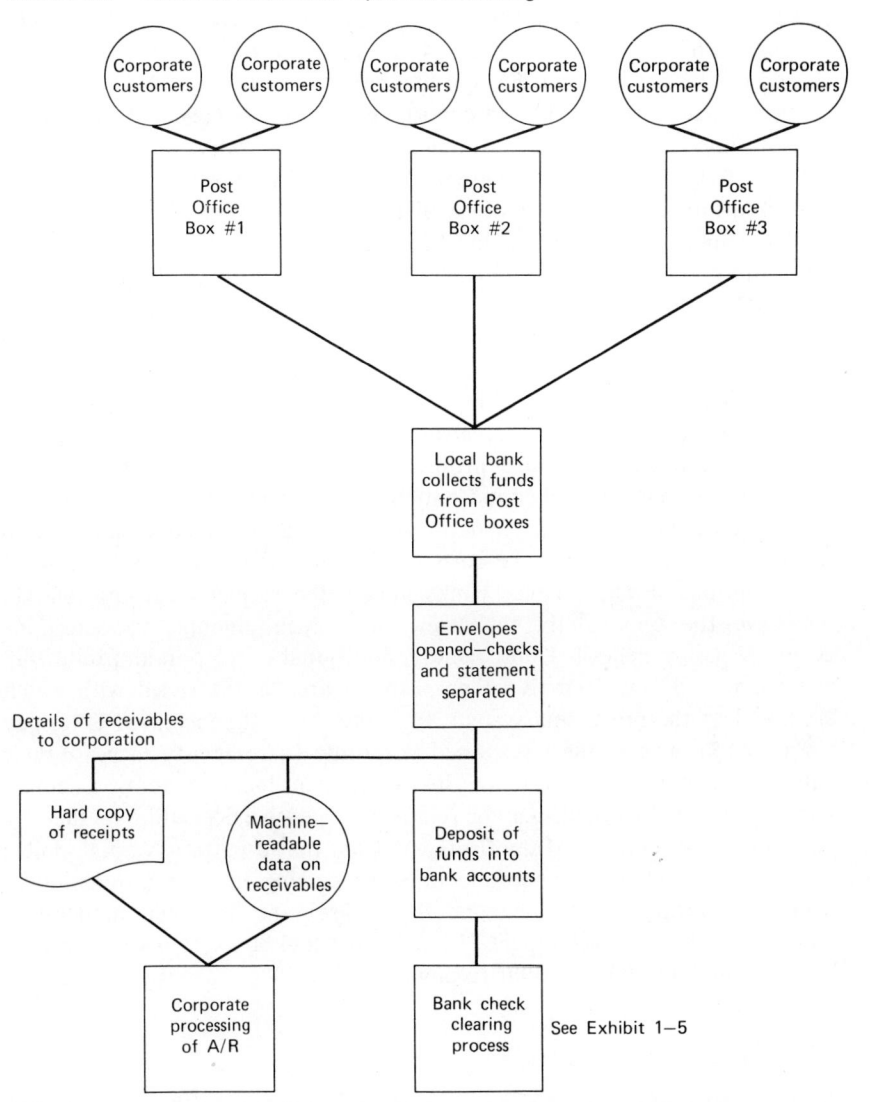

```
                Corporate customers ...
                        |
        ┌───────────────┼───────────────┐
   Post Office     Post Office     Post Office
    Box #1          Box #2          Box #3
        └───────────────┼───────────────┘
                        |
              Local bank collects funds
                from Post Office boxes
                        |
              Envelopes opened—checks
                and statement separated
                        |
   Details of receivables
      to corporation
        ┌──────────┬────────────┐
   Hard copy   Machine-      Deposit of
   of receipts readable      funds into
               data on       bank accounts
               receivables       |
        └──────┬──────┘       Bank check
               |              clearing      See Exhibit 1-5
          Corporate           process
         processing
           of A/R
```

Use of a lockbox system reduces the time required for a corporation to physically handle receivables and to deposit checks for collection. Additionally, collection time is reduced because checks are received at the post office, which reduces mail delivery time. Lockbox services can increase the availability of funds for corporate cash management by 1 to 4 days over in-house remittance processing. This can provide significant additional earning power to the corporation. For example, the interest earned on $1,000,000 for 2 days at a 6% annual rate is $333.34. This is additional income that can be earned by the corporation through lockbox processing, which reduces mail delivery, check processing, and deposit time. If funds collected by lockbox receipts are not used for investment, they are available as compensating balances to banks in support of credit and noncredit services performed.

In addition to increasing the availability of funds to the company by reducing internal mail-processing time and reducing the check collection time, the company often benefits by a reduction in receivables-processing costs. This can occur because banks specialize in high volume lockbox processing and can often provide the service for lower per item cost than the corporation. The company further benefits because its receivables data can be captured in machine-readable form by the bank and made available to up-date corporate accounts receivable records faster than the company using conventional in-house processing methods. Automated lockbox processing systems, described in Chapter 4, describe the processing flow.

Lockbox services are efficient in accelerating funds collection and in reducing clerical work for the corporation, although there are operational considerations. First, because banks handle the receipts, corporations do not have the opportunity to review remittance amounts to determine accuracy before deposit. Consequently, additional correction and follow-up expense can be involved. Another problem area is the speed with which checks clear the processing system. In many cases, the increased efficiency from lockbox processing has caused corporate customers to increase their balances at banks because of the loss of float in local accounts. Lockbox services provided by banks can be relatively expensive depending on the corporations requirements. Many firms point out that if patterns of high-dollar payments are not experienced, lockbox processing may be uneconomical from the corporation's viewpoint. This viewpoint has been moderated, however, with the development of automated lockbox systems designed to handle high-volume, low-dollar receipts.

Pre-authorized Checks

A pre-authorized check (PAC) is a signatureless demand deposit instrument that is used to accelerate the collection of fixed payment types. Exhibit 3-2 illustrates the flow of a typical pre-authorized check system.

Under this collection technique, the corporation's customer is required to sign an authorization agreement with the company that allows checks to be drawn against his account at specified intervals. The company typically signs and sends an indemnification agreement to the customer's bank to

Exhibit 3.2 Pre-authorized Check System. Reprinted by Permission of Crocker National Bank, San Francisco, California

PRE-AUTHORIZED CHECK SYSTEM

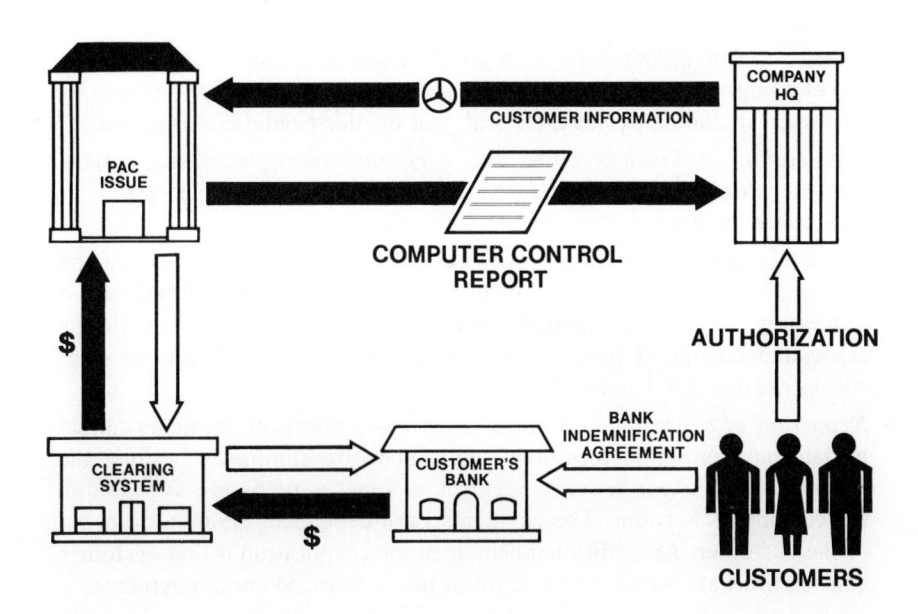

notify it that signatureless checks are issued against some of the bank's accounts. The company takes responsibility for the checks issued and presented to the banks in most situations. The banks are the only receiving parties to the transaction. Following the completion of authorization and indemnification agreements, the company or its PAC service bank produces the PACs on the specified payment dates. Although companies can create the PACs, often cash management service banks provide this corporate service. Under this scenario, the corporation fowards to the bank its file of customers and dates when PACs are to be produced. The bank maintains the files provided by the company and up-dates them based on corporate-generated instructions. Based on computer-based files, the bank issues and deposits the PACs on the specified payment date. Computer control reports, along with deposit and availability information for funds drawn, are forwarded back to the corporation. The checks, often deposited by the PAC service bank, then pass through the normal check clearance process eventually being presented to the customers bank.

The advantages accruing to a company from using a PAC system include:

- *Increased cash inflow predictability*—Through PACs, the dollar amount generated by day is known in advance to facilitate daily cash flow forecasting.
- *Elimination of billing costs*—Corporate-based accounts receivable costs are eliminated because no repetitive notice is necessary to the corporate customer, including postage, clerical, and invoice-production expenses.
- *Elimination of lockbox costs and corporate receipt-handling costs*— Because checks are produced and deposited by the bank, no costs for receipt are involved.
- *Reduction of collection float*—As a result of direct check production and deposit by the cash management service bank, the company-based processing float is eliminated. Additionally, the mail float with the associated receipt of funds from mailed remittances is eliminated since checks are directly deposited.
- *Reduction of corporate collection expenses*—Collection problems caused by late payments and forgotten remittances are eliminated because the pre-authorized check assures payment as long as funds are available in the customer's account. The payment is not dependent upon an overt act of the customer. An additional benefit to the corporation is that customer cancellations are reduced as a result of pre-authorized check payments.

For the corporation using a cash management bank to provide this service, the most important selection considerations include:

- Ability to make timely PAC customer file changes
- Ability to consistently print checks on specified due dates and deposit in a timely manner
- Provision of a competitive collection schedule since many PACs may be drawn on distant points

The type of business transactions susceptible to the PAC application are fixed-dollar repetitive types of payments such as those experienced by insurance, cable television, and leasing and mortgage companies. Pre-authorized checks are also applicable to budget payment plans for utility or other household bills. Pre-authorized checks are issued for 11 months for a constant amount with provisions for a twelfth month variable payment. Through this method, fixed payments may be generated based on historical experience.

Pre-authorized Debits

Pre-authorized debiting (PAD) is defined as a system whereby a customer's account is automatically *charged* for funds due, on an agreed upon date. Pre-authorized debits are also known as "checkless" or "paperless" transactions and are effected through the use of automated bank processing of both the customer's and the creditor's accounts. As a result of this process, funds are automatically transferred from one account to another. Record of payment appears on the next bank statement of both parties. Although there has been much publicity regarding the potential of this method of payment and subsequent collection as an electronic funds transfer application, it has failed to gain widespread acceptance for retail transactions. The pilot program named SCOPE (Sub-Committee for Paperless Entries) in California discovered that even though the system accelerates the flow of cash and eliminates paperwork, there has been significant consumer resistance to this cash control tool because the accelerated payment and clearing of obligations significantly reduces the float available to corporate customers thus requiring larger than desired balances. The transfer of funds is accelerated because "in-transit" mail time, late payments, and physical check processing is eliminated through the use of computer files to directly effect the required debit and credit account entries to the appropriate accounts. Although automated pre-authorized debits are efficient and are touted as the trend of the future, current experience indicates that significant modifications are required to gain consumer acceptance. The flow of pre-authorized debits and their place in the emerging electronic funds transfer environment is described in detail in Chapter 12. The advantage to the corporations using this PAD system are essentially the same as those under a PAC system. However, elimination of PAC production expenses can be considered an additional benefit. The per item charges under PAD systems are significantly lower than the PAC-based charges that include:

- PAC file maintenance—name, address, bank account number, and so on
- Printing charges per PAC produced
- Deposit charge to corporation
- Per item collection charges
- Returned item charges

The use of pre-authorized checks and pre-authorized debits both represent valuable collection techniques in meeting the cash management objective of accelerating the collection of receipts.

Concentration Banking

Even though lockbox services and PACs are commonly used techniques of accelerating receipts, concentration banking techniques are a valuable cash control approach being used today by sophisticated cash managers. Under an area concentration banking system, the corporation's sales offices are often responsible for the collection and processing of customer receipts. This approach places the collection and disbursement function close to the customers it serves. In recent years, this has expanded to include lockbox-processing services provided by local banks to improve cash management techniques. At times, both methods are used by the corporation: that is, large accounts are handled by lockbox services and smaller accounts are processed by local sales offices. From these local servicing banks, funds are either reported to the corporate cash manager or automatically transferred to a central or "concentration" bank.

The primary purpose of concentration banking is to mobilize funds from decentralized receiving locations, whether they are banks or company operational facilities, into a central cash pool. The cash manager may then monitor only a few cash pools to obtain maximum use of funds. The cash manager would then use these regional concentration cash pools for short-term investing or allocations of funds to other required areas within the company.

Exhibit 3-3 is a representative flow of concentration banking. Under this scheme, the sales offices report to the corporate headquarters the amounts deposited each day. Similarly, local banks also provide processing and balance information based on lockbox receipts. At that point, the corporate cash manager effects a transfer of funds by wire transfer or depository transfer check (DTC). The local bank accounts may be concentrated in a regional area first then further moved to the corporate concentration account.

Use of concentration accounts facilitate better cash control. If centralized disbursements are used, the corporation can forecast available cash for investment from the concentration account and invest surplus cash in short-term investments to increase company profits. Additionally, this permits greater overall distribution control of the corporations assets. As funds become available to the corporate cash manager, the allocation of cash resources can be executed according to: required daily disbursements, maintenance of compensating balances requirements, cash reserve for corporate contingencies, and investment of surplus funds in the short-term money market.

Exhibit 3.3 Automated Cash Management Control Systems

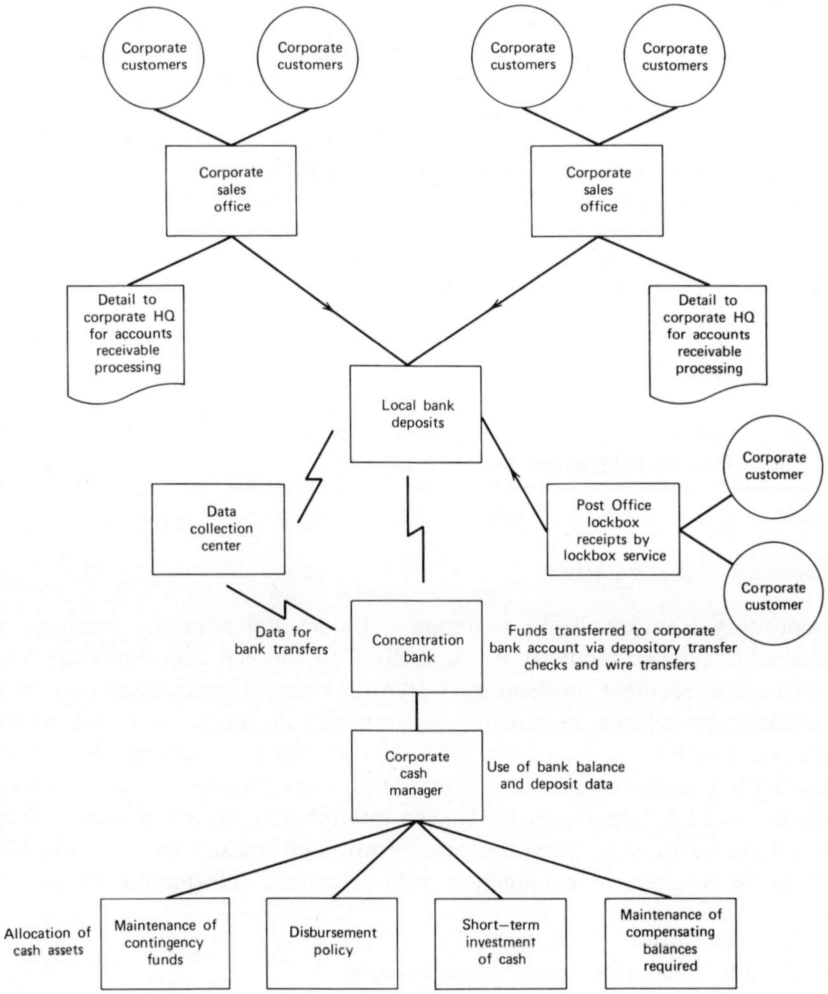

Funds Mobilization

Essential to concentration banking as a cash management technique is the ability to effectively and efficiently move the locally collected funds to the concentration cash pool bank. The two techniques commonly used to concentrate funds are depository transfer checks and wire transfers.

Exhibit 3.4 A Pro Forma Guide in Authorizing the Use and Acceptance of Depository Transfer Checks

"RESOLVED FURTHER that, anything in this Resolution or in any other Resolution of this Corporation to the contrary notwithstanding, any funds of this Corporation on deposit in any account maintained by this Corporation with any bank may be transferred to any other account maintained by this Corporation with such bank, or with any other bank, by use of unsigned depository transfer checks, and any bank in which this Corporation maintains an account is hereby authorized to honor and pay such unsigned depository transfer check, provided only that:

(a) it is labeled "Depository Transfer Check";
(b) it bears the printed name of this Corporation as drawer;
(c) it is payable to the order of a bank for credit to this Corporation or for credit to an account of this Corporation; and
(d) it is presented for payment through regular banking channels by or for the account of the bank named therein as payee."

Depository Transfer Checks

Depository transfer checks represent a simple and relatively inexpensive method of moving funds from one location to another. Since no corporate signature is required on depository transfer checks, banks often require a corporate "resolution statement" to authorize the acceptance of transfer checks. Exhibit 3-4 is an example of a corporate resolution form and Exhibit 3-5 is an example of a DTC. Depository transfer checks are commonly issued automatically by concentration banks against a local collection bank in order to speed the concentration of funds. This concentration of funds is often in conjunction with a deposit information collection

Exhibit 3.5 Depository Transfer Check Example

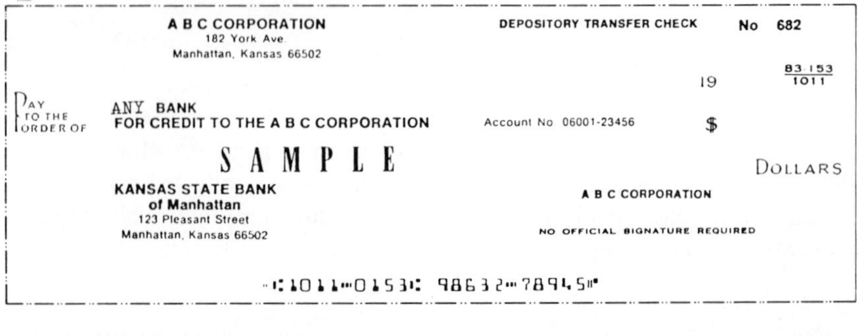

```
  A B C CORPORATION              DEPOSITORY TRANSFER CHECK     No  682
      182 York Ave.
  Manhattan, Kansas 66502
                                                                    83 153
                                                           19       1011
 PAY
 TO THE    ANY BANK
 ORDER OF  FOR CREDIT TO THE A B C CORPORATION   Account No 06001-23456   $
                     S A M P L E                                     DOLLARS
           KANSAS STATE BANK                          A B C CORPORATION
               of Manhattan
             123 Pleasant Street
           Manhattan, Kansas 66502              NO OFFICIAL SIGNATURE REQUIRED

               ⑈1011⑈0153⑈ 98632⑈78945⑈
```

system. Exhibit 3-6 illustrates the operational flow and use of DTCs in a typical application. As illustrated, several areas of a company located in dispersed geographic locations make deposits at local depository banks. The deposit amounts are reported daily into a central data collection service. Usually the data collection center is a nationwide data-processing network operated either by a bank or an independent service bureau. The time-sharing vendors offering automated deposit reporting service include:

- Automatic Data Processing Corporation
- General Electric
- Interactive Data Corporation
- National Data Corporation
- Rapidata Corporation

For corporations using an automated DTC system, the data collected by the service bureau is transmitted at a specified time to the corporation's concentration banks. The concentration bank, based on stored data that identifies each corporate reporting location's bank account, automatically produces a DTC that is deposited for collection the same day. As the DTCs complete the collection process and are presented at the local deposit banks, the checks deposited by the local collection office are also becoming collected funds to the local depository bank. The use of DTCs to concentrate funds is an effective and cost justified method for funds concentration. Cash managers are typically provided by the concentration bank with control reports that are used to determine projected funds availability.

Even though the automated DTC system described is the most commonly used, some firms prefer to internally generate DTCs. Under this approach, each corporate location calls the cash manager daily with the amount deposited, and depository checks are generated by the cash management department. The disadvantages associated with a manual concentration system include:

- *Increased clerical costs for check production*—This is an important consideration when the number of locations are significant.
- *Risks of late deposits*—Bank cut off times for deposits may be missed if manual production of deposits are delayed, resulting in the loss of the funds for one day.
- *Suboptimization of concentration funds*—Because the company must physically deposit the manually generated checks to the bank prior to the bank's daily deposit cut off time, corporations may not be able to collect funds reported later in the day by its reporting location. The earlier the

Exhibit 3.6 Typical Concentration Network Processing Using Depository Transfer Checks

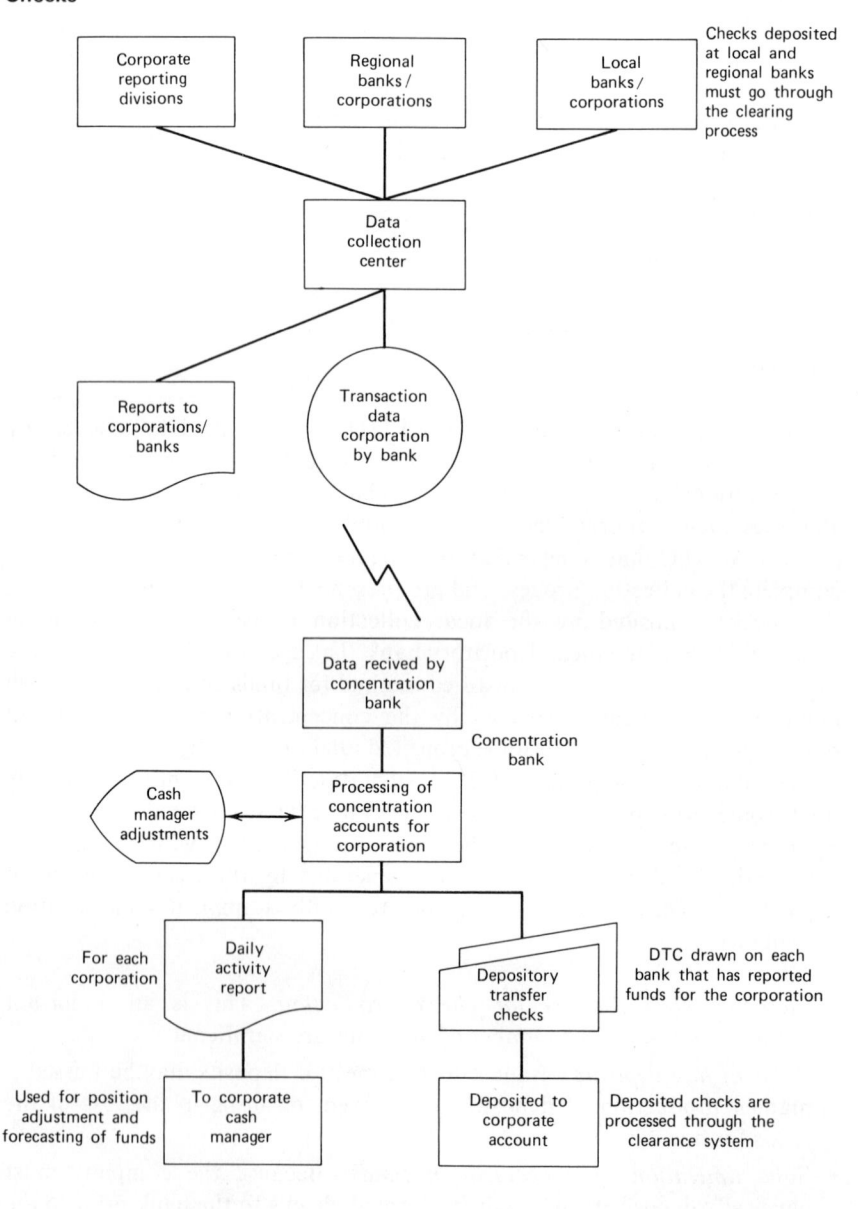

cut off time imposed to reporting locations, the lower the average daily concentration amount.

Although manual systems can be effective, experience indicates that the bank-controlled automated DTC systems are more effective and less costly because the bank controls its deposit cut off times. Therefore, while a company-operated DTC system is required to physically deposit checks for collection by 4 P.M. daily, the bank may be able to process DTCs internally for collection up until 8 P.M. or as late as 10 P.M. before closing its books for the day.

Wire Transfers

The primary purpose of wire transfer is to increase funds availability. It is a viable alternative to the depository transfer check as a money mobilization technique.

Even though the most popular concentration vehicle is the DTC, there is a perceptive movement toward the use of wire transfers to concentrate funds. The primary reason for this shift is the increasing awareness of the value of funds to the corporation.

There are two basic wire services available—the Federal Reserve wire service, which is operated by the Federal Reserve Bank system, and the Bank Wire system, which is operated by a cooperative of bank members. Both wire services are described in more detail in Chapters 12 and 13. In determining the best funds-mobilization technique (DTC versus wire transfer), the cash manager needs to perform a cost/benefit analysis to define the optimum transfer mechanism (wires versus DTCs) and the frequency for transfers. Daily transfers may not be cost justified because deposit amounts may be too small on a daily basis but justified on a twice or three time per week frequency. For this reason, the cost of the wire transfer is being more carefully evaluated by cash managers against the value of funds available for investing. A typical wire transfer cost could be $6.00 in total, which is comprised of a $3.00 charge by the originating bank and a $3.00 charge by the receiving bank. To the cash manager who can earn 6% annual return on funds, this represents a 1-day transfer value of approximately $36,000 in order to break even on funds transferred if only 1 day's acceleration can be realized. This suggests that any transfers in excess of $36,000 are profitable to the corporation. Additionally, the $6.00 wire charge can be reduced by the savings in DTC production costs charged by the concentration bank.

The Bank Wire transfer system operates between banks that choose to subscribe to the system. Usually banks with large corporate accounts use this system to effectively service their clients. The transfer is initiated by the corporate cash manager who requests a movement of funds from one bank to another, possibly a concentration bank in a distant city. The local bank sends a wire transfer of funds to the concentration bank advising it to credit the corporate customer's account and to debit the local bank's balance at the concentration bank. Under this arrangement, the local bank maintains an account with the correspondent concentration bank. These accounts are maintained with the concentration bank to insure that wire transfers are covered by available funds in the concentration bank. Funds are also required in the concentration bank to cover any special handling charges necessary to service the local bank. The concentration bank commonly maintains a cash balance account with the local bank to effect funds transfers back to the local bank when required. In effect, use of bank wire transfers makes funds available immediately because of bank-related accounting transfers.

The integrity and security of bank wire transfers resides with the banks involved in the transaction. Occasionally, banks make wire transfers without available funds in the correspondent's bank account. In this instance, it is possible for a firm to draw on its account the same day presuming the presence of transferred funds only to be notified of an overdraft the next day. To avoid this situation a federal funds wire transfer can be requested. The federal funds wire transfer does not affect the bank account relationship between correspondent banks. Rather, the request for movement of funds is directed through the Federal Reserve wire service. The Federal Reserve maintains cash balances for all member banks. The local bank requests a transfer of funds from its Federal Reserve account to the concentration bank's account. At the same time, the local bank notifies the concentration bank that federal funds are transferred to its account and should be credited to a specified corporate account. The Federal Reserve wire is not executed if the sending bank does not have sufficient funds to cover the transfer. Consequently, with a Federal Reserve wire, the security of the funds is guaranteed by the Federal Reserve and not by the participating banks.

Wire transfers are used extensively though the cost is higher than other funds transfer instruments such as depository transfer checks. However, the same day availability of funds and resulting earnings more than offset the wire transfer expense. Even though the bank wire transfer of $1,000,000 from a Denver bank to a San Francisco bank may cost approximately $6.00, the corporation saves approximately $222.22 in interest by paying down its 8% loan for a day. The larger the amount of funds transferred, the less significant the transfer expense.

Use of the wire transfer system permits the same day use of funds. That is, on the same day that a regional depository realizes collected funds for checks, they are moved to the central depository and made available to the corporation. Wire transfers are often made on predefined criteria. For example, all funds in excess of a base amount (for required balances, etc.) could automatically be transferred from a local bank to a concentration bank account. Because of the expense of wire transfers, they are often used a few days a week rather than on a daily basis. This is an important consideration for the cash manager since the expense of transferring funds must be deducted from his earnings on those funds.

Concentration System Design

Developing concentration systems is an important consideration in any cash management program. It is the area of cash management where maximizing availability of funds is most significantly affected. While no one concentration system works best for all companies, general types of concentration system designs seem more applicable to certain industry types and sizes. Of course, the specific design for a corporation essentially rests on its approach to centralized versus decentralized control of receipts and disbursements, geographic dispersion to be controlled, and the size of the company.

A comprehensive illustration of a fully decentralized concentration system is depicted in Exhibit 3-7 and illustrates a full expansion of a complex concentration system. In constructing a system, a cash manager needs to consider internal corporate constraints including:

- Manageability of concentration points to be controlled
- The number of financially controlled divisions or profit centers to be included in the design
- The degree of financial control over geographically dispersed divisions
- The concentration of large dollar amounts into various locations of the system

In constructing a concentration system appropriate for the cash manager's needs, a decision must be made at each of the three levels indicated in Exhibit 3-7.

Design Considerations. Essential to the concentration design is the definition of the degree of interface between the corporation and its lead bank. If the credit and concentration service lead banks are the same, it is possible to eliminate level B concentration banks if strong financial relationships and simplified control are required. Under this scenario, all local banks

54   Cash Management Techniques

Exhibit 3.7   Concentration System Design Architecture

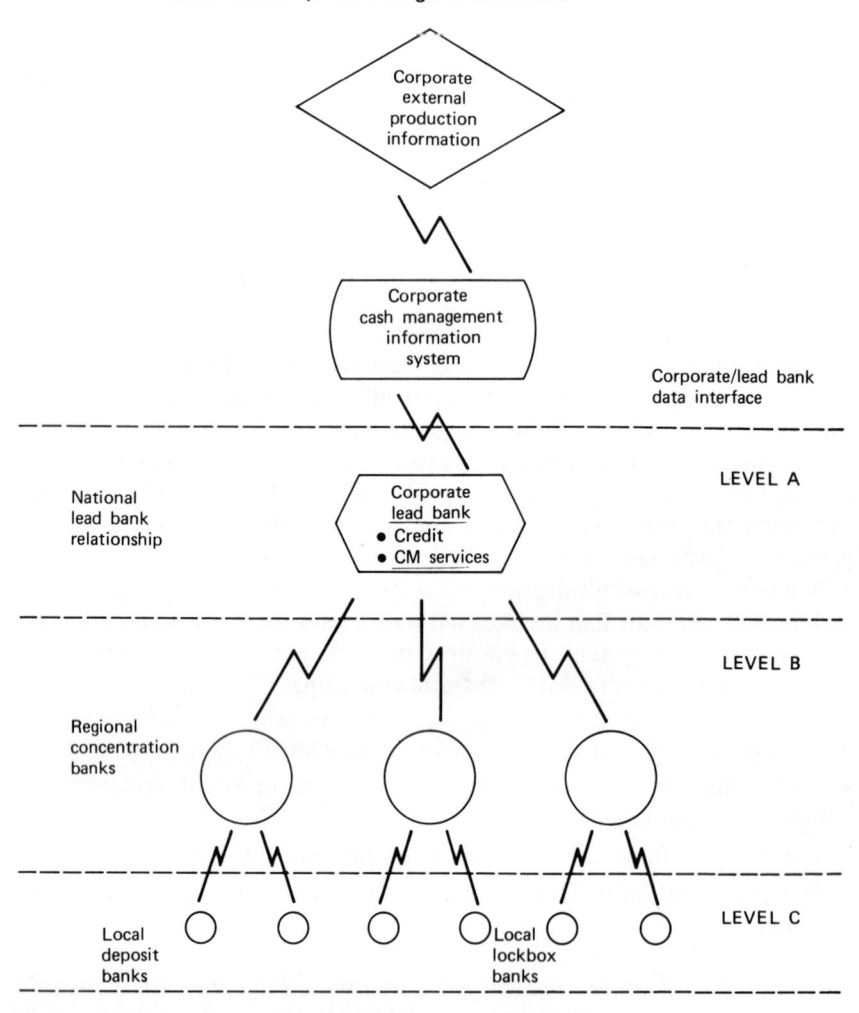

transfer funds directly to the corporation lead bank. This single node approach is the simplest for the cash manager since account monitoring and interface is required with only a one-lead bank. If a national network is involved, a two-lead bank design might be appropriate. A limited-lead bank/corporate interface design would appeal to corporations that:

- Maintain limited cash management staffs
- Support a limited number of local lockbox or depository banks nationally

- Exercise highly centralized financial control over all corporate locations (funding and disbursement)
- Generate limited requirements for credit services in local communities

Although use of a single or dual node interface for corporate concentration systems is rare, its use is increasing as credit and corporate operational services are separated in the cash manager's approach to bank interaction. Though not widely used, limiting concentration nodes represents the simplest control mechanism because the cash manager controls a limited number of accounts in a central location. The primary disadvantage is the diminished contact with local banks, which is an important consideration if financing is required by local operating units.

Regional concentration banks illustrated in level B represent another decision level for the cash manager. Traditionally, regional concentration banks have been used to concentrate funds using DTCs from local deposit accounts. The regional deposit banks are also used for credit services, depending upon the corporations geographic distribution. Regional concentration banks have traditionally been used to increase the concentration of funds into useable cash pools. With increasing use of wire transfers (for amounts of approximately $40,000 or more), use of regional banks for concentration are of less importance. In deciding on the use of regional concentration banks in the system, the cash manager evaluates the pattern and amounts of local deposits so a cost/benefit analysis may be performed to determine the optimal use of wire transfers that may simplify the concentration system by eliminating regional concentration banks. The elimination of regional concentration banks:

- Reduce the bank account monitoring by the cash manager
- Reduce overall cash management expenses
- Increase contact with local depository banks

The number of regional concentration banks, if required, should be determined by the geographic location of corporate profit centers.

Local depository and lockbox banks illustrated in level C are essential because physical proximity to deposits made by locations or receipts collected affects funds availability and the physical size of the cash pool. Consequently, in defining the number of local banks to be used, emphasis should be placed on overall system optimization. If several local banks can be combined, the total periodic deposit may justify a wire transfer for funds concentration as opposed to DTCs. If this occurs, a regional concentration bank may be eliminated along with its attendant expenses. As described later, there are several cash management lockbox-optimization models offered by banks to assist cash managers in defining the optimal selection of lockbox locations. Defining the number of required local banks, however, is more involved because of possible requirements for credit services by various profit centers.

Disbursement Control Techniques

Accelerating collections represent one side of cash management, and delaying funds outflow is the other side of the coin. Cash managers today are viewing the delay of cash outflow as a cash management tool as aggressively as they have approached the increased efficiency of funds collection. It is through the combination of both approaches that optimization of the cash position can be realized. Optimization must take into account fair compensation to banks as well as maximization of the use of funds. Maintaining control over cash is accomplished both through acceleration of receivables collections and delay of payments in order to earn income or provide cash liquidity.

Centralization of Payables

No single corporate action can more effectively control cash outflow than centralization of corporate payables. This allows the cash manager to evaluate the timing of payments coming due for the entire corporation and schedule payments based on system-wide needs. Centralized disbursement activity also permits more efficient and effective monitoring of account balances and current float positions. Payables deceleration occurs, for example, when the payables department centralized in California pays suppliers in Massachusetts with checks drawn on California banks.

Payables centralization also allows the cash manager to take the optimal economic time in settlement of obligations. This is accomplished by evaluating the terms of the purchasing agreement or industry standard and disbursing only as required to optimize the financial benefit to the company. Early disbursements can be as wasteful and uneconomical for a corporation as can late payments that result in loss of discounts or penalty charges. For example, by paying an invoice amount of $20,000 in 15 days rather than taking the full 60 days, a company loses potential investment income of $150, assuming those funds could be invested at 6% in a short-term instrument. Conversely, delayed payment can also be costly to a cash management-minded firm if it results in loss of cash discounts. For example, if a corporation buys on terms of 1/10 net 30 and does not pay within the discount period, he has in effect paid 18% per year for the funds (amount due) for the 20 days used. Through use of centralized accounts payable, corporations are able to better control and execute the corporate philosophy regarding funds payment. Additionally, the responsibility for this function is centered in one accountable person—the cash manager.

Playing the Float

Float is the sum of the outstanding corporate checks (checks not presented to the bank) at any time. Even though the collected balance in the bank's account may be $500,000, the company's book balance may only be $200,000 because it has issued $300,000 in payments. The disbursement float of $300,000 is available to the corporation to use until those checks are presented for payment. Float on the collection side is the difference between the bank's ledger balance and the collected balance in an account. The float difference is that amount banks are in the process of collecting. Playing the float or "riding the float" is becoming more important as a cash management technique used in conjunction with the deceleration of cash outflows. The object of a corporate strategy that slows cash outflows (lengthening payment times) is to provide funds for short-term investment. Under this concept, money can be used in three places at once. That is, a company can issue payment and receive credit for the firm's receivable account with the payee while the uncollected funds are invested in a short-term, income-producing instrument. These same funds can also be used by the local bank as compensating balances for the corporation's lines of credit if a dynamic float analysis is not used or double counting is used, even though depository transfer checks have been issued.

Float in terms of decelerating payables is affected by 1) mail delivery, 2) check-processing time, and 3) collection of funds. Exhibit 3-8 illustrates the disbursement flow and how each area can affect the outflow of funds from the company's account. Float can be increased first by issuing the payables check against a distant bank. In this manner, the maximum check clearance time is realized by the corporation. Although the maximum Federal Reserve clearance time stated is 2 days, in reality it often takes longer for the physical check to be presented against the issuing account. Consequently, issuing checks on small country banks that do not enjoy frequent delivery schedules from the Federal Reserve results in longer clearances.

Another method sometimes used by corporations is delayed postmarks. This is important because discounts are based generally on postmarked dates not the actual date received. Consequently, a company could postmark a payable on Friday, have it mailed on Monday and gain three days float on the funds as well as gaining the cash discount. This technique is not generally recommended since credibility with suppliers is jeopardized.

Cash Management Techniques

Exhibit 3.8 Techniques Used to Increase Corporate Float Funds

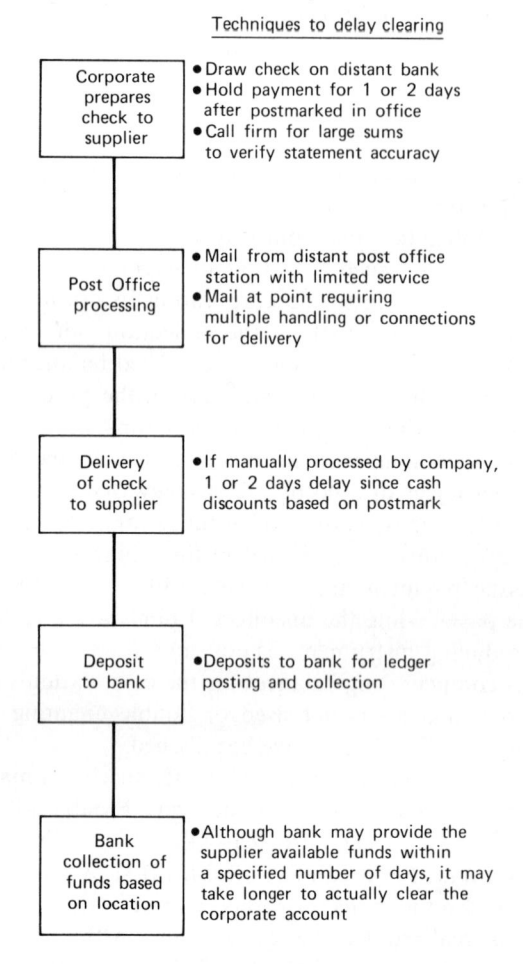

Techniques to delay clearing

Stage	Techniques
Corporate prepares check to supplier	• Draw check on distant bank • Hold payment for 1 or 2 days after postmarked in office • Call firm for large sums to verify statement accuracy
Post Office processing	• Mail from distant post office station with limited service • Mail at point requiring multiple handling or connections for delivery
Delivery of check to supplier	• If manually processed by company, 1 or 2 days delay since cash discounts based on postmark
Deposit to bank	• Deposits to bank for ledger posting and collection
Bank collection of funds based on location	• Although bank may provide the supplier available funds within a specified number of days, it may take longer to actually clear the corporate account

Mailing funds from remotely located post offices (see Chapter 4) can also help to maximize the length of time it takes payments to reach vendors. This provides additional mail system-supplied time for cash utilization, but is not generally used or encouraged by cash managers.

When funds are received by suppliers they must be processed, usually resulting in a 1-day utilization of funds for the corporation if a lockbox system is not used. Finally, the bank must collect the funds through the clearance system described in Chapter 1. Issuing checks on banks in remote locations results in the maximum time for funds collection.

The objective in playing the float is to track disbursements through central bank accounts and not through company books, while only maintaining balances sufficient to cover bank services and daily transactions. Consequently, the company's books can often show a negative cash balance.

It must be noted that in some states it is illegal to write checks unless sufficient funds are on hand to cover the obligation. The cash manager must work with collected bank balances and not the bank's ledger balance, which reflects deposited but uncollected checks. Otherwise a cash manager could easily find himself drawing on uncollected funds as a source for making short-term investments. Most banks charge a firm for use of uncollected funds at a rate in excess of the company's loan agreements; consequently, the penalties outweight the short-term investment opportunities.

Disbursement Services

Zero Balance Accounts. Zero balance accounts (ZBA) are special disbursement accounts having a zero dollar balance on which checks are written. As checks are presented to this account (Exhibit 3-9) for payment (causing a negative balance), funds are automatically transferred from a central control account. From a bank's viewpoint, zero balance accounts require special attention because of a 1-day delay in funds collection at some banks. This occurs because the automated posting systems often used post credits to accounts first and then records the daily charges. This posting sequence is reasonable for normal demand accounts; however, with a zero balance account, the transfer of funds to the account is often for yesterday's overdraft. A negative balance is, therefore, registered until funds are deposited when the balance returns to zero. Current daily charges are incurred causing an overdraft for payment the next day. Often use of zero balance accounts requires that an equivalent day's charges be on balance in the account to reduce the "overdrawn" status of the account. When a 1-day balance is not required and the "control" account is not at the zero balance account bank, funds may have to be wire transferred to the receiving bank. Although some banks require the average daily deposit amount, more sophisticated banks operate a true zero balance accounting system whereby all debits to zero balance accounts are automatically funded from the concentration account on a same day basis. Zero balance accounts are helpful in cash management because cash balances can be reduced to only that required to cover all daily transactions presented for payment. Additionally, it provides centralized and current data on transactions made by geographically dispursed operating units.

Exhibit 3.9 Zero Balance Disbursement Flow, Alpha Corporation

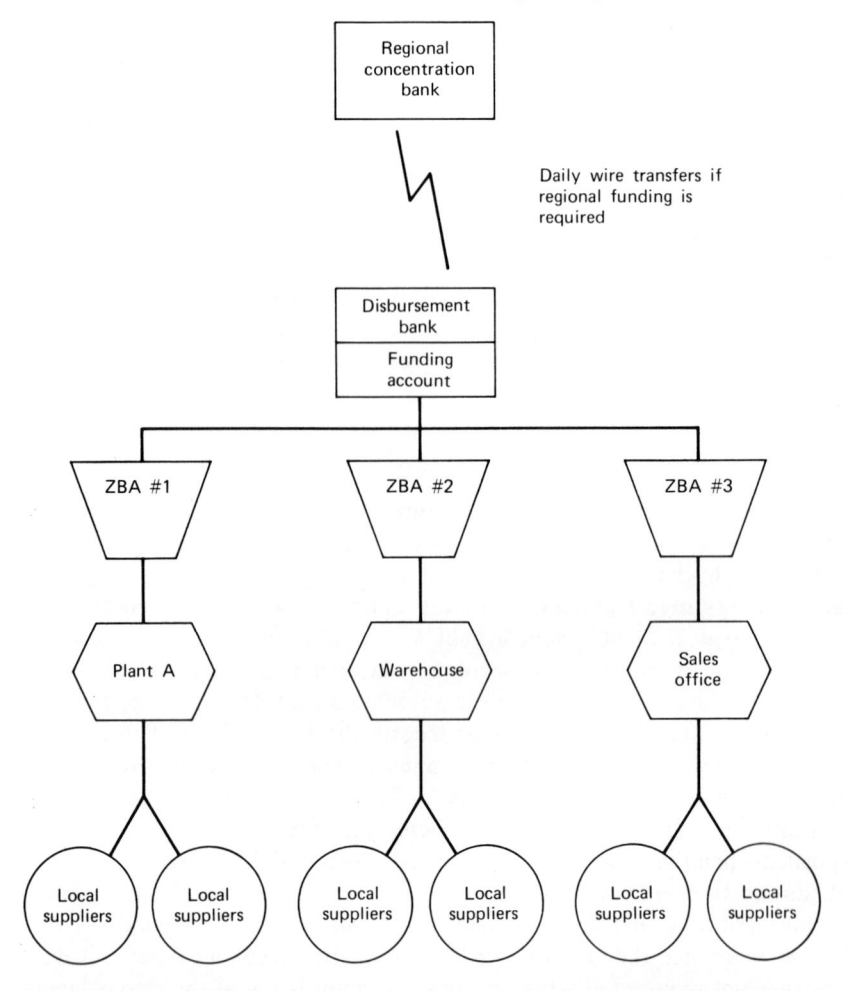

Zero balance accounts facilitate the decentralized disbursement of cash in the cash management system. The major benefits of zero balance accounting include:

- Centralized cash control but decentralized disbursements
- Elimination of imprest accounts or balances at outlaying banks thus freeing funds
- Extension of disbursement float thereby increasing the available cash pool

The primary benefit to the cash manager of zero balance accounts is the simplification gained by dealing with one main control account, while permitting each division or profit center to maintain its disbursement autonomy. Exhibit 3-9 illustrates how a ZBA account can be used to reduce the number of bank accounts monitored by the cash manager, thus providing increased centralized control while permitting remote corporate locations to maintain their independence. Use of ZBAs can also result in reduction of required imprest balances at a multitude of local disbursement locations and concentrate control in one major bank.

Imprest accounts are demand deposit accounts in which a fixed amount of funds are deposited with a bank by a corporation in order to compensate a bank for services performed. The balance in such an account is never to go below a predetermined level. When it does, funds are automatically transferred by the bank in order to maintain the required balance. Imprest accounts can be used in conjunction with zero balance accounts to compensate a bank for its services. It is a common method of bank compensation at both the regional and concentration levels of banking.

Payable-Through-Drafts. Through the use of payable-through-drafts, a cash manager gains the benefits of playing the float without running the risk of overdrafts or inadvertently using uncollected funds. Additionally, any legal problems involving insufficient funds are circumvented since the drafts are not "obligations" against the corporation until presented for payment. Drafts differ from checks to the extent that they are not drawn on a bank but on the issuer and are payable by him, even though they may physically resemble one another. The bank acts only as an agent in the clearing process presenting it to the issuer for final payment. Although payable-through-drafts are used as an administrative device for legal consideration where there is third-party involvement in the payment process, they are drawing more attention as cash management interest grows. Though banks dislike the substitution of drafts for checks, the use of payable-through-drafts as a cash management technique is still utilized in the financial community.

Although a company using payable-through-drafts should only be required to keep a token balance in its clearing bank, this does not work in practice. The additional operational problems encountered by banks in handling drafts coupled with the respective need to transfer funds to cover drafts coming due has led to many banks requiring a 1-day balance of funds equal to the largest draft amounts being collected. In this manner, banks collect income for the services they perform.

A serious deterrent to the use of drafts must be high-lighted. Banks take no responsibility for the final payment of the draft and consequently do not maintain stop payment or special instruction records; therefore, the company must establish and maintain this process.

Remote Bank Disbursements. As outlined previously, remote bank disbursement points can play a significant role in controlling cash outflows. In the past 5 years, the growing trend of many corporations is the use of remotely located banks for check issuance.

The objective is to lengthen the time required to clear a check through the bank. For example, a check written in California on a New York bank may take up to 2 days to be collected. That same check issued on a bank in Guam or the Virgin Islands may take 4 to 5 days to clear. The additional 2 to 3 days are used to produce income for the corporation. This trend has contributed to the resistance of electronic funds transfer systems in the United States because cash managers are reluctant to give up control of their cash asset faster than necessary because of its detrimental impact on the corporation's cash position. Although cash managers are beginning to distinguish between low-dollar high-volume and high-dollar/low-volume transactions in order to reduce low-dollar payable expenses, the use of remote disbursement is expected to continue until the Federal Reserve can effectively reduce actual clearance times. The issue of remote disbursement has moral implications as described by many corporations, since the local suppliers are the parties most often injured by the holding of checks by banks until funds are collected. However, the Federal Reserve, because of the Fed float created, is the party most affected. The Federal Reserve is involved in a continuing program to reduce or eliminate the Fed float created by remote disbursements.

The techniques discussed in this chapter should be viewed as tools with which a corporate cash manager may construct the system that best meets the philosophical tenor of his company. Some firms choose to accelerate receivables but not alter prompt disbursements policies because of supplier considerations. One Los Angeles equipment manufacturer increased his receivables payments and invested surplus funds. However, because of the dependence of his supplies on prompt payment, he felt it unfair to stretch out payments that could cause economic hardship on specialty suppliers. Available techniques must be artfully blended together to conform to the corporate philosophy related to cash management. The corporation must evaluate the possible effects of decelerating payables on their suppliers and any potential credit utilization gaps that might cause future problems. If the potential effect is significant, it could outweigh the profit gained by the cash management program. Conversely, these techniques are valid tools in the efforts of management to use cash as a working asset on which a suitable return must be realized.

CHAPTER 4

LOCKBOX BANKING—DEFINITION, METHODS, AND TRENDS

DEFINITION AND PURPOSE

Acceleration of receivables is an integral factor in cash management programs. The objective is to speed the receipt and processing of receivables and effect a quick conversion to cash. Subsequently, cash is mobilized for cash management utilization. The timely production of accounts receivable statements is of course, the responsibility of the accounting department; however, the methods used to speed collection of funds reside with the corporate cash manager. Lockbox systems are the oldest and most extensively used method of achieving this corporate goal. Through minimization of in-transit funds, corporations can reduce their total annual borrowing expenses. Use of lockbox systems does not alter the cash availability schedule of banks but does reduce mail and corporate processing float time.

Lockbox services are defined as the use of special post office boxes to intercept accounts receivable payments and accelerate deposits for cash utilization. Post office boxes are special to the extent that a bank is authorized to collect corporate mail.

Lockbox processing was initiated in 1947 by Bankers Trust of New York and the First National Bank of Chicago. The stimulus for the development of this service was provided by the Radio Corporation of America, which was seeking new techniques to accelerate receivables collections while reducing corporate paperwork.

The primary purpose of a lockbox system is to collect funds faster; consequently, bank selection and lockbox locations are critical to successful implementation.[*]

[*] Searby, Fredrick, "Use Your Hidden Cash Resources," *Harvard Business Review*, March–April 1968.

The selection of a lockbox bank includes the following criteria:

- The size of the city in which bank operates
- The location of the city in relation to where receipts originate
- Reliability of mail service to the selected city from originating points
- Availability schedules offered by selected lockbox bank
- Availability of wire transfer systems
- Payment flexibility for lockbox services
- Bank ability to provide additional services required

The size of the city is significant to the selection criteria to the extent that lockbox locations in Federal Reserve bank cities usually provide faster and more reliable funds availability. Additionally, the size of the bank operating area may provide special expertise in the development and operation of lockbox services.

Since the purpose of using decentralized collection points for receivables is to reduce mail float time, a careful analysis of required days for mail to reach destination lockbox points is essential. This is the most critical factor in assuring a successful lockbox operation. Determining the mail and float days saved is required to develop a valid cost/benefit analysis. Additionally, the evaluation of mail times is required periodically to determine the economic change resulting from changing mail times. The increasing mail times over the past 5 years have altered the economic viability of some lockbox applications. Exhibit 4-1 is a mail times matrix developed in 1970, and Exhibit 4-2 is a mail times matrix for 1975. A contrast of these exhibits indicates an increase in mail time between many major cities. The longer mail times result in increased lockbox feasibility, which was previously uneconomical because intercepting funds results in increased utilization. As mail times change over time, so does the economic size of items handled through lockbox systems. An item that is economically justified through the saving of 2-days mail float may not justify handling if 1-day float is reduced.

Although funds may be *deposited* faster through local and regional lockbox banks, faster availability is a function of each lockbox bank and requires close examination. Most items handled by local or regional lockbox banks should be available funds in 1 day. If a major bank is used for regional collections, checks have same-day availability if drawn on the lockbox bank.

The cash manager's objective is to consolidate all funds received in a cash pool for better control. To achieve this goal, the lockbox bank should be on the bank wire system or the Federal Reserve wire service. The advantage of

Exhibit 4.1 Matrix of Mail Times Between 12 Federal Reserve Cities (in days)

Sending points \ Receiving points	BOS	NYC	PHI	CLE	RIC	ATL	CHI	ST.L	MIN	KC	DAL	SF
BOSTON	1.1	3.1	2.0	3.7	2.6	2.2	3.0	2.3	2.8	2.5	2.0	2.6
N.Y.C.	2.3	1.5	1.8	2.9	2.2	2.1	2.0	1.8	2.6	2.3	2.	2.3
PHIL.	2.0	1.7	1.2	3.0	1.5	2.0	2.1	2.1	2.4	2.9	1.6	2.1
CLEVELAND	2.3	2.9	2.3	1.0	2.9	2.1	2.2	1.6	2.9	1.9	2.1	2.7
RICHMOND	3.1	2.9	2.3	4.1	0.8	1.8	2.5	2.7	4.2	3.4	3.1	3.0
ATLANTA	2.8	2.4	2.2	4.7	1.7	0.9	2.2	2.3	2.6	2.6	1.8	2.
CHICAGO	2.4	2.0	2.0	0.9	2.5	1.6	1.1	2.1	2.1	2.0	1.8	1.9
ST. LOUIS	2.5	2.6	2.7	3.6	2.7	2.7	2.2	1.4	2.2	1.8	2.9	2.5
MINNEAPOLIS	3.0	3.2	2.9	4.8	2.9	3.1	2.3	3.9	0.5	2.3	1.8	2.8
KANSAS CITY	3.0	2.7	2.5	4.8	2.9	2.1	2.4	1.6	2.9	0.8	2.1	2.3
DALLAS	3.4	3.0	2.7	4.0	2.9	1.7	2.1	2.3	3.0	2.4	0.9	1.6
SAN FRAN.	3.0	3.6	3.2	3.2	3.3	2.3	2.5	3.0	3.1	2.4	2.0	1.6

Source: Reprinted with permission, Phoenix-Hecht Inc., Chicago. Study, 1970.

Exhibit 4.2 Matrix of Mail Times Between 12 Federal Reserve Cities (in days)

Sending points \ Receiving points	BOS	NYC	PHI	CLE	RIC	ATL	CHI	ST.L	MIN	KC	DAL	SF
BOSTON	1.4	2.2	2.0	2.5	1.9	1.9	2.0	1.8	2.6	2.3	2.5	2.8
N.Y.C.	2.5	1.2	1.9	2.1	1.8	1.7	1.7	2.3	2.8	3.1	2.1	2.8
PHIL.	2.2	1.9	1.2	2.1	1.9	1.5	1.8	1.8	2.6	2.2	2.0	2.5
CLEVELAND	2.6	2.3	2.3	1.1	2.0	1.8	2.1	1.7	2.1	1.9	2.1	2.6
RICHMOND	2.0	2.1	1.9	2.2	0.8	1.8	2.0	1.7	3.1	3.2	2.2	3.0
ATLANTA	2.2	2.1	1.9	2.2	1.7	0.5	1.9	1.7	3.0	2.3	1.9	2.4
CHICAGO	2.5	2.4	2.0	2.1	1.7	2.0	0.8	1.4	1.6	1.9	2.3	2.3
ST. LOUIS	2.5	2.2	2.5	2.3	2.2	1.6	1.4	.5	1.6	0.8	1.6	2.1
MINNEAPOLIS*	2.5	2.6	2.6	2.4	1.9	2.2	1.5	1.1	.7	1.9	2.0	2.6
KANSAS CITY	2.6	2.8	2.8	2.5	2.4	1.5	1.6	1.0	1.4	0.5	1.8	2.2
DALLAS	2.5	2.2	2.3	2.0	1.8	1.4	1.7	1.7	2.5	1.5	0.6	2.7
SAN FRANCISCO	2.8	2.8	2.8	3.3	2.5	2.5	2.1	2.4	2.9	2.2	2.4	1.2

* St. Paul is the sending point.

Source: Reprinted with permission, Phoenix-Hecht Inc., Chicago. Study 2, 1975.

wire transfers is to provide same-day funds pooling. Knowledge of deposit amounts is usually available through the deposit reporting systems previously described.

Reporting corporate deposits is essential to decentralized lockbox systems. At the conclusion of the day's lockbox collection and deposit activities, the data collection system generates a magnetic tape for the concentration bank. The data includes the amount of deposits made at lockbox location banks. Total daily deposit amounts are used to automatically produce depository transfer checks against each of the local lockbox or depository banks. Through this method, no additional mail time is lost because DTCs are ledger balances the next morning for the corporation in their concentration bank. While the checks are being collected by the concentration banks, they are also being collected by the regional depository bank. Collection float exceeding availability schedules accrues to the corporation at the regional depository bank. Float funds can be used for credit toward services, whereas the same funds may be already working in the concentration account as collected balances.

An alternative to DTCs is maintenance of accounts with regional lockbox banks and movement of funds as required. The availability of a wire system is essential to this approach to funds concentration. After identifying the location and amount of available funds, the cash manager may mobilize funds later in the day to cover balance requirements, pay down loans, or make short-term investments in the money market.

The payment method is another selection criteria. For low-volume lockbox accounts, payment in balances may be painless and efficient, whereas high-volume low-dollar (high-expense) services can adversely affect a cash management program. Traditionally, many banks offer lockbox services for cost alone or as loss leaders based on individual account importance. Recently, a cash manager in San Francisco received lockbox services free, even though the funds maintained with the service bank were imprest by law. The cash manager's position was that although he did not have an investment option, he did have control over which bank held the imprest funds. As a result, the deposit bank agreed to develop and operate a lockbox service with no service charges.

Inadequate servicing is never worth serious consideration. This is especially true in relation to lockbox processing. Corporations today require direct interfaces between lockbox receipts and automated accounts receivable systems. Increasingly, the ability to provide machine interfaces in transmission capabilities and customized corporate formats will affect lockbox decisions made by cash managers. While the trend toward automated support is growing, the bank must be responsive to corporate processing methods. Concurrently, the corporate cash manager must be cognizant of the inverse relationship that exists between customized servicing and standardization. Regardless of the requirements, the net effect is reflected in corporate expenses.

In recent years, lockbox services have become increasingly complex for many banks, with the attendant result that many banks are less responsive to customized lockbox requests. Problems are aggrevated because many custom-designed systems exist that lack a framework within which to operate. Consequently, inadequately defined operating philosophies have resulted in the design implementation and maintenance of inefficient and expensive lockbox services.

LOCKBOX PHILOSOPHIES

Lockbox requirements developed by corporate cash managers have often opened a bankers' Pandora's box. Banks have often initiated lockbox services without defining objectives to be attained and a general operating philosophy. Consequently, banks allowed the market to dictate the directional development of lockbox services. The requests and approaches developed by corporate cash managers are many and varied. Historically, banks have not given lockbox services the attention initially required; consequently, corporations found willing vendors anxious to provide customized services for lockbox processing.

Although many banks still operate under the customization approach, more innovative banks are developing initial requirements for "uniform" or "standard" lockbox processing. Recently, one of the nation's three largest banks notified customers that hereafter only standard lockbox-processing services would be offered because of the prohibitive processing expense. Although the jury is still out on the bottom line effect, the bank feels that the loss of unprofitable business is a net gain to the bank overall. The controversy over offering a "uniform" versus "custom" lockbox processing is a central operational consideration. Many banks feel that standards beyond the three basic types of manual lockbox processing (covered later in this chapter) are impossible because of corporate requirements. Although many corporations have developed divergent standards, no major effort has been made to establish the price elasticity of demand for "uniform" lockbox services. Exhibit 4-3 illustrates a design for a standardized lockbox service.

Even though customization provides advantages to the corporation, it results in more expensive processing costs and longer processing times. Standardization, conversely, can provide lower costs, although some flexibility may be required by the corporation in use of information produced.

Exhibit 4.3 Uniform lockbox service.

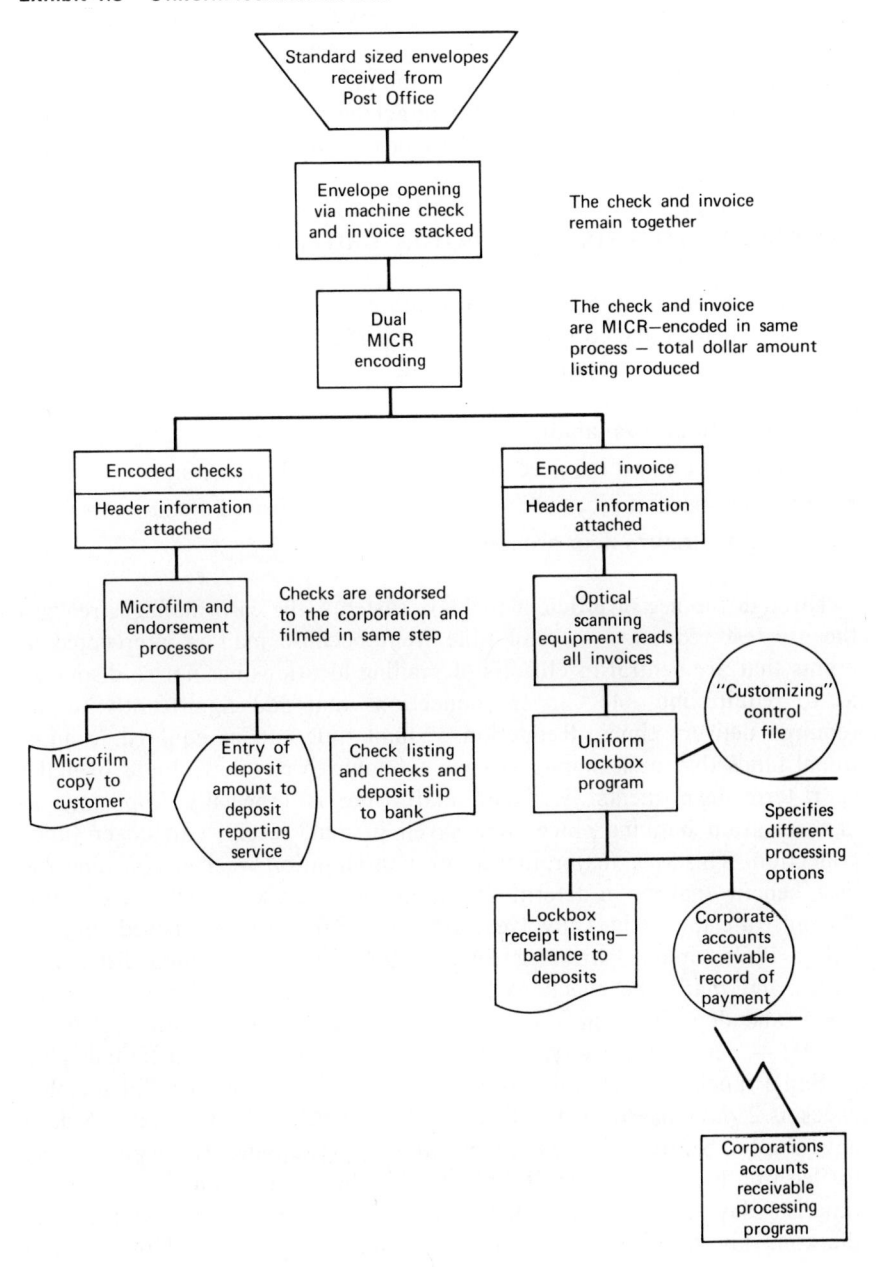

Standardization as a processing philosophy is attainable if requirements are quantified. Regardless of current systems used, most major elements of data are common from one firm to another. An example of common data elements include: previous balance, amount due, amount paid, and late charges. The most significant factor in achieving lockbox uniformity is use of computer-based systems for lockbox processing.

CORPORATE LOCKBOX EVALUATION CRITERIA

The primary motivation for a corporation to use lockboxes is to reduce internal expenses and to increase its earnings on available funds. The basic benefits gained by the corporation include:

- Increased funds availability
- Elimination of staff required for manual receivable processing
- Increased speed of receivables processing and improved credit control
- Accelerated return item processing

Through the use of efficient lockbox systems, the cash manager realizes the greatest reduction in mail time float because mail is intercepted at points that are central to clusters of mailing locations but not so dispursed as to require multiple carrier connections that add significantly to the required delivery times. Reduction of mail time can be equated to additional funds that cash managers have available to pay down loans or make short-term investments. Reduced mail time is especially important in concentration banking since time saved in mail receipt can cover funds collection. This is a major factor for consideration when performing the cost/benefit analysis in determining the economic use of lockbox systems. To illustrate the savings involved, assume a San Francisco-based supplier bills a Philadelphia distributor for $100,000. The Philadelphia distributor writes and mails the check to San Francisco. The supplier receives the check and deposits it in a local bank. Based on the mail time chart in Exhibit 4-2, it takes 2.8 days for the remittance to travel from Philadelphia to San Francisco. The time required to physically clear the Philadelphia check is 2 days based on the Federal Reserve schedule. In total, 4.8 days have elapsed before the funds are available to the supplier. If the check were mailed to a lockbox located in Philadelphia the maximum mail and deposit time is 1 day. The deposited check would thus clear the Philadelphia bank the same day for a saving of 3.8 days. Since the funds are available 3.8 days faster, they may be wire transferred by the supplier for use. At an annual return of 7% on these funds, the cash manager realizes $72.85 from the 3.8 day earlier availability. As the illustration demonstrates, the size of the remittance and the number of days saved are essential considerations in determining lockbox applicability.

Staff reduction, the second benefit to the company, can be an important consideration for retail oriented corporations. Large volumes of receipts require dedicated personnel to handle manual opening, sorting, and balancing functions. Often significant reductions can be realized when banks assimilate these responsibilities. Corporate personnel are always required to check bank-performed functions and to reconcile erroneous items, make adjustments, and answer customer complaints and inquiries.

Corporate processing speed can be an important factor in the retail area. Since credit files are updated to authorize purchases through on-line credit checking, delays in payment recording may result in lost sales and aggravated customers. If a corporate customer pays off high-dollar short-term charges to free credit, the payment receipt may not be reflected on the credit files for days subsequent to payment receipt. Corporate accounts receivable notification may be made by either transmission of magnetic tape files or through facsimile transmission of large item payments.

THE COST/BENEFIT ANALYSIS

The cost/benefit analysis performed by the cash manager determines company lockbox justification. Although the analysis is performed based on company requirements, essentially the same critical elements are evaluated. The analysis by the cash manager may require the cooperation of several departments as well as banks under consideration.

The factors requiring definition and the sources of information include:

- *The average face value of checks received*—This information is required to develop processing expenses for evaluation on a per item basis by bidding banks. Data can be developed and supplied by the accounting section of the corporation.
- *Identification of corporate personnel currently performing functions that would be eliminated by using lockbox services*—The accounting department is the source for this information as well as per hour expenses. These are needed to determine potential corporate cost savings if bank supplied services were used.
- *Identification of overhead expenses that can be reduced or eliminated through bank operated lockbox operations*

- *Definition of the corporate money utilization rate*—This factor is important because it determines dollar value of accelerated funds collected because of reduced mail float.
- *Reduced mail float days*—This factor must be carefully evaluated based on nonlockbox corporate experience versus published mail study times. It controls the time factor in the earnings formula.
- *Processing expense per item*—This expense is the amount submitted by the banks under consideration.

Once these factors are developed, the cash manager is prepared to analyze the cost/benefit analysis. Often the cash manager finds it beneficial to establish the evaluation on a time-sharing system so sensitivity analysis may be performed while providing a standard for future corporate lockbox evaluations. The formulas used to develop the lockbox cost/benefit analysis report are

$$LBXE = LEI * \frac{100,000}{AFV}$$

$$GI(x)_{x=1,7} = 100,000 * \frac{D(x)_{x=1,7}}{365} * R$$

$$NI(x)_{x=1,7} = GI(x) - LBXE + TCS$$

Variables Entered

LEI = Lockbox-processing expense per item provided by service banks
AFV = Average face value of checks received—Developed from analysis by the cash manager, this value can be pre-set at various dollar values.
R = Money utilization rate—This is the rate that the available funds are valued by the corporation. At a minimum, this rate is the corporation's cost to borrow funds. Often the rate used is the same as the internal corporate opportunity cost. When performing a similar analysis recently, a large west coast conglomerate used its 25% required return on investment factor to evaluate the viability of east coast lockboxes. The basic reasoning was that the freed money could be used in corporate expansion projects where capital was at a premium and the payoffs large.
TCS = The total cost saving realized by the corporations through use of a vendor supplied service—This figure is a composite of staff reduction expense and overhead expenses required for internal handling of receipts. This total cost savings can be computed on a volume basis if the fixed and variable expenses are relatively stable over

large-volume ranges. The application of per unit expense reduction varies considerably by company and type of processing.

Constants

The amount of annualized savings in the example is $100,000. This amount must be modified to accomodate the characteristics of each corporation's receivable patterns.

Float days reduced—In this example a matrix report is produced (Exhibit 4-4) illustrating the varying net savings and breakeven points based on the number of days saved. This model uses 1 to 7 days as factors.

Exhibit 4.4 Lockbox simulation analysis: annual savings on $100,000.

	AVERAGE FACE VALUE OF CHECKS				
	$10	$50	$100	$500	$1000
MAIL FLOAT DAYS REDUCED					
ONE DAY VALUE	(475.34)	(75.34)	(25.34)	14.66	19.66
TWO DAY VALUE	(450.68)	(50.68)	(0.68)	39.32	44.32
THREE DAY VALUE	(426.03)	(26.03)	23.97	63.97	68.97
FOUR DAY VALUE	(401.37)	(1.37)	48.63	88.63	93.63
FIVE DAY VALUE	(376.71)	23.29	73.29	113.29	118.29
SEVEN DAY VALUE	(327.40)	72.60	122.60	162.60	167.60

MODEL ASSUMPTIONS					
CAPITAL RATE	0.09	9.00	–	–	–
LBX EXP PER ITEM	0.05	–	–	–	–
CORPORATE SAVING	–	–	–	–	–

ENTER CAPITAL UTILIZATION RATE ?9.00

ENTER LBX EXPENSE PER ITEM ?.10

ENTER AMOUNT OF CORPORATE SAVINGS ?0.00

SET PAPER THEN TYPE C/R ?

Exhibit 4.4 (*Continued*)

| | AVERAGE FACE VALUE OF CHECKS |||||
	$10	$50	$100	$500	$1000
MAIL FLOAT DAYS REDUCED					
ONE DAY VALUE	(975.34)	(175.34)	(75.34)	4.66	14.66
TWO DAY VALUE	(950.68)	(150.68)	(50.68)	29.32	39.32
THREE DAY VALUE	(926.03)	(126.03)	(26.03)	53.97	63.97
FOUR DAY VALUE	(901.37)	(101.37)	(1.37)	78.63	88.63
FIVE DAY VALUE	(876.71)	(76.71)	23.29	103.29	113.29
SEVEN DAY VALUE	(827.40)	(27.40)	72.60	152.60	162.60
MODEL ASSUMPTIONS					
CAPITAL RATE	0.09	9.00	–	–	–
LBX EXP PER ITEM	0.10	–	–	–	–
CORPORATE SAVING	–	–	–	–	–

Derived Factors

GI = The gross income derived from the dollar savings for 1 to 7 days.
NI = The net income for 1 to 7 days given the variables input.
$LBXE$ = The total lockbox expense based on the annualized dollar amount and the average face value of the check received.

An example of the lockbox analysis report using three different cost per item and money utilization rate estimates is presented in Exhibit 4-4. As

Exhibit 4.4 (*Continued*)

	AVERAGE FACE VALUE OF CHECKS				
	$10	$50	$100	$500	$1000
MAIL FLOAT DAYS REDUCED					
ONE DAY VALUE	(1975.34)	(375.34)	(175.34)	(15.34)	4.66
TWO DAY VALUE	(1950.68)	(350.68)	(150.68)	9.32	29.32
THREE DAY VALUE	(1926.03)	(326.03)	(126.03)	33.97	53.97
FOUR DAY VALUE	(1901.37)	(301.37)	(101.37)	58.63	78.63
FIVE DAY VALUE	(1876.71)	(276.71)	(76.71)	83.29	103.29
SEVEN DAY VALUE	(1827.40)	(227.40)	(27.40)	132.60	152.60
MODEL ASSUMPTIONS					
CAPITAL RATE	0.09	9.00	–	–	–
LBX EXP PER ITEM	0.20	–	–	–	–
CORPORATE SAVING	–	–	–	–	–

indicated in the reports, the higher the value of the checks received, the lower the breakeven point. Of course, the amount of savings that the corporation realizes is another significant factor in the evaluation.

By implementing this model or one similar, a cash manager can quantifiably demonstrate the benefits of establishing a lockbox service and realize increased use of otherwise dormant funds.

Exhibit 4.4 (*Continued*)

	AVERAGE FACE VALUE OF CHECKS				
	$10	$50	$100	$500	$1000
MAIL FLOAT DAYS REDUCED					
ONE DAY VALUE	(2975.34)	(575.34)	(275.34)	(35.34)	(5.34)
TWO DAY VALUE	(2950.68)	(550.68)	(250.68)	(10.68)	19.32
THREE DAY VALUE	(2926.03)	(526.03)	(226.03)	13.97	43.97
FOUR DAY VALUE	(2901.37)	(501.37)	(201.37)	38.63	68.63
FIVE DAY VALUE	(2876.71)	(476.71)	(176.71)	63.29	93.29
SEVEN DAY VALUE	(2827.40)	(427.40)	(127.40)	112.60	142.60
MODEL ASSUMPTIONS					
CAPITAL RATE	0.09	9.00	–	–	–
LBX EXP PER ITEM	0.30	–	–	–	–
CORPORATE SAVING	–	–	–	–	–

OPTIMIZING CORPORATE LOCKBOX LOCATIONS

Essential to the efficient operation of a lockbox system is the optimal selection of lockbox location cities. Since many firms are involved in national receipts, it becomes an involved problem to determine optimal location points for establishing lockboxes. Since this is part of the evaluation criteria banks can often be of assistance in the selection process. Many banks have developed elaborate optimization models with regularly scheduled up-dates on mail time surveys. The fact that a bank is involved in this level of development is a strong indication to the cash manager that the bank is professional and understands how to evaluate the lockbox location problem. In some cases, banks lacking internal model capability can perform analysis on a purchased time-sharing facility. The number of cities involved nationally and varying mail times make the use of these types of services necessary in order to be assured of an optimal lockbox location configuration.

One model offered by many banks nationally is the Phoenix–Hecht lockbox location model. The data is prepared by the cash manager to include:

- *Monthly receipts*—These are the monthly receipts by state for the corporation.
- *Cost of capital*—Similar to the previous example, this is the internal ROI or the annual short-term money rate.
- *Receiving city*—The city where receipts are currently sent receives this designation.
- *Processing time*—This is the time required to currently process receipts in order to be deposited in a bank
- *Average bank clearing time*—The average availability offered by most banks is reflected here. For example, the Federal Reserve offers clearance schedules of 1 to 2 days.
- *Special city considerations*—This permits the use of a specified city

Exhibit 4-5 is an example of the matrix developed from this model. This model is extremely useful in determining the number of lockbox locations after the lockbox decision has been made based on the economic factors. Based on the receipt patterns, the point of diminishing savings can be

Exhibit 4.5 Output example of lockbox optimization location. Reprinted with permission, Phoenix-Hecht Inc; Chicago, Illinois.

```
*** ANALYSIS OF LOCK-BOX SYSTEMS
    THE BEST 1 LOCK-BOX SYSTEM IS:
        ST. LOUIS

    MAIL FLOAT............  41,630,542    (DOLLAR-DAYS)
    TOTAL FLOAT...........  78,347,994    (DOLLAR-DAYS)

    COST OF MAIL FLOAT....     11,406
    COST OF TOTAL FLOAT...     21,465

    SAVINGS OVER CURRENT SYSTEM    2,022

    AVERAGE MAIL TIME.....          1.87   DAYS

    SAVINGS OVER CURRENT SYSTEM     .33

    ***DESTINATIONS

            *** 1 LOCK-BOX ***
        ALL STATES SEND TO ST. LOUIS

----------------------------------------------------
COMPUTE
```

Exhibit 4.5 (*Continued*)

```
*** ANALYSIS OF LOCK-BOX SYSTEMS

   THE BEST 2 LOCK-BOX SYSTEM IS:

        ST. LOUIS
        SAN FRANCISCO

MAIL FLOAT............    38,885,822    (DOLLAR-DAYS)
TOTAL FLOAT...........    75,603,273    (DOLLAR-DAYS)

COST OF MAIL FLOAT....    10,654
COST OF TOTAL FLOAT...    20,713

SAVINGS OVER CURRENT SYSTEM    2,774
SAVINGS OVER 1 LOCK-BOX
    SYSTEM............          752

AVERAGE MAIL TIME.....         1.75   DAYS

SAVINGS OVER CURRENT SYSTEM     .45
SAVINGS OVER 1 LOCK-BOX
    SYSTEM............           .12


***DESTINATIONS

          *** 2 LOCK-BOXES ***

                          STATE                        SENDS TO

    AL  AZ  AR  CA  CO  CT  DE  FL  GA  ID  IL  IN
    XX  XX  XX      XX  XX  XX  XX  XX      XX  XX    ST. LOUIS
                XX                      XX            SAN FRANCISCO


    IA  KS  KY  LA  ME  MD  MA  MI  MN  MS  MO  MT
    XX  XX  XX  XX  XX  XX  XX  XX  XX  XX  XX  XX    ST. LOUIS
                                                      SAN FRANCISCO


    NE  NV  NH  NJ  NM  NY  NC  ND  OH  OK  OR  PA
    XX      XX  XX      XX  XX  XX  XX  XX      XX    ST. LOUIS
        XX          XX                      XX        SAN FRANCISCO
```

Reprinted with permission, Phoenix-Hecht Inc; Chicago, Illinois.

```
    RI  SC  SD  TN  TX  UT  VT  VA  WA  WV  WI  WY
    XX  XX  XX  XX  XX      XX  XX      XX  XX  XX    ST. LOUIS
                        XX          XX                SAN FRANCISCO

------------------------------------------------------------------
COMPUTE
```

Reprinted with permission, Phoenix-Hecht Inc; Chicago, Illinois.

Exhibit 4.5 (*Continued*)

*** ANALYSIS OF LOCK-BOX SYSTEMS

THE BEST 3 LOCK-BOX SYSTEM IS:

    FORT WORTH
    ST. LOUIS
    SAN FRANCISCO

```
MAIL FLOAT............    37,524,292   (DOLLAR-DAYS)
TOTAL FLOAT...........    74,241,744   (DOLLAR-DAYS)

COST OF MAIL FLOAT....        10,281
COST OF TOTAL FLOAT...        20,340

SAVINGS OVER CURRENT SYSTEM    3,147
SAVINGS OVER 1 LOCK-BOX
  SYSTEM..............         1,125
SAVINGS OVER 2 LOCK-BOX
  SYSTEM..............           373

AVERAGE MAIL TIME.....          1.69  DAYS

SAVINGS OVER CURRENT SYSTEM     .51
SAVINGS OVER 1 LOCK-BOX
  SYSTEM..............          .18
SAVINGS OVER 2 LOCK-BOX
  SYSTEM..............          .06
```

***DESTINATIONS

    *** 3 LOCK-BOXES ***

```
                       STATE                         SENDS TO

    AL  AZ  AR  CA  CO  CT  DE  FL  GA  ID  IL  IN
                XX                                   FORT WORTH
    XX  XX      XX  XX  XX  XX  XX      XX  XX       ST. LOUIS
            XX                      XX               SAN FRANCISCO

    IA  KS  KY  LA  ME  MD  MA  MI  MN  MS  MO  MT
                XX              XX                   FORT WORTH
    XX  XX  XX      XX  XX  XX  XX      XX  XX  XX   ST. LOUIS
                                                     SAN FRANCISCO
```

Reprinted with permission, Phoenix-Hecht Inc; Chicago, Illinois.

```
    NE  NV  NH  NJ  NM  NY  NC  ND  OH  OK  OR  PA
                    XX              XX               FORT WORTH
    XX      XX  XX      XX  XX  XX      XX           ST. LOUIS
        XX                              XX           SAN FRANCISCO

    RI  SC  SD  TN  TX  UT  VT  VA  WA  WV  WI  WY
        XX          XX                               FORT WORTH
    XX      XX  XX          XX  XX      XX  XX  XX   ST. LOUIS
                    XX              XX               SAN FRANCISCO
```

determined. With this knowledge, the cash manager may then proceed to establish a national lockbox system to satisfy corporate objectives.

Models are often available free of charge from cash management-oriented banks. However, some cash managers may require more customized service. Spanning the gap between the model described and the custom requirements, there are a host of specially designed linear programming models.*

CURRENT LOCKBOX SYSTEMS

Banks offering lockbox services have developed three basic systems over the years. Since there is very little standardization between corporations, these methods offer a framework within which to operate. From this starting point, special operational instructions are usually developed to accomodate corporate customers. The three basic methods are:

- The envelope system
- The photocopy system
- The data transmission system

The first to be developed and the most commonly used lockbox method is the basic envelope system. The functional flow of information is illustrated in Exhibit 4-6. The purpose of this system is to provide the corporate customer with the original envelope and invoice for record-keeping purposes. Since the checks and invoices are separated early in the processing, the probability for loss is high. Significant balancing problems are often encountered with this method because it is almost entirely a manual process. The processing costs charged by the bank tend to be directly proportionate to the volume because of the manual effort required. Since the information required by corporations can vary and processing steps are often dissimilar, training of new personnel is often required because high turnover is experienced in low-skill level personnel areas that usually perform this type of processing. This method is recommended for low-processing volumes where large dollar amounts are involved. Processing peaks and valleys must be evaluated using the envelope method because cycles of billing are not always spaced causing the bank to be inundated with volumes it is ill-equipped to handle. This method is useful for wholesale

---

* An example of an alternative model may be found in: Maier, Steven, and Vander Weide, James, "The Lockbox Problem: A Practical Reformulation," *The Journal of Bank Research*, Summer 1974.

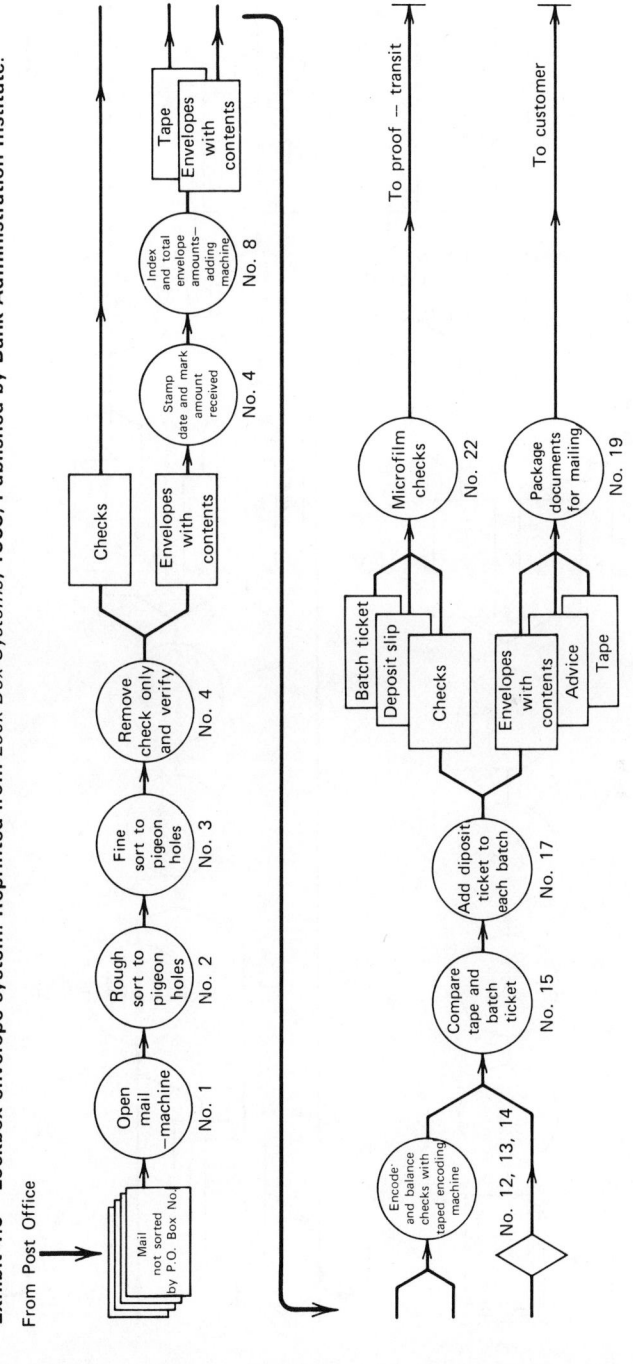

Exhibit 4.6 Lockbox envelope system. Reprinted from *Lock Box Systems*, 1968, Published by Bank Administration Institute.

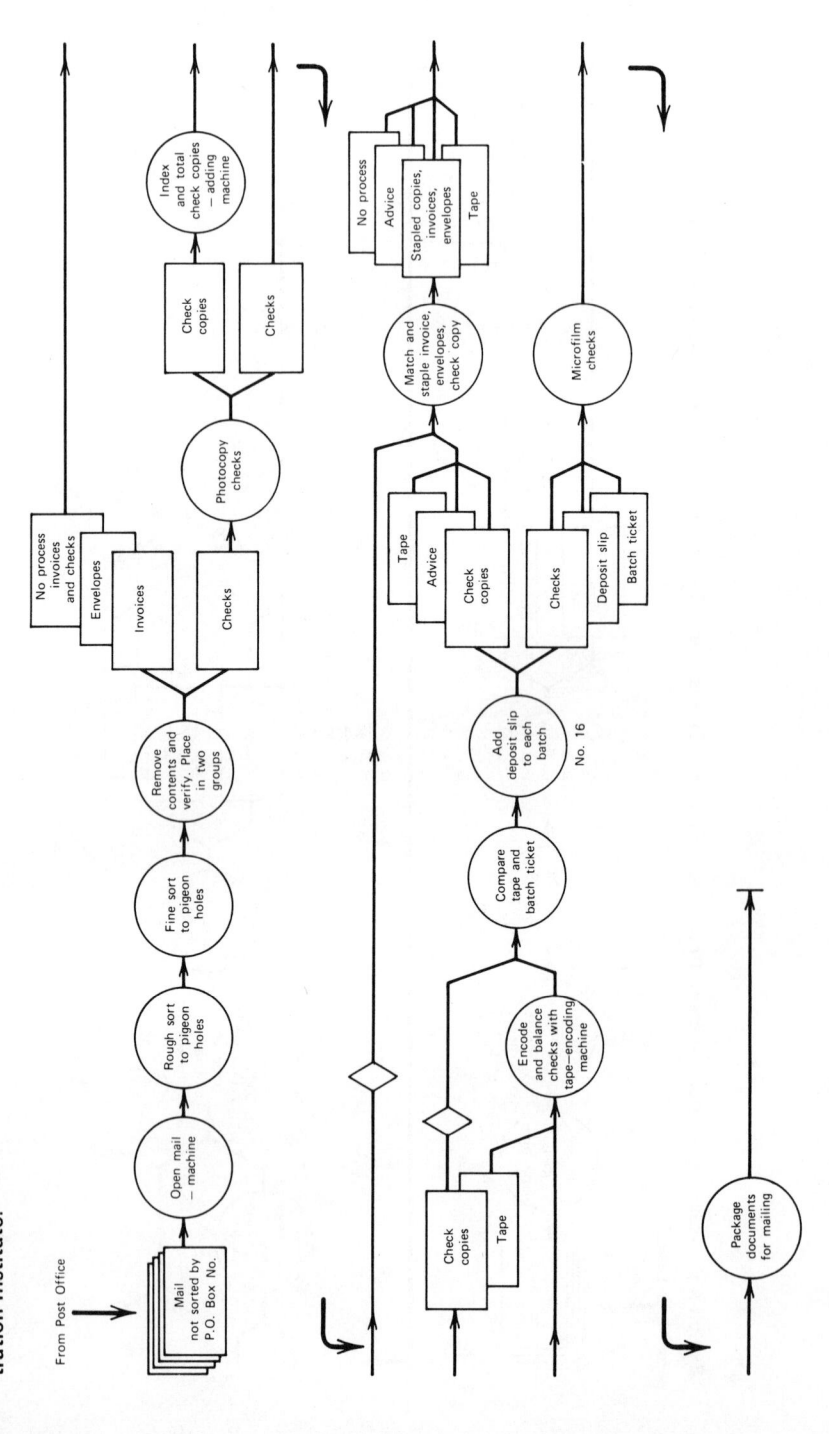

Exhibit 4.7 Basic flow of the lockbox photocopy system. Reprinted from *Lock Box Systems*, 1968, Published by Bank Administration Institute.

82

Exhibit 4.8 Magnetic tape transmission lockbox system. Reprinted from *Lock Box Systems*, 1968, Published by Bank Administration Institute.

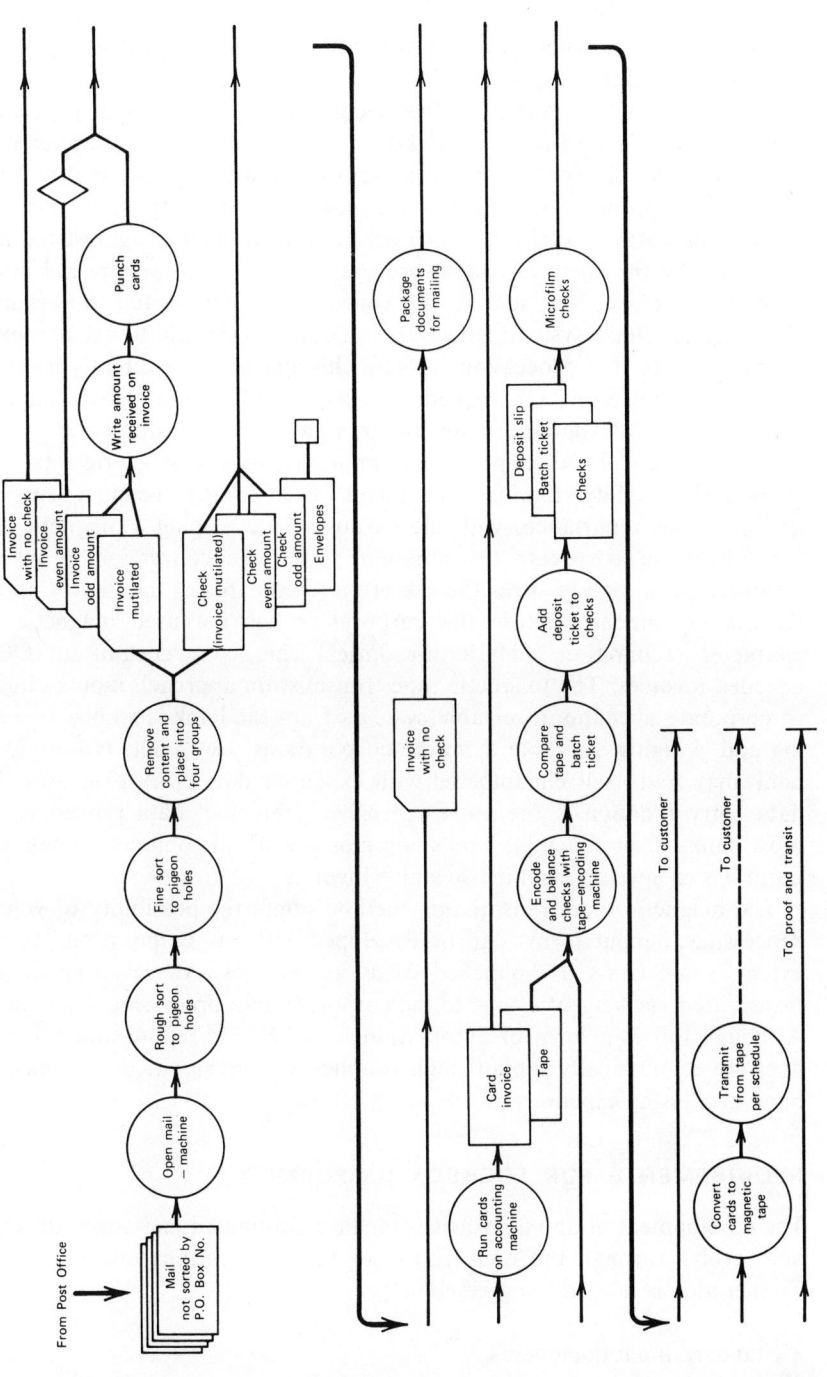

types of accounts where volume and patterns are predictable and dollar amounts significant.

The photocopy method is the second most often used processing approach and is illustrated in Exhibit 4-7. The object of the photocopy approach is to provide the corporate customer with a copy of the check. Under this approach, the corporation pays for the check photocopy and bank labor costs. The check copies are totaled to balance against the tape developed by the check-encoding process. The check copies are assembled with the envelopes and sent to the corporation. This system differs little from the envelope system; however, it does provide additional corporate documentation. The processing costs for this approach are directly based on the volume processed. Consequently, it lends itself to the high-dollar/low-volume market as opposed to low-dollar/high-volume remittances.

The last basic lockbox processing approach uses a magnetic tape data transmission facility (Exhibit 4-8). Under this approach, the bank separates and processes remittances with the purpose of developing a magnetic tape for subsequent corporate transmission. Often the conversion of invoice information to tape involves the use of punched cards or data entry on key to disk equipment because the corporation has not used magnetic ink character recognition (MICR) or optical character recognition (OCR) encoded invoices. The magnetic tape transmission approach inputs directly to corporate accounts receivable systems from the banks lockbox processing and is highly desirable from the corporations' viewpoint. However, the bank may find itself encumbered with expensive data entry processes. The data entry function is the most expensive element of data processing for most banks. Consequently, banks commonly work in conjunction with corporations to develop machine-scanable invoices.

The magnetic tape transmission method offers the possibility of volume processing if input forms can be developed with the corporation. To this extent, some firms use punched cards as invoices. All resulting data is transmitted via magnetic tape to the corporate data processing department. Although this is a form of automation, it is basic in nature and generally does not economically support high volumes without significant increases in bank-processing expenses.

REQUIREMENTS FOR LOCKBOX UNIFORMITY

The development of an inexpensive standard automated lockbox system can only evolve through the cooperation of the corporations and the banks. Cooperation is needed to agree upon:

- Standard input documents
- Standards for machine-readable input formats

- Common elements of input data
- Common set of required output data
- Standards for output media
- Standards for transmission of data to corporate customers

Every company is proud of its particular accounts receivable system. With developmental pride, the data processing department stresses the advantages the system offers over other alternatives. It is this philosophy that must be modified if standard lockbox approaches are to be developed. The use of standard input documents is an essential consideration because equipment can only be developed to handle a finite range of document sizes. The type of equipment includes automatic envelope openers as well as MICR and OCR readers. The reduction of manual work involved in handling input documents and initial entry into the system is essential to effective cost reduction through an automated service. Exhibit 4-9 is an example of a standard input document. Achieving agreement on input and output standards is essential so that a standardized automated lockbox system can be developed. In order to receive substantial cost savings, corporations need to agree upon a set of common data elements to be included on the receivables statement. Since needs vary from one industry to another, flexibility is required to serve the needs of each industry area.

Output developed must, in a "standardized" system, be defined to accomodate flexibility similar to input data elements. The files must contain

Exhibit 4.9   Standard optically scannable input document.

Statement			Company of California P.O. Box 500 San Francisco, California 94150 Please return this portion with your payment.
Unpaid Minimum	Minimum Due	New Balance	Indicate Amount Paid
$	$ 30.69	$ 306.94	$

Please print change of address between lines below

R   MRS LOIS T HILL

P08   RT 5 BOX 3

         OBELIKA AL 36801

Revolving Credit Plan allows you to pay monthly, within 25 days of the Closing Date, either the New Balance (to avoid additional FINANCE CHARGE) or an amount not less than the Minimum Due (which will result in an additional FINANCE CHARGE). See reverse side and accompanying statements for additional information.

335134763 003069400030692 010025

information required by corporations to effectively process its accounts receivable accounting records while remaining within agreed upon structures. Additionally, the reporting media required by corporate customers, for example, printed output reports and tape or punched cards, needs to be defined so that standards can be established. Communication of the lockbox-captured information can be effectively handled by telecommunication between the lockbox bank and the corporation either through tape-to-tape transmissions or direct computer-to-computer data exchange.

Efforts to establish standards for remittance processing are being actively pursued by the National Standards subcommittee and through development of GIRO payment systems. When successful, the standards for data elements and physical characteristics of remittance documents facilitate accelerated development of automated lockbox methods.

UNIFORM LOCKBOX SERVICES—AN AUTOMATED APPROACH

Often the implication exists that a "uniform" approach to problem solution precludes individual options. Uniformity allows for individuation but within specified limits. "Uniform" is defined as limits established in an automated lockbox system that provide required market flexibility. In order to accomodate the market flexibility, a "custom control file" philosophy may be used. Essentially, this approach takes a basic or "standard" set of processing steps and allows for use of options as part of the corporate conversion process. Through this approach, an automated lockbox service can define degrees of corporate customization while maintaining processing "uniformity." Essential to success under this philosophy is that customization is confined to the automated portion of the system. The areas of customization facilitated by a control file philosophy include:

- *Input file definition*—Although the physical dimensions of the input document must be fixed within certain limits to develop a standard service, the number of fields of information received may be variable. This offers the corporate customer the flexibility of capturing some information that can be indigeous to the efficient operation of the corporations' accounts receivable system. As the input document in Exhibit 4-9 illustrates, several additional elements of information may be encoded on the basis of the scanable document. Therefore, while there is format uniformity for input information, there is also flexibility in the amount of data captured for corporate customers.
- *Report formatting*—The basic function of column listing of information received is flexible within the framework of the custom-control-file

approach to lockbox processing. The amount of information reported and the levels of totals developed can be specified by corporate customers. This is a required feature because analytical information, often required by the corporate customer, includes:
  - Amount of daily lockbox receipts by payment type—amount of full invoice payments, number and amount of partial payments, and number and amount of minimum payments received
  - The distribution of lockbox receipts by customer type that is encoded on the invoice—This information can be useful in establishing credit profiles over a period of time.
  - The distribution pattern of receipts from varying corporate geographic areas—These types of reports can also be used to isolate average increases in mail times so physical lockbox locations may be adjusted.
- *Corporate receivables formats*—Using the custom-control-file approach a corporation, within limits, can specify the informational order of elements captured on input and the interfaces between the bank and corporate data processing facilities. This reduces the amount of modification required by the corporation to use a uniform bank offered automated system. In many instances, it reduces input expenses of the corporation because conversion of input documents to machine-readable formats is no longer necessary.

DEVELOPING TREND IN AUTOMATED LOCKBOX SYSTEMS—THE PROTOTYPE

The previous sections have discussed current lockbox-processing systems and suggested that increased automation of the lockbox function results in better cost/benefit performance. Although there are several approaches to automating lockbox functions, most are a combination of automated techniques with a heavy involvement of manual processing. The type of optimal lockbox processing that can be achieved has been custom developed by a large west coast bank and serves as the prototype system for developing lockbox systems over the next several years. The purpose of this section is to:

- Define the development motivation
- Identify lockbox-processing objectives and philosophy
- Define hardware configuration
- Specifically view the processing scenario
- Discuss the features and benefits of the system

The system described in this section reflects an increasing trend in sophisticated automation of the lockbox function by major commercial banks. This is not to suggest that future automated systems will be structured as described, but the system designed is a reality and represents a major breakthrough in lockbox-processing techniques. This section provides a basis for comparing specific processing steps described earlier with fully automated systems.

Development Motivation

Innovation is primarily motivated by objectives. Such was the situation that developed in a large west coast commercial bank. Although the bank was traditionally a major factor in both the retail and wholesale lockbox markets, it felt pressures to change. Although traditionally profitable, the bank found that the profitability of the lockbox operation had dramatically declined during a 4-year period. Declining profits were directly attributable to increased personnel processing costs. Other competing banks in the area discovered the same situation. The basic decision for lockbox-processing banks was whether or not to continue to offer lockbox services because of shrinking profit margins and the increased inclination of companies to perform the lockbox functions themselves if per item prices exceeded certain limits. Although several banks decided to eliminate or significantly reduce involvement in lockbox processing, this major west coast bank decided that expanded involvement in the lockbox market was imperative to achieving cash management service objectives.

Recognizing that a dramatic change would be required to restore reasonable profit margins, the bank decided to establish primary objectives and to view the traditional lockbox function as a new function to be evaluated using modern technology. The desired results of the system included:

- Restoration of lockbox profit margins—wholesale and retail
- Lower total per item lockbox cost
- Allowance for increased volumes without proportionate increase in variable costs
- Increased base of high-volume low-dollar lockbox businesses being discarded by competitors
- Increased lockbox work environment and improved service quality

Achievement of the stated objectives could not be attained using traditional methods reviewed by bank personnel. Realizing that an innovative approach was required, an independent consulting group was used to evaluate the requirements and recommended an optimal solution. During the evaluation stages, the consulting firm, which had no previous lockbox experience, reviewed all existing and announced systems and surveyed banks and corporate customers procedures in order to fully evaluate an optimal approach. The conclusion and recommendation was the development of a unique, fully automated lockbox-processing system.

Design Philosophy

The consulting firm in recommending a unique solution based their approach on a philosophy where existing technology from a number of technical fields could be integrated to produce a problem solution. As the system developed, this meant an equipment synergy to develop a unique lockbox-processing system. Placing the overall bank objectives in perspective in order to define the hardware requirements was the next essential development step.

Implementation of the design philosophy placed heavy emphasis on the hardware configuration. The primary considerations in designing the hardware configuration were to provide:

- A wide range of volume growth with little additional hardware requirements
- High reliability
- Equipment redundancy to provide backup
- System expandability
- Flexibility to satisfy a wide range of customer requirements
- Internal management reporting flexibility

While all the design considerations were important, the reliability of the system and expanded volume capability were of prime importance to meeting the bank-stated objectives. Increased growth was anticipated from expansion into the retail lockbox market so maintaining low variable costs was an essential consideration. Because increased funds availability is a prime factor for companies using lockbox services, any disruption in service would have traumatic effects on customer relations. These effects can be compounded when accounts receivable records are posted late, thus affecting customer credit availability.

Automated Lockbox System Components

In order to achieve the bank's objective, the automated system designed centered around reduction of manual document handling coupled with reduced processing steps by operators. The number of functions performed manually was reduced from 10 to 2. To accomplish this, a great deal of equipment dependence evolved. In evaluating the existing systems, it was determined that no single supplier could configure a system to meet the requirements in an optimal mode. Consequently, a synergy of equipment was configured to satisfy the processing objectives with the intricate interfacing of equipment being performed by the consulting firm. The equipment configuration developed is illustrated in Exhibit 4-10.

The specific equipment custom interfaced included:

- *Reader/sorter* by Cummins-Allison—This equipment was fitted with an OCR and MICR read heads. It was modified by the addition of:
  ◦ *Audit Trail Imprinter* by A. B. Dick Company—This was used to sequence spray processed data.

The reader/sorter is used as the primary input device and as a sorter after processing is complete. To satisfy reliability requirements, two reader/sorters are used, one for input and the other for output. Both are identically configured so that the redundancy requirement is satisfied.

- *Custom designed TV video camera*—This unit was custom designed by the consultants to record a picture of each check and remittance document as it passed the input process. The two video discs used were also custom engineered. Eight television-type terminals were attached to the disc subsystem to provide access.

- *Mini computer and periferials by Data General*—Modified to meet special processing functions, the main frame minicomputer controls the overall system functions and all hardware. The periferials include:
  ◦ *Operator Terminals*—These display video-retrieved images as well as digital data captured on input. Additionally, the key boards reflect the system-defined functions. Each terminal is independent of the other and can act as a direct back-up if needed.
  ◦ *Master terminal console*—This terminal is similar to the operator terminals and can operate in a back-up mode if necessary. Its primary purpose is work scheduling and system monitoring.
  ◦ *Line printer*—Used to print operational control reports (batch control, etc.) as well as management information reports and required customer reports, the master terminal, having a hard copy capability, can operate as a back-up unit if necessary to accomplish the goal of system reliability.

Exhibit 4.10 Lockbox system: hardware components. Reprinted by permission of Teknekron Inc. Berkeley, California.

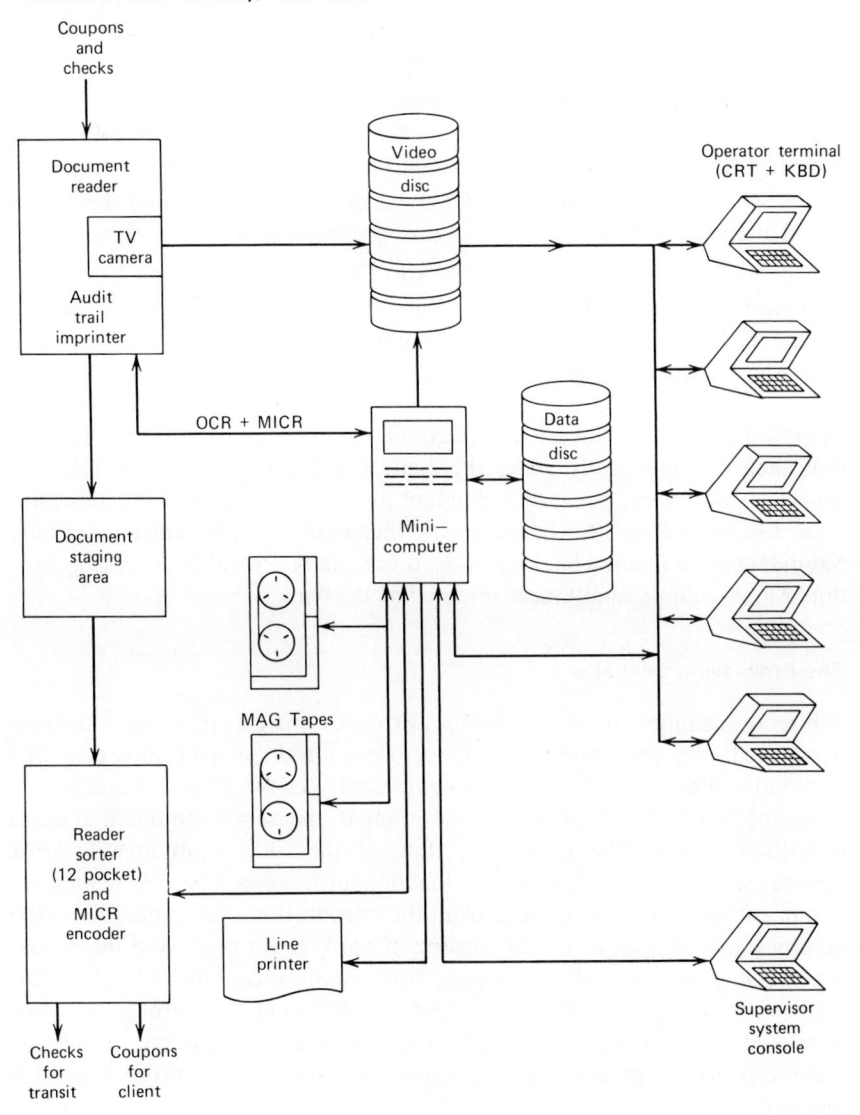

- *MICR check encoder* by Burroughs—With a capacity of 7000 items per hour, this encoder is also interfaced to the system. After processing the checks and remittances, this minicontrolled equipment MICR encodes the remittance checks prior to deposit.
- *Two dual density tape drives*—Operating independently, the goal of system redundancy is satisfied. The purpose of the tape drives is to:
  - Provide machine transmittable data to lockbox customers
  - Generate a direct interface between lockbox processing and the bank's demand deposit accounting systems to eliminate check handling
  - Establish history files in a convenient machine-processable format
- *Digital disc*—In addition to the video disc, a digital disc was directly accessable to the minicomputer to record the MICR and OCR-read data from the remittance documents.

Interfacing between the various equipment was effected by the consultants so that each unit is directly under the control of the minicomputer. The only aspect of the system not fully redundant as the main frame of the minicomputer because of cost considerations. Other than this, all elements are fully redundant as functional back-up. This is especially critical in processing low-dollar high-volume remittances targeted by the bank.

The Processing Scenario

While the equipment configuration provides insight into the functions performed, the processing flow described in Exhibit 4-11 illustrates the interaction between operator and equipment. As the flow is described, a comparison can be made with those manual and semi-automated systems described earlier. The processing flow of the fully automated lockbox service described here focuses on lockbox processing where a remittance document and check is received from the corporation's customer. This type of processing applies to the processing of bank credit cards and the receiving of oil company and department store remittances where balance forward accounts receivables are common. Although the processing flow described is based on this example, the system can accomodate wholesale lockboxes where greater customization is required. The processing flow includes:

- *Document staging*—Documents are received by clerks and opened using Docutronics letter-opening equipment. The remittance coupon and check are separated from the envelope at a rate of 900 to 1000 per hour. The checks and coupons are placed together in a batch tray with checks

Exhibit 4.11 Automated processing system. Reprinted by permission of Teknekron Inc. Berkeley, California.

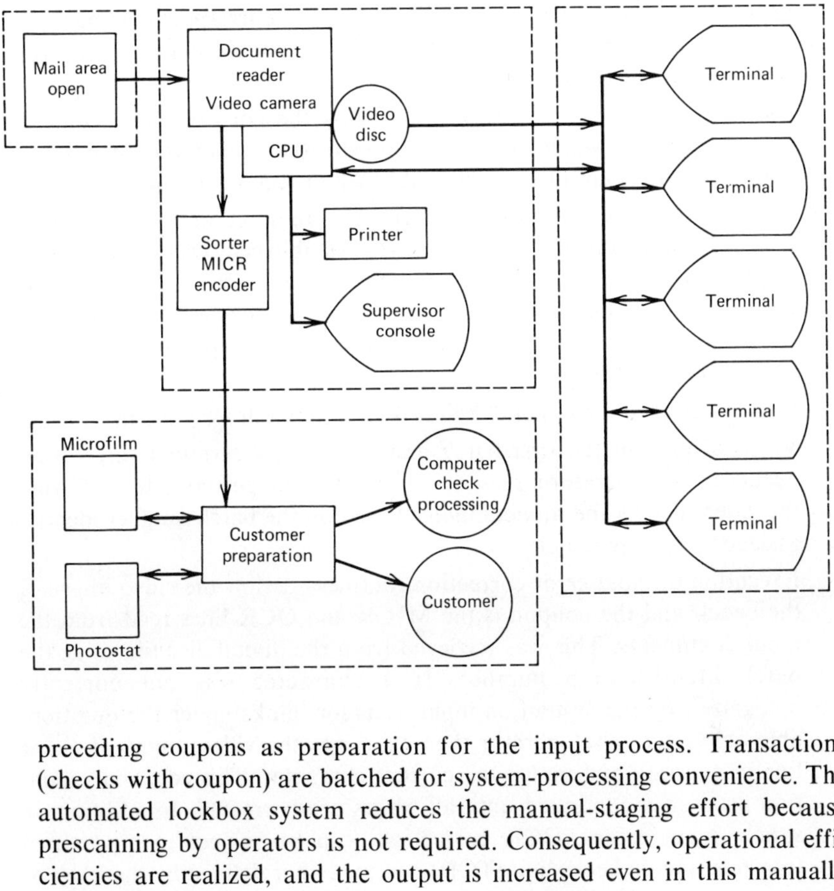

preceding coupons as preparation for the input process. Transactions (checks with coupon) are batched for system-processing convenience. The automated lockbox system reduces the manual-staging effort because prescanning by operators is not required. Consequently, operational efficiencies are realized, and the output is increased even in this manually intensive function.

- *Remittance batching*—After remittances are batched the data entry function is performed through the Cummins-Allison reader/sorter at a rate of 30,000 items per hour. Specifically:
  ○ The MICR line of the remittance coupon (if it contains one) is captured and recorded on the digital disc.
  ○ The MICR line of the check is captured and recorded on the digital disc.
  ○ The OCR line of the remittance document (if present) is recorded on the digital disc. This includes the amount of minimum and full payment for the corporate customer.

- ○ An image of the check and coupon (still in sequence) is taken by the video camera and recorded on the video disc.
- Sequence spraying of the checks followed by the corresponding coupon is accomplished so that a batch audit trail is available if items are accidentally separated or for later inquiry.
- *Outsorting checks*—The checks followed by the corresponding coupons are outsorted in a single pocket. Operators then place the checks and coupons into trays until the functional batch processing is complete.
- *Processing control*—Terminal operators are next in the processing scenario. Overall control of the schedule is established through the master terminal console, which results in batch assignment to operators. As operators process the remittances, the system records performance statistics that are used later in management information reports. Specific terminal processing includes:
  - ○ Log-on procedure by operator that results in batch assignment

    Video display of the first batch item on the TV terminal screen that occurs at the operator's request—The video image was retrieved from the video disc by the minicomputer based on the batch number identity assigned by the batch clerk.
  - ○ Execution of input error correction routines—Below the video image of the check and the coupon is the MICR and OCR lines read from the input documents. This was retrieved from the digital disc file using the batch identification number. If a character was not correctly recognized by the system on input a cursor blinks under the questionable character. The operator then examines the video image of either line in question and inputs the correct character. This edit and validation process is continued until all errors are corrected. In addition, in simple input errors, OCR corrections can be subject to a specified transpositional-check-digit (TCD) routine either defined by the bank or the customer. The use of customer control files provides flexibility in this area. If an OCR line does not pass the TCD check performed by the minicomputer, the operator depresses a special function process key.
  - ○ After edit and validation review, the operator is then ready to process the remittances and check on the display at the video terminal. The operator usually examines the check amount on the screen and the OCR field on the remittance document to identify the payment as a full payment, partial payment, or minimum payment. If a partial payment is received, the operator enters the amount of this payment twice to insure accuracy. The amount of the partial payment is recorded on the digital disc to be used later in the encoding process. If the "full" or

Developing Trend in Automated Lockbox Systems—The Prototype

"minimum pay" function keys are depressed the item is considered completed.
- Before moving to the next batch item, the operator examines the remittance coupon to check for changes of address. If there is a "change of address" key is depressed on the terminal. The operator then continues to the next item until the batch is completed.
- *Entering checks and coupons*—After all batch items have been completed by the operators, the checks and coupons, which still maintain their transaction integrity, are entered into the redundant Cummins-Allison sorter. Based on the function defined by the operator during batch processing, the system separates the checks for MICR encoding to one pocket and the coupons to separate pockets based on functions defined at the terminal by the operator. The function defines which coupons are outsorted to include:
  - Full payment coupons—This classification requires only two key strokes to complete (one to depress key and one to advance).
  - Partial payments—Only four key entries of which two are entry of the amount paid.
  - Minimum payment—Here only two key strokes are necessary since the amount paid is recorded in the coupon document, which is recognized by the minicomputer.
  - Change of address—This classification provides for automatic outsorting of all customers identified by operators in processing.
  - Messages—Special messages written by corporate customers are out sorted so they may be separately identified.
  - Special process function—This classification causes the check and the coupon to be outsorted in the same sequence as received, these will be returned to the customer because something about the document failed on the input edit and validation test.
  - Do not process—This function key also causes the check and coupon to be outsorted together, to be returned to the corporate customer. This is used based on customer instructions for payment refusal.
- In final processing steps, the checks for deposit are entered into the 7000 item per hour MICR encoder. The minicomputer identifies the batch and extracts the amount to be encoded on the check from the digital disc file. To insure accuracy, image verification is performed by checking to see that the position of each item (based on ABA bank number) in the batch is correct.

Following the process described here, any special customer-required services such as photostating is accomplished. Additionally, if the customer requires data transmission of the accounts receivable data, it would be accomplished by creating a tape based on the OCR information off the digital disc file. As a by-product of the check-encoding function, a tape is created for input to the bank's demand deposit system so that the receipts are deposited that day to the corporate customers account. As described, the only manually oriented tasks in the system in order of magnitude are:

- Remittance opening
- Machine entry
- Machine outsorting
- Check entry
- Document return to corporate customers

Special Features and Benefits

Although the prototype system is very sophisticated, many other automated systems can achieve similar results while providing to both processing banks and corporate customers features and benefits that exceed those possible through manual processing. The special features provided by services such as the prototype described include:

- *Single-step processing*—Through the unique use of video techniques applied to lockbox processing, the manual functions required are significantly reduced resulting in lower costs.
- *Control file philosophy*—Each customer using the service has a separate control file identified on the minicomputer by account number. On the control file, special TCD routines are recorded along with indigenous customer-processing instructions.
- *System redundancy*—Each piece of equipment except the minicomputer is fully backed-up, resulting in a high degree of reliability.
- *Input/output flexibility*—This special feature is provided because not only can a variety of different signed documents be read but various positions of OCR and MICR readable data can also be accommodated.

Even though the special features of the system provide for customization and flexibility, the special benefits derived by banks and corporate customers include:

- *Cost reduction*—Reduced requirements for manual processing results in direct cost reductions to the banks using systems such as the prototype described. This permits restoration of diminished profit margins.

- *Price reduction to corporate customers*—Because variable costs can be reduced from increased use of automation, the per item processing costs can be reduced by banks while maintaining profit margins.
- *Increased funds availability*—This benefit occurs to both the bank and the corporate customer through the use of automated systems. Increased throughput results in more items processed in less time. Consequently, deposit cut off times can be extended since input is from machine-readable tape. Additionally, large-dollar items can be segregated out automatically and collections expedited.
- *Improved management information*—Both the corporate customer and the bank enjoy better information because data captured by the minicomputer can be used to produce a variety of custom management reports for both the bank and corporate customer. Reports can range from production and individual account profitability to profiles of remittances from corporate customers.

SUMMARY AND CONCLUSION

Increased involvement of corporate cash managers in direct lockbox processing results in banks' seeking new and innovative approaches to lockbox services to maintain corporate income. The best opportunity for banks to remain competitive in this area is to provide high-volume/low-dollar processing capability that would be difficult for corporations to justify. Scale economies applied to lockbox servicing can only be efficient if banks develop fully automated systems to replace manually oriented functions. Flexibility and customization are essential considerations since corporate customers still have indigenous processing requirements. Both can be achieved as illustrated in the prototype system. As banks become more automated in providing lockbox services, the number of banks participating in the market diminishes because the capital requirements limit the number of participants generating the high volumes required to achieve scale economies. Evolution in the bank-servicing area includes "ghost" processing services offered to banks with individually insufficient volume to justify highly sophisticated lockbox systems similar to the described prototype.

Further establishment of standards in the remittance document area is required for expansion of automated lockbox processing. As scale economies become evident to corporations, greater acceptance will spread. The expansion of GIRO-type payment systems, which will alter the traditional lockbox services, results from the high-volume capability described here. The same high-volume systems used in the prototype can be used to capture machine-readable data in a GIRO environment where credit transfers from a corporate customer's account to a corporation can be efficiently handled. (See Chapter 12 for a definition of GIRO.)

Trends in Lockbox Processing

Although the way in which lockbox services have developed in the past years has been checkered in design, a real business service is performed. The attentive bank can attract and maintain profitable lockbox accounts, retail and wholesale, even though most approaches are manual in nature. Most lockbox services offered by banks tend to increase in expense proportionate with volume, offering little in the way of scale economics. However, many corporations have found that they benefit from bank lockbox services through reduction of clerical help and faster availability of otherwise dormant funds.

Because most banks have evolved a "custom" approach to the lockbox market, most services are manually oriented. In this regard, lockbox services are Neanderthal compared with other bank-offered business services. Additionally, most bank-offered lockbox services do not offer the potential of scale economies. Consequently, many banks find themselves without growth capacity in lockbox processing, which results in staffing inefficiencies to meet market commitments.

The current trend in the lockbox development area for major banks is in the research and development of "uniform" lockbox services. There is a growing awareness that a completely integrated approach is required as the demand for low-dollar/high-volume lockbox processing increases. Additionally, many banks are experiencing profit squeezes in other areas of operation as personnel expenses rise. The evolving environment suggests that the more definitive, clearer cost analysis, currently under development by banks, illustrates that marginal costs for banks to manually process volume lockboxes exceeds corporate expenses for similar functions. Because banks lose lockbox business to corporations, banks interested in providing a full range of lockbox services are dependent upon the development of automated lockbox systems. As increased emphasis is placed on the low-dollar/high-volume remittances, banks will be required to increase significantly automated lockbox processes to reduce variable costs. If increased processing efficiency does not develop, banks can expect lower lockbox volumes as corporations develop more efficient internal systems.

Currently, both banks and corporations are gravitating toward uniformity in lockbox operations. The corporations desire to use lockboxes extensively for retail as well as wholesale applications, while banks can benefit by performing needed services profitably using scale economics.

The embryonic state of uniform development is currently without the required ingredient for success—central coordination. While thinking by both banks and corporations is toward uniformity, the movement soon falters without the cooperation and coordination of efforts. During the next few years, the development of fully automated lockbox services capable of handling large retail corporate accounts will provide scale economics to the progressive banks involved in this development effort and lower per unit processing expenses to the corporations.

Chapter 5

SPECIALIZED BANK-BASED CORPORATE SERVICES

An important bank selection criterion for many corporations is the specialized services offered by banks to aid corporate cash management functions. The growing trend is toward consideration of services that extend beyond the standard financial services described in Chapter 3. The importance of these services is increasing in relation to the profit center responsibility placed on the corporate cash manager. As the cash manager is increasingly required to produce tangible and profitable contributions, increased assistance from the corporate banking institution is desired. The types of services currently offered and under development by banks include:

- Cash management consulting services
- Centralized cash management information systems
- Automated business services
- Investment services

CASH MANAGEMENT CONSULTING SERVICES

Resulting from increased emphasis on corporate cash management, major banks have developed professional corporate cash management staffs. The purpose of these staffs is to evaluate procedures used by corporations for receivables collection and disbursements and to formulate system-wide optimization recommendations.

The bank's philosophy is often to become involved in large corporate fund management systems in order to establish a solid position as a concentration or lead bank. If consulting services are effective, the bank may generate additional revenue through expansion of the bank relationship or initiation of new bank customers. Banks also benefit by becoming involved in the formation of corporate cash management programs so that adequate fee income or compensating balances are assured in the planning stage. Inability to provide sophisticated consulting services may jeopardize the banks chances to attract and hold large corporate accounts. Providing consulting facilities for corporate cash management is a growing trend on the part of banks nationally. Small banks often offer these services even though they do not intend to be a concentration bank because they can function as regional facilities or as remote disbursement points for corporations. This is frequently a marketing strategy used by small banks to attract large corporations. For example, a small bank located in a non-Federal Reserve city can provide a corporation with a longer check clearance time (described in Exhibit 1-5), thus making funds available for short-term investment. This is a technique that has been gaining popularity both by the corporations and by some small banks to promote increased bank revenue while establishing account relationships with large corporations.

Consulting services provided usually take the form of reports or proposals made to the corporate treasurer or the financial vice president. Generally, the onus for implementation of proposals is placed on the corporation. However, a developing trend is for banks to develop implementation teams that execute, on a fee basis, approved cash management plans both within the corporation and with affected banks. Use of consulting services are initiated by corporate financial officers by contacting several banks for proposals. A request is made to evaluate the firm's current cash handling methods and to produce cash management recommendations. Review of several banks' approaches provides the corporation with several viewpoints to evaluate while affording a closer look at the sophistication, thoroughness, and interest of potential study banks. Through evaluation of several proposals, a financial manager may find that a combination of several proposals provides the best solution.

Overall control and responsibility for the implementation of cash management proposals should remain within the corporation because only corporate personnel are able to evaluate fully the effects of specific implementation recommendations. Consequently, any internal modifications must be effected by the corporations. The essential consideration in the implementation phase is modification of existing office procedures or systems to realize the desired proposal results without distorting processing accuracy. If significant permanent disruption of office procedures results in additional expenses, these results could outweigh income produced by extricated funds.

CASH MANAGEMENT INFORMATION SERVICES

Banks are becoming increasingly involved is cash management-related information services. The purpose of designing and offering information services is to develop specialized techniques to attract and hold large corporate relationships. In many cases, these bank-developed, nation-wide information services are in competition with third-party deposit and balance reporting systems. Several of the country's largest banks have implemented programs for cash information gathering with separate identifiable features.

Exhibit 5-1 pictorially describes a typical system. The object of the bank is to develop an information network that is compatable with other banks nationally in consolidating funds for large corporations and providing cash management information to cash managers. Under this system, the bank performs the corporate lockbox receivables function while receiving additional deposit information from the company's local sales office. Based on an established daily cutoff time, the sales offices call the bank with the amounts of payable checks issued that day. In addition to remittance reporting, account balance data is also collected. The local bank at the prescribed time calls a centralized reporting telephone number. A voice-response (computer-controlled) device or telephone operator then requests the location identification and: 1) the collected balance at the start of the day, 2) lockbox deposits made by the local bank, 3) deposits made by corporation offices, 4) disbursements made by local corporate offices,* and 5) the required compensating balance, if any, by the local bank. This information is received over multiple phone lines and recorded within a 10-minute period on a central computer file. At this point, the consolidated information is available to the corporate cash manager for inquiry.

Once data is available to the central computer file (4:40 P.M.) a bank deposit-reporting program, which produces a summary by corporation (in machine-readable format) of local bank activity and required balances for that day, is initiated. Activity information is input to the concentration banks "concentration account analysis" programs. These systems analyze the net effect of daily transactions in each of the local banks. Based on guidelines (parameters) established by individual corporate cash managers, the system then generates depository transfer checks, which transfer local bank funds (after clearance) to the concentration account. It also up-dates corporate ledger balances, which reflect the effect of the daily corporate activity, and provides activity reports to the corporation. Because of growing information requirements and an accelerated "need to know," there is a

---

* In many cases, all disbursements must be handled centrally. However, some funds control and check-writing abilities are usually maintained at local offices.

Exhibit 5.1 Developing bank-offered cash management services.

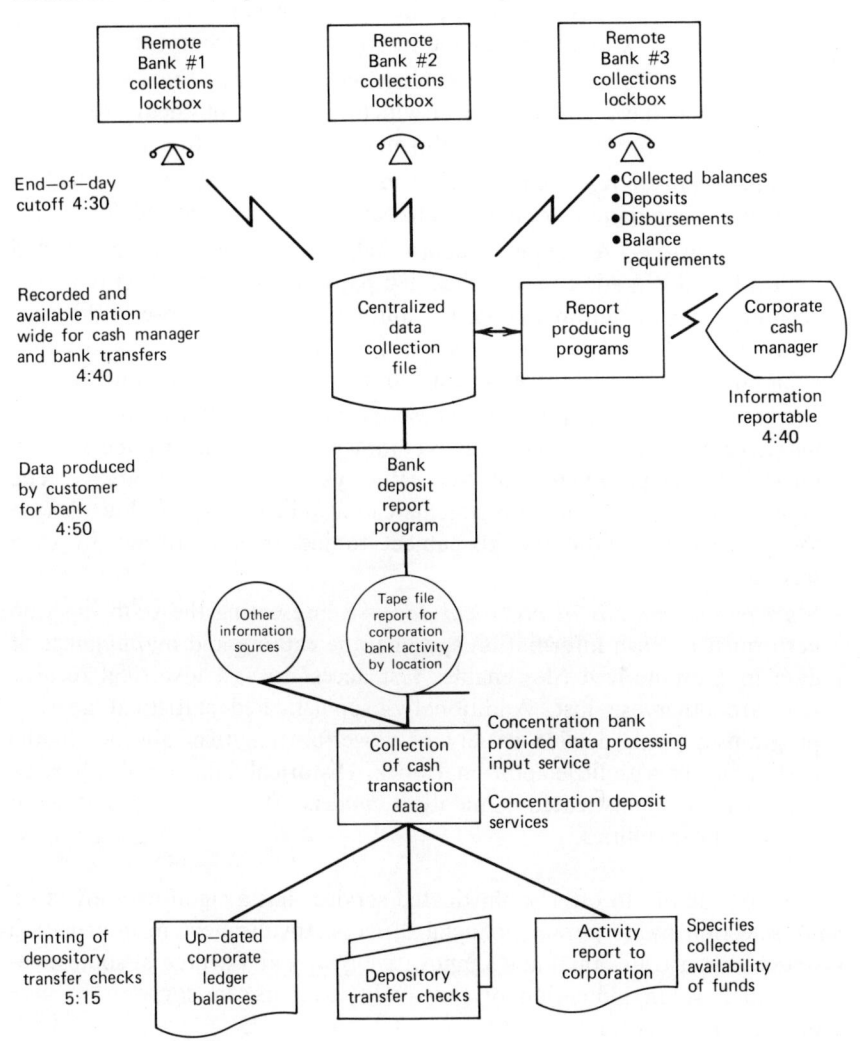

```
   ┌──────────┐      ┌──────────┐      ┌──────────┐
   │ Remote   │      │ Remote   │      │ Remote   │
   │ Bank #1  │      │ Bank #2  │      │ Bank #3  │
   │collections│     │collections│     │collections│
   │ lockbox  │      │ lockbox  │      │ lockbox  │
   └──────────┘      └──────────┘      └──────────┘
```

End–of–day
cutoff 4:30

• Collected balances
• Deposits
• Disbursements
• Balance requirements

Recorded and
available nation
wide for cash manager
and bank transfers
4:40

Centralized data collection file ⟷ Report producing programs ⟷ Corporate cash manager

Information reportable 4:40

Data produced
by customer
for bank
4:50

Bank deposit report program

Other information sources

Tape file report for corporation bank activity by location

Collection of cash transaction data

Concentration bank provided data processing input service

Concentration deposit services

Printing of depository transfer checks 5:15

Up–dated corporate ledger balances

Depository transfer checks

Activity report to corporation

Specifies collected availability of funds

recognizable trend toward development and implementation of this type (as well as other types) of cash information sytems. Development of responsive systems of this type take time because of the national (and eventually international) cooperation required. However, all systems of this type will be developed toward meeting the following six major corporate support functions:

- *Deposit consolidation*—The initial thrust of cash information systems to bring together the cash asset availability of the corporation in a time-related framework in a national and international environment.
- *Balance reporting systems*—This function accelerates the reporting of activities that have taken place in widely dispersed physical areas of a corporation and provides timely information on useable funds.
- *Required balance reporting*—A cash manager knows daily how much in compensating balances are required to pay for services used each day.
- *Cash forecasting*—A computer-controlled system based on data reported by local banks in addition to scheduled payables is modified daily by the cash manager for unforeseen cash requirements. The purpose of this type of system is to provide the cash manager with time frames and dollar values that can be used for short, medium, and long-term investments.
- *Investment recommendations*—These systems are interfaced to computerized investment services to recommend specific instruments based on established parameters of risk value, yield, and convertability. The actual purchase order for investments can also be generated, thus making the process automatic though subject to judgemental review by cash managers.
- *Storage and analysis of historical data*—Representing the sixth function performed by cash information systems, the capture and maintenance of data in computerized files enables fast access to vast historical records that are otherwise lost. Additionally, sophisticated statistical analysis programs provide a wide variety of powerful analytical abilities to the cash manager with little additional work. Historical data can also be used as input to sophisticated simulation models, thus offering additional analytical capabilities.

A bank's ability to offer sophisticated services has a significant effect on bank selection by corporate financial officers. Involvement in information systems demonstrates the bank's innovative ability and degree of sophistication, which is an indication of the quality response a corporation may expect in a long-term relationship.

AUTOMATED BUSINESS SERVICES

Another factor often affecting bank selection is the availability of automated business applications. The objective of offering automated business services is to provide a "service bureau" type of data processing facility to firms at economical rates. Frequently, this can be accomplished economically by banks because required processing can usually be scheduled at off-peak processing times. Consequently, these types of services often represent money-saving corporate services. Processing fees charged for automated business services may be charged against the corporate earnings allowance for funds on deposit. Additionally, banks offering these services de facto demonstrate a signficiant working knowledge of the corporate problems related to the services offered and can provide assistance (based on their broader experience) in the solution of internal corporate processing problems. One common problem that may arise in using banks for automated business processing is that the funds required are often debited immediately (computerized). In this way, low service fee charges are offset by transfer of the float availability from the corporation to the bank. Banks often have two charging schedules that provide a corporate payment option based on a fee basis or the combined fee and float basis. The corporate cash manager must decide, in conjunction with accounting officers, whether it is more economical to invest the funds and pay higher fees or to consider the float a reasonable opportunity cost in relation to the effort saved in monitoring these funds.

The automated services most offered by banks include:

- Payroll services
- Accounts payable services
- Accounts receivable services
- Inventory services

Payroll Services

With the exception of indigenous, special industry requirements, the internal processing of payrolls is generally not economical. Competition for payroll processing by service bureaus and banks in the past 5 years has accelerated, while costs to the users have fallen. The expense to internally process payroll on corporate data processing sometimes exceeds that which a bank or service bureau can supply. To use a payroll service (as shown in Exhibit 5-2), a corporation transcribes payroll information onto bank forms (or some other input media, e.g., data cassette or phone input of data). Data is converted into machine-readable formats and processed according to parameters established by the corporation. Resulting from the specified processing are:

- *Employee payroll checks*—These checks are disbursed on payday, an alternative is direct deposit of payroll amounts to employees checking accounts.

Exhibit 5.2 Automated payroll system flow.

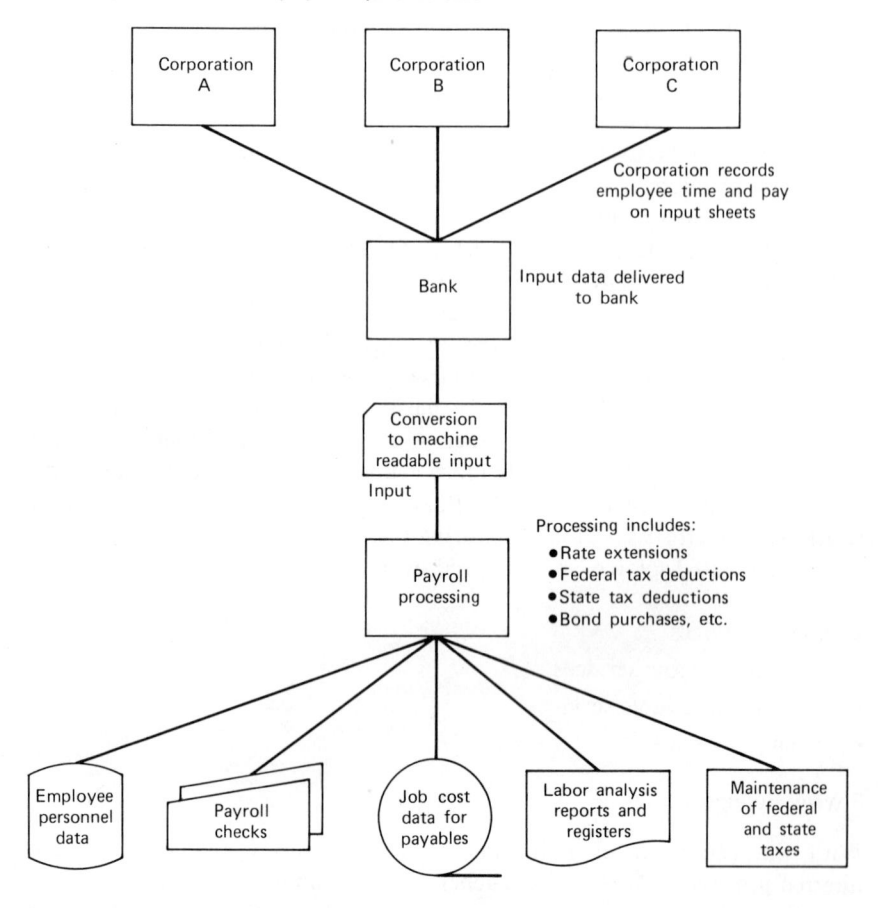

```
    Corporation      Corporation      Corporation
        A                B                C
         \               |               /
          \              |              /
           \             |    Corporation records
            \            |    employee time and pay
             \           |    on input sheets
              \          |          /
               \         |         /
                +--------+--------+
                |      Bank       |   Input data delivered
                +-----------------+        to bank
                         |
                         |
                +-----------------+
                |  Conversion     |
                |  to machine     |
                |  readable input |
                +-----------------+
                       Input
                         |
                +-----------------+    Processing includes:
                |     Payroll     |    • Rate extensions
                |   processing    |    • Federal tax deductions
                +-----------------+    • State tax deductions
                /    /   |   \    \    • Bond purchases, etc.
               /    /    |    \    \
    Employee  Payroll  Job cost  Labor analysis  Maintenance
    personnel checks   data for  reports and     of federal
    data               payables  registers       and state
                                                 taxes
```

- *Job cost data*—These files, which are created by breaking down the employee hours worked by job classifications, are used in conjunction with payables-supplied data (e.g., material expenses for jobs).
- *Labor analysis reports and payroll register*—These documents provide the corporation with labor details by department, product produced, or job allocation. The payroll register lists gross sales deductions and net pay amounts to provide adequate corporate record keeping.
- *Tax record maintenance*—These are records of bank-held funds for state and federal tax payments on required due dates. The bank assumes liability for effecting timely corporate tax payments and for filing required corporate tax reports. Banks maintain highly trained staff to assure compliance with tax-filing dates for corporations using payroll services on a nation-

wide basis. Bank compensation for service is obtained by retention of tax funds accounts until taxes actually are due. Thus each pay day, the corporation is charged for taxes that are due at some future time. The corporation must decide the significance of handling tax reporting and funds investment measured against the cost of bank services.

- *Personnel data collection*—This service represents the last major service performed by many bank payroll systems. Data is maintained on file regarding corporate employees. This data can be used to generate skill inventory listings, historical compensation records, schedules of compensation reviews, required career counseling schedules, educational backgrounds, and areas of special employee interests.

Through the use of these payroll-related services, corporations can free personnel to perform tasks that are directly profit related. Consequently, many firms use banks where cash management objectives can be blended with support of payroll services.

Automated Accounts Payable

Another service frequently offered by large banks is an automated accounts payable service. Through this service, a corporation may reduce clerical work associated with tracking and timely vendor payment. Exhibit 5-3 is a typical processing flow. In lieu of corporate handling of payables checks, processing can be accomplished by the bank's business services section, which converts the data to machine-readable format and places it on computer files until required for payment. Under such a scheme, payable checks are automatically produced on customer instruction based on recorded discount dates or the "net" due date. Through an automated system, cash discounts are not inadvertently lost by the company. Production of vendor analysis reports for the corporations is an additional benefit. A major benefit to cash managers from this service is the production of schedules of accounts payables (by discount due date) that can be used for short-term cash requirement forecasting. Cash managers are, consequently, provided a practical tool for use in payment decisions. Through this type of automated system, disbursements by time periods can supply valuable historical information to cash managers for future forecasting. As a by-product of this process, vendor expenses can be assigned to departments or job classifications for use in conjunction with payroll data in integrated job cost reports.

Establishing an automated payables service using a bank's automated business service requires a clear definition regarding payment methods. In

Exhibit 5.3 Automated payables processing system.

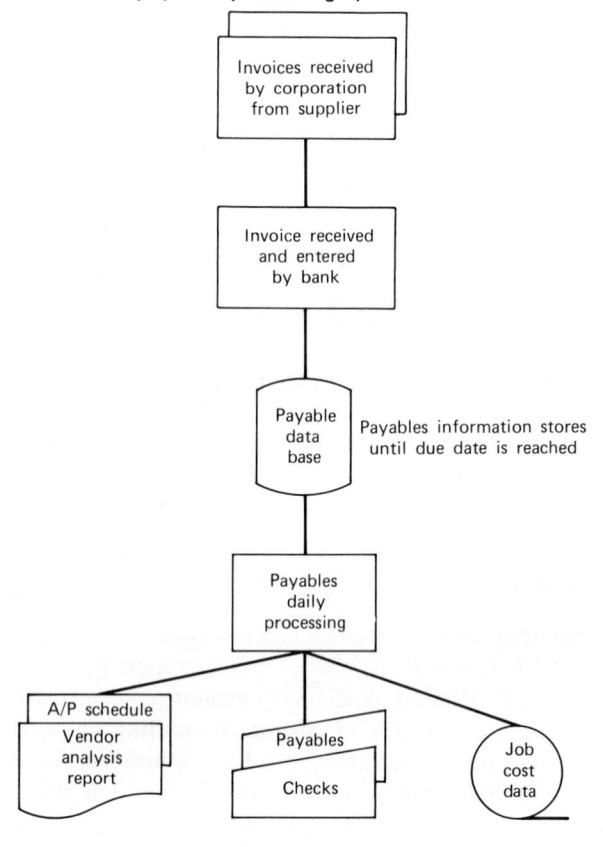

```
        ┌──────────────┐
        │ Invoices received
        │ by corporation
        │ from supplier │
        └──────┬───────┘
               │
        ┌──────┴───────┐
        │ Invoice received
        │ and entered
        │ by bank      │
        └──────┬───────┘
               │
        ┌──────┴───────┐
        │ Payable      │   Payables information stores
        │ data base    │   until due date is reached
        └──────┬───────┘
               │
        ┌──────┴───────┐
        │ Payables     │
        │ daily        │
        │ processing   │
        └──┬────┬───┬──┘
           │    │   │
   ┌───────┘    │   └────────┐
   │            │            │
A/P schedule  Payables     Job
Vendor        Checks       cost
analysis                   data
report
```

many banks, stated processing fees for such services are low because banks charge the corporate accounts for payables checks issued the day the check is written. Consequently, the corporation loses all float benefits. The bank often considers the use of float as partial compensation to offset processing expenses. Corporations may, if float is significant, negotiate a straight fee structure for processing that returns float control to the cash manager.

Accounts Receivable

Use of automated accounts receivable processing by corporations is increasing as a result of expanded bank service activity. Both the open item and balance forward type of accounts receivables systems can be efficiently processed by the more sophisticated banks. The general flow of activity is outlined in Exhibit 5-4. Banks receive customer payment directly, and the corporation fowards records of customer credit purchases to the bank. The bank converts both sets of data to machine-readable formats that are stored

Exhibit 5.4 Accounts receivable bank service.

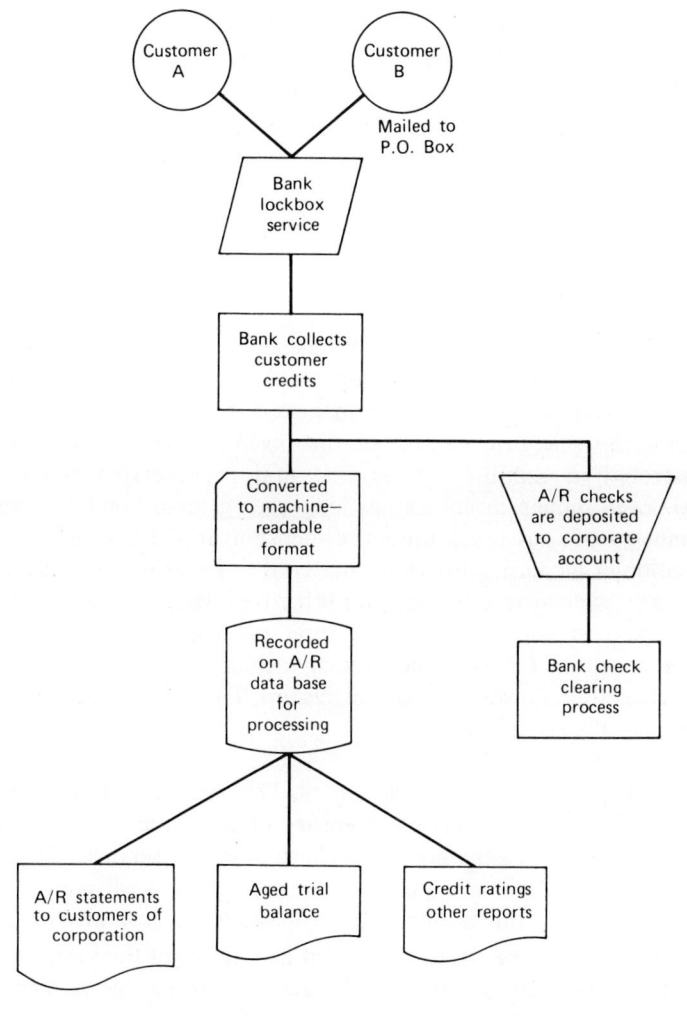

```
        Customer        Customer
           A               B
                         Mailed to
                         P.O. Box
              Bank
             lockbox
             service

           Bank collects
             customer
              credits

           Converted           A/R checks
           to machine—         are deposited
            readable           to corporate
             format              account

           Recorded
           on A/R              Bank check
           data base            clearing
             for                 process
          processing

  A/R statements    Aged trial    Credit ratings
  to customers of    balance      other reports
    corporation
```

for use in accounts receivable processing. Checks received through lockbox services are deposited to corporate accounts and travel through the normal clearing process. The bank's automated accounts receivables service then produces:

- *Monthly customer statements*—These statements show the customer's current charges due, stating any special conditions. Also displayed on the invoice are any interest charges that may be assessed for past due amounts with the required regulation "Z" disclosure statement printed on the statement.
- *Aged trial balance*—This is produced as a by-product of examining each customers account when preparing the monthly billing statement. This commonly used accounting tool enables the cash manager to expedite tardy payers and better control cash flows.
- *Other reports*—Some reports are customized to the special needs of the corporation. Charging for automated accounts receivables is usually on a fee only basis. Many corporations find it beneficial to use these services rather than incur custom-programming expenses.

Inventory Control

The newest entry to automated bank business services is inventory control and management services. More sophisticated than previously examined business services, it offers cash managers a readily useable information source for the scientific control of the inventory-related cash drain. As demonstrated in Exhibit 5-5, several major processing functions are affected. Even though inventory has long been a focus point for aggressive cash managers, it has taken on new dimensions in the past few years. The combination of increasing prices for material and soaring interest rates have dramatically underscored the need for effective inventory control. Inventory systems vary in capability by the type of bank offering the service. However, essential functions performed include the control of all related input sources to the inventory control system. The types of output produced include:

- *Automatic purchase order generation*—This type of output is based on minimum/maximum levels of inventory or an economic order quantity (EOQ). The system generates a purchase order for services. Through the centralized production of purchase orders, better cash control can be achieved. This centralization can be achieved on a corporate-wide basis.
- *A/R customer information*—Produced as a result of the sales order, this data can be entered directly into the accounts receivables system, which produces reports for the cash manager.
- *On-line stock status reporting*—This service provides instant access to the total inventory picture. This tool can be used as a quick information

source for a cash manager who is attempting to pledge his inventory for a required short-term loan.
- *Inventory demand forecasts*—The cash manager uses this service, which can be generated using historical data modified by management, for cash forecasts for the next planning period. Consequently, seasonal fluctuations may be anticipated and appropriate funds made available to the business without disruption of the cash management program.
- *Historical demand*—Data bases can be created to maintain and report on historical peak and valley demand cycles for the company. With this data, the corporate cash manager has a compendium of data available for use in short- and long-range cash requirement forecasts.

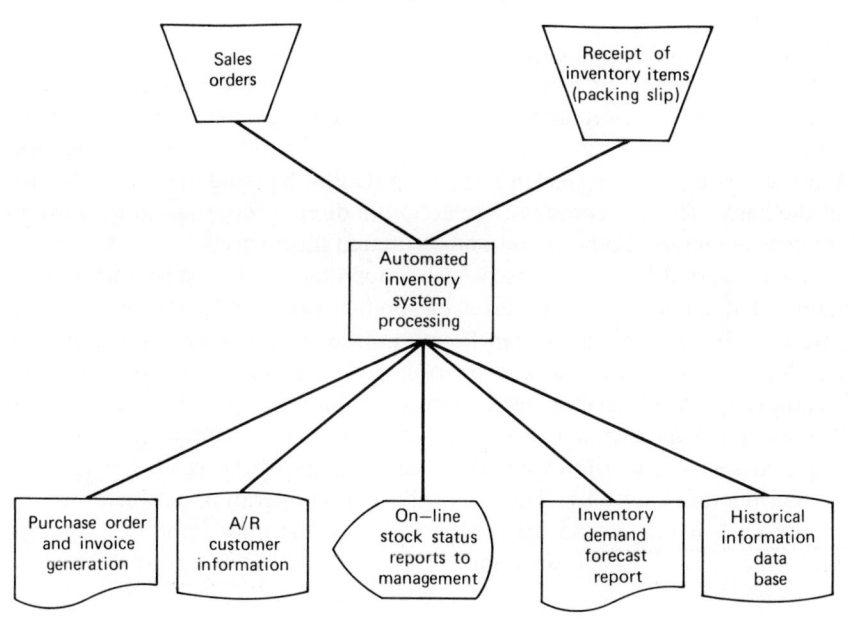

Exhibit 5.5   Automated inventory management system.

```
         Sales                    Receipt of
         orders                   inventory items
                                  (packing slip)
              \                  /
               \                /
                \              /
                 Automated
                 inventory
                 system
                 processing
            /    |      |      |      \
           /     |      |      |       \
   Purchase   A/R    On-line  Inventory  Historical
   order and  customer stock   demand    information
   invoice    information status forecast data
   generation         reports to report   base
                      management
```

Automated inventory processing, through the newest of the bank-offered business services, promises to be a powerful, full-service tool. Corporate cash managers can benefit from improved inventory monitoring because computer control reduces both raw materials and finished goods inventory for manufacturers, wholesales, and distributors. Pricing for inventory services is usually on a fee basis. Processing fees must be evaluated in relation to the cost of maintaining excess inventories. Excess inventory is indicated when a corporation does not maintain an inventory turnover rate equal to or greater than the established industry averages. The dollar cost of additional inventory must be reflected in the interest expense for borrowing funds and lost opportunity costs.

Wisely used automated business services offered by banks can represent an untapped source of assistance to the cash manager. By dealing with banks offering automated business services, cash managers can be assured that the banks' levels of sophistication are significant and that comprehensive industry knowledge exists within the banks' structures.

SUMMARY

Corporate banking relationships usually involve several banks. However, the selection of banks can be equally important whether it is a large concentration bank or a regional center for use by local offices. The corporation must carefully analyze and fit its required processing needs to the banks under consideration. Financial stability and sound business reputations are essential consideration for all potential banking partners. The size of the bank affects a company's selection in direct proportion to its borrowing requirements—both present and estimated future needs.

Since internal bank skills vary, it is imperative that corporations choose banks that coincide with its level of sophistication and aggressiveness. In this way, future frustration can be minimized if corporate innovations are developed that require bank cooperation. Establishing a sound, equitable relationship with several lead banks is essential to the corporation. Although a bank may not satisfy all the requests of a firm, it must perform required services to the extent that major areas of the cash management system operate smoothly. The atmosphere of cooperation between the corporate cash manager and his banker is one of the most important intangibles in bank analysis and selection.

BIBLIOGRAPHY

Conference Board, *Cash Management,* Report #580, 1972.

Hill, Roger W., *Cash Management Techniques,* American Management Association, 1970.

Lorden, James F., *The Banking Side of Corporate Cash Management,* Financial Publishing Company, 1973.

Axford, Clifton, "Bank-Corporate Sales for Improving Cash Management," *Burrough Clearing House,* May 1968.

Lake, Fie, "Cash Management in the 70's—Those Dancing Dollar Bills," *Journal of Commercial Funding,* October 1974.

Beehler, Paul J., "Corporate Cash Management: The Banking Dilemma," *Baylor Business Studies,* May–June 1976.

Reed, Walter, "Cash, The Hidden Asset," *Financial Executive,* November 1970.

Emory, John, "Managing Cash for Profit," *Financial Executives,* April 1968.

Searby, Frederich, "Use Your Hidden Cash Resources," *Harvard Business Review,* March–April 1968.

PART III

FORECASTING CASH FLOWS

CHAPTER 6

CASH FORECASTING: THE ENVIRONMENT

Although forecasting is often used in areas of management science and business planning, its definition is often lost in contextual use. Forecasting can be defined as the ability to plan, calculate, or predict future events or conditions. Related to the business environment, the forecasts are usually based on the analysis of pertinent current or historical data. With particular regard to cash management, the application of forecasting techniques takes on the characteristics of a heuristic art form. Often forecasting, no matter how it is approached, tends to ward off many cash managers. The purpose of this chapter is to place forecasting in a working context for later application. The second portion of this chapter defines and reviews basic elements that affect forecasting as related to cash management.

FORECASTING IN PERSPECTIVE

The growing complexity of business, coupled with the increasing capital requirements for business expansion has placed increasing pressure on forecasting techniques as a common sense tool in business planning. The basic purpose of forecasting is to provide "best" approximations for future events or to estimate ranges for conditions in the business environment. Central to the use of forecasting for cash management, or any other purpose, is the recognition that it provides information on which to base reasonable decisions. Forecasting does not, and is not designed to, make the decision or basically alter events. Over the past few years, forecasting methods have been used in marketing, production, personnel, and finance. Of all these areas, finance is the business environment where the greatest returns have been realized. Projections of cash flows, revenues, and expenses assist the corporate treasurer in maintaining corporate liquidity.

The impact of forecasting on the corporation's daily operating environment has been accelerating during the past decade. Today, many profit centers are governed by forecasts of one type or another. For example, sales forecasts are translated into salary budgets for the coming year and used as a base for production schedules in many corporations. Consequently, production schedules dictate the timing and quantity of materials required for budget year forecasts. These quarterly requirements are used by the finance department to project required cash positions by month. Similarly, cash inflows from receivables can be projected from the forecast of sales. In an environment of rising interest rates and growing vulnerability in international markets, the forecast of business elements takes on added dimensions.

Although each functional area of business contains elements indiginous to itself, there are three common elements related to forecasting. The first element is the futurity of the forecast and the decisions based on forecasting. A forecast deals with a specific point in the future. The second element, which is almost synonymous with forecasting, is uncertainty. The primary contributors to uncertainty are trends, cycles, and random occurrences. Although trends may be detected and projected (even though their changing characteristic cannot), random occurrences can usually only be observed. The third common element that varies, based on circumstances, is the applicability of historical data to future occurrences. Usually, forecasts are based on data obtained from historical data. This is especially true when forecasting is applied to the various areas of cash management. Because forecasts are based on past data, the distinction between forecasting and planning is often lost. Forecasting is used to estimate with varying degrees of accuracy what most probably will occur in the future, based on past experiences, if no positive action is taken. Planning is the function of taking positive action to change the expected results of a future event. Therefore, it is only through an adaptive type of forecasting model that forecasting can reflect a long-term change as a result of a single period decision.

Forecasting Methods

There are two basic categories of forecasting—qualitative and quantitative. The essential difference is the degree to which mechanical forecasting methods can be applied to historical data to produce functional results.

Using a qualitative approach to forecasting requires the direction and orchestration of an "expert" in the field, since the object is to *anticipate* changes in basic long-term trends. A recent and successful application of this forecasting approach has been the use of product life-cycle predictions. Although this area of forecasting is receiving ever greater attention, its application to short and intermediate-term cash forecasts is generally regarded as inappropriate.

Quantitative forecasting techniques are generally used today because of the reasonably high degree of reliability that can be achieved by making model modifications over time. Some of the more widely used techniques include moving averages, regression analysis, and exponential smoothing. These techniques have in common the fact that they use historical data for a base period and make projections to a specific future point. The future point is usually projected in a strictly linear fashion, unless more sophisticated variations are included in the model. Since situations vary widely, the choice of forecasting methods appropriate to the application is often more of an art than a science. In considering the factors that influence the choice of an appropriate method, managers must consider six basic factors:

- *The time horizon*—All forecasts must relate to time. It is the time frame that has a major bearing on the accuracy of forecasts using different techniques. Consequently, the time horizon affects the appropriate method selection.
- *Level of detail*—This element specifies the level of response the forecast must address. A macroeconomic forecast is useless to a production line foreman in planning labor allocation for auto production for the coming week.
- *Number of elements*—The number of elements affects the cost of developing and maintaining any forecasting model and must be considered in the composition of the forecast methodology. The greater the number of elements, the more expensive the forecast may be.
- *Data volitility*—This element affects the accuracy of the model, and the expense of maintaining such a model because of the cost of error correction and related bad decisions based on the model.
- *Existing planning methods*—Existing planning must always be considered since most firms are at best reluctant to make dramatic changes in operational procedures, especially when they are understood by only a few of the management team, as is often the case with the introduction of forecasting techniques into the corporation.

Although consideration of the environment in which the forecast is applied is extremely important, knowledge of the characteristics of the forecasting methods available is also critical. A careful analysis of different techniques better enables the manager to apply the most appropriate technique to the problem area. The major factors affecting the selection of forecasting techniques are:

- The time dimension is particularly relevant to cash forecasting since time spans vary from next-day balance forecasts to 2-year funds flow forecasts. Different techniques must be evaluated and used for each situation. Similarly, the *number of periods* into the future for which the forecast is required also affects the technique chosen.
- The pattern of cash related elements affects the techniques chosen since many techniques are based on the assumption that an overall pattern exists in the futurity of the elements being forecast. For this reason, it is essential that historical data be carefully examined so that the appropriate methods are chosen to coincide with the historical patterns of the cash information elements.
- The type of model refers to the selection of a model type such as the applicability of a simple time series approach using regression or correlation to adequately describe the environment, or if a causal model is required. If the causal approach is chosen, several attributes require a definition so that reliable results are obtained. Because it contains many variables, the causal model is more expensive to develop and maintain. (This is discussed later.)
- Expense relates to the development, operational, and maintenance costs related to the model. The variation in development and operational expenses inversely affects the desirability of a model.
- Accuracy, is affected by the amount of data maintained and analyzed. The required accuracy of cash forecasts varies, based on the corporate situation. In daily cash forecasts, inaccuracy results in overdraft expenses to the corporation and adversely affects their banking relations.
- Practicality relates to the degree of understanding and acceptance that exists on the part of the user. Without a significant level of personal conviction regarding the forecasting technique, the manager is reluctant to place a high degree of confidence in the method chosen by others, regardless of their qualifications. The techniques chosen must be effective and understandable.

As with any other business decision, the cost/benefit relation must be defined. This approach provides the manager a framework within which to make technique choices. The manager should also be aware of the relative change in value and cost when the level of accuracy changes. Essentially, whenever a simple forecasting technique can be defined to satisfy forecasting requirements, it should be chosen over more sophisticated approaches. The more involved the approach, the fewer the number of people who understand or subsequently are able to lend support if required.

Another consideration in the development of a forecasting method for cash managers is the amount of historical data available and the time frame within which the forecast must be available. If the method chosen is complicated and the response time lengthy, then computer models are required if the forecasts are to be timely.

The final and major consideration in the selection of a forecasting method is the environment within which the model operates. If the method is not understood, then important elements of up-dated data may be routinely ignored or the accuracy of data reported may be less than required to make the forecasting technique valuable. In this regard, support of the forecasting method is more than providing data through mechanical data collection methods. Without correct historical data, not only is the forecast inaccurate and costly to the corporation because of incorrect decisions, but also because the integrity and credibility of forecasting methods is made questionable in the corporation.

Data Patterns

Forecasting, whether daily, weekly, monthly, or annually, is subject to basic data patterns. Because patterns often exist in cash elements requiring forecasts, it seems reasonable that quantitative methods can often be applied to the forecasting of related cash items. Using quantitative methods, which are outlined later, assumes that definite long-term patterns in the data can be defined. This pattern identification is not to ignore the presence of random occurrences but only to recognize an overriding trend or movement for the variables being forecast. The ability of a given technique to forecast effectively in a specific situation depends on matching the pattern in that environment with a method that can relate to the pattern in the data. There are, essentially, four patterns that affect cash forecasting, which must be considered: horizontal, seasonal, cyclical, and trend.

- *Horizontal patterns* exist where the data is void of any trend. When this situation occurs, it is referred to as a static environment because the only variance from the average experience is caused by random occurrences. The time aspect is an important consideration because in the short run, patterns that may take on long-term significance may be considered stable for purposes of short-term forecasting.
- *A seasonal pattern* exists when a series of data fluctuates with some definable regularity such as the seasons of the year. However, this seasonality may occur within any recognizable time frame. Daily, weekly,

monthly time frames may possess seasonal elements. Once identified, data may be deseasonalized.
- *Cyclical patterns* are actually a variation of seasonal fluctuations except that they generally refer to a time period greater than 1 year. Cyclical patterns have significance to longer-term forecasts such as economic-based data. Its relation to cash management forecasting is minimal at best.
- *Trends* can be defined as a general increase or decrease in a variable over time. Trends have direct application to cash forecasting since many of the variables that may be included in the forecast model developed can have long-term trends contained within them.

Classification of Forecasting Models

Before examining the elements to be considered in a cash forecast, a brief overview of the different types of models is appropriate. Models may be classified into four general categories: time series, causal, statistical, and nonstatistical models.

The basic assumption of a time series model is that there are only two variables involved—the time or forecast period and the element being forecast. This could be the corporation's collected balance or amount of lockbox collections from a given point on a given day. By identifying the pattern and starting point, as well as the number of periods into the future, a model can be defined. An advantage of time series models is that the basic rules of accounting are directed toward sequential time periods. Consequently, most firms have data readily available from historical files on which to initiate this type of forecasting.

The causal model is defined in terms of the techniques that assume that the values of certain variables are directly related to the performance or results of other variables. An example is the weekly sales projections for a corporation that may be based not only on historical data for this week, but also on the dollar level of advertising the company performs. An advantage of the causal model is that the manager can develop a range of "what if" situations by changing the value of different variables. The causal model is more sophisticated than the time series type of modeling and, consequently, requires more definition and data to establish the operating parameters. Additionally, the intricacies of this type of model may often confound all but the designer of the particular model.

The statistical models can be defined following the rules and procedures of statistical analysis in the process of identifying patterns on the variables being forecast. Because statistics speak of the degree of confidence that can be associated with a forecast, it is often construed to be the most accurate of the forecasting models. Nevertheless, it may be the one that has exerted the least impact on managerial decision making. The primary reason is the somewhat difficult terms within which statistics are expressed. Because of its means of expression, few business people effectively use this method.

The last type of model is the nonstatistical model. All models not adhering to the strict rules of statistical analysis and probability theory can be classified as nonstatistical techniques. These approaches are often a combination of quantitative methods intermixed with some statistical techniques. They are generally the result of what the manager intuitively feels should be considered in a forecast, rather than a rigid set of mathematical steps. In Chapter 8, we define and discuss a specific example of this intermixed approach. Often this approach is more practical than following established rules that may not apply to a known and familiar environment. The most important element in cash forecasting is understanding the variability in the elements being forecast and establishing the managerial familiarity with the approach. The accuracy of the approach can be refined, based on experience, to achieve the required performance level.

This portion of the chapter has been an overview of forecasting, placing it in a general framework for cash management reference. Next we must examine the specific elements involved in the development of corporate cash forecasts.

CASH MANAGEMENT AND FORECASTING

The previous section has presented an overview of forecasting. The approaches to forecasting have been placed in a structure to assist in identifying essential elements to which forecasting techniques and models may be applicable in a corporate environment. This portion of the chapter develops the bridge between general forecasting approaches and their applications to cash management. A basic context or philosophy is developed to provide a framework within which to approach and identify the elements to which forecasting techniques and models need to be applied. In succeeding chapters, specific techniques and models that currently exist or can be developed for cash forecasting are reviewed.

The Time Horizon and the Cash Forecast

Forecasting is basically used in financial areas of corporations as a planning tool. The concept of cash management planning is an extension of this approach. The planning motivation needs to be separated from and identified with the control aspects of cash management because both suggest distinctly different time frames. The planning aspect of cash management refers to longer-term time horizons. Since the time horizon is a key element in the selection of the type of forecasting technique, a brief definition of the time horizon is appropriate. As related to cash management, three time horizons or terms can be identified:

- The capital period
- The budget period
- The immediate period

The capital period is any planning period beyond 1 year. In terms of the planning functions, this is important because longer-term forecasts of this nature often deal with permanent financing decisions of the firm. Additionally, the immediate actions resulting from this forecasting time horizon do not have a direct daily impact on the cash managers' functions or performances. It is essential to identify the degree of accuracy required in the capital period forecasting term so that forecast methods (and related costs) can be developed to meet the planning requirements of the corporation. The budget period forecast is defined as quarterly cash-related forecasts which are developed into the annual corporate budget. The purpose of this forecast time horizon in cash management is for both planning of reserves and funds allocation and control over the inflow and outflow of funds. An example of this time horizon for forecasting is the projection of interest expenses for inclusion in the higher level budget planning function of the corporation.

The planning function involved for this time frame is concerned with the resources required for the next year to meet established goals. This planning function is communicated into cash management terms through the requirement of capital for expansion, which results in long-term debt requirements and possible short-term funding for developmental products. Using the budget period time horizon, the cash manager can plan for the amount of credit required to support the corporation during the year and estimate the interest expense for providing capital funds. The control objective of this time horizon forecast is to establish limits or ranges for the expenses incurred in acquiring the required capital. In concrete terms, the budget period forecast allows the cash manager to negotiate for required funds in advance of capital requirements. This is advantageous in periods of rising interest rates so that a borrowing rate significantly lower than the rising short term investment rate may be realized. The use of the budget period forecast can also result in an overall lower cost of working capital for the corporation for the year and provide some measure of short-term income.

Forecasts of economic conditions by the corporate cash manager are essential since this type of future budgeting can work to the company's detriment if adequate "pay down" provisions are not available with the lending bank. "Pay down" provisions refer to the ability of a borrower to pay down the outstanding loan amount for a period of time to reduce the overall interest expense. The budget period is important to the cash manager both in terms of the elements that are forecast in this time span and because the resulting cash flows are used in cash management for both planning and control. The forecasts resulting from this time period have much more "immediacy" in action required by the cash manager than capital period forecasts.

Of all the time horizons, none has such a direct impact as the immediate period time horizon for the cash manager. The immediate period time horizon in cash forecasting is defined as the daily and weekly forecast of cash receipts and disbursements for the corporation. The maximum time usually encompassed in this time horizon is 8 weeks. The results of this type of forecast are immediate in nature and are action oriented. Forecasts and subsequent actions are known and visible in a short time frame. For example, an insurance company forecasting available funds of $10 million in excess of daily needs can draw down those funds and invest them overnight in repurchase agreements for a reasonable profit. However, if the forecast was in error, and, in fact, the insurance company's account was overdrawn by $1 million, not only would charges be made for the overdrawn amount but sanctions may also be applied by the insurance commissioner since by regulation, insurance companies (and other industries) are prohibited from account overdrafts. Conversely, if funds were in excess on a given day, an opportunity cost would have been incurred. Achieving the appropriate balance for the company on a daily basis is the most volatile area in cash forecasting because of the blend of controllable and uncontrollable factors.

The immediate period cash forecast affects corporate activities in the monitoring and maintenance of required balances with lending banks. Although this monitoring can be averaged out monthly and annually, the balance between banks can best be achieved on a daily basis. By shifting excess funds from one bank to compensate for deficient amounts in another bank, an equitable balance can be maintained during the month. This approach is also preferred by the banks.

Although the total credit requirement may not exceed budget period expectations, the total amount required at one time may be greater than anticipated if planned receipts and cash flows are not as originally forecast.

The monitoring and modification of capital forecasts as performed by the cash manager serves as an early warning signal to other areas of the corporation that significant variances are occurring in the immediate period time horizon that may affect achievement of overall corporate goals for the budget period.

Forecasting Cash—The Need

Perhaps the most basic question to be addressed is defining why cash forecasting is required as part of the cash management function. Corporations have conducted and many still do conduct business daily without formal cash forecasting programs. To be sure in some situations, the immediate period forecast may not be used by a firm; however, the management of a firm without budget or capital period planning tools is untenable.

By the time the need for funds is apparent, the required lead time to acquire the funds is generally inadequate. While the budget and capital period time horizons are essential to planning for corporate growth and expansion, the immediate period horizon attracts more concentrated attention. Without the careful scheduling of incoming and outgoing funds on a daily basis, corporations soon lose credibility with the banks since overdrafts would be commonplace and vendors would soon demand payment in advance. The matching of current assets to current liabilities is the life blood of the daily market dealings for corporations. To cover transactional requirements, a firm must approximate its required cost to maintain bank balances equal to or greater than current booked obligations. To a large extent, this was for many years the modus operandi for many corporations. Daily account tracking as a required element of cash management has developed extensively only in the past 10 years because of the increasing cost of money. Consequently, corporate cash managers are much more aggressive in pursing daily control over the major corporate accounts. Immediate period cash forecasting is required because of the lag time of banks in reporting corporate bank account activity. The control aspects of immediate period forecasting translates into short-term action on a daily and weekly basis for the cash manager. The cash manager needs to know his cash position for each account being controlled early enough in the day to take definite action to effect the end of day position. The use of cash forecasting in this context provides the cash manager with an approximation of what the account end of day position will be if no modifying action is taken.

Exhibit 6-1 pictorially describes the timing and the flow of basic bank processed information. Here daily corporate deposits and account charges are received by the corporate bank. The deposits originate from corporate depositing locations and lockbox services (described in Chapter 4) provided by banks.

Exhibit 6.1 Basic flow of daily cash forecasting.

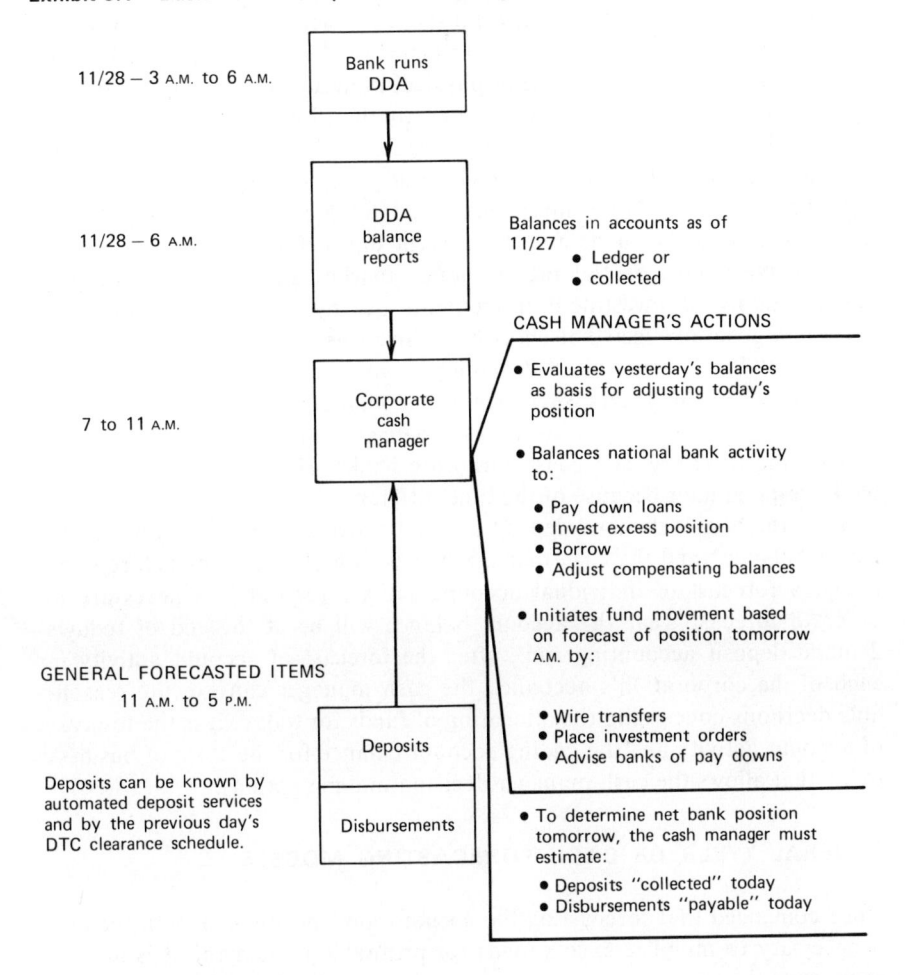

Time	Process	Details
11/28 – 3 A.M. to 6 A.M.	Bank runs DDA	
11/28 – 6 A.M.	DDA balance reports	Balances in accounts as of 11/27 • Ledger or • collected

7 to 11 A.M.	Corporate cash manager	**CASH MANAGER'S ACTIONS**
		• Evaluates yesterday's balances as basis for adjusting today's position
		• Balances national bank activity to:
		  • Pay down loans
		  • Invest excess position
		  • Borrow
		  • Adjust compensating balances
		• Initiates fund movement based on forecast of position tomorrow A.M. by:
		  • Wire transfers
		  • Place investment orders
		  • Advise banks of pay downs

GENERAL FORECASTED ITEMS
11 A.M. to 5 P.M.
 	
Deposits can be known by automated deposit services and by the previous day's DTC clearance schedule.
	Deposits
	
	Disbursements
		• To determine net bank position tomorrow, the cash manager must estimate:
		  • Deposits "collected" today
		  • Disbursements "payable" today

The change to the corporate account arises from the cashing of accounts payable and payroll checks issued by the corporation. The bank after its closing time (about 3 P.M.) balances the deposits and cash receipts and reconciles the checks cashed. The deposits to the corporation's account (credits) and the checks cashed against the account (debits) are then processed by the bank's demand deposit accounting system, which up-dates the corporation's account. Since banks have several thousands of accounts to process each night, the processing cycle is not completed until approximately 5:30 A.M. This is the earliest time that the up-dated ledger balance for the corporations account can be known. The output of the demand deposit accounting system must then be sent to branch or reporting service officers where reports can be made to the corporation. Often the earliest this is available because of physical limitations is 7:30 A.M. To clarify a point—the ledger balance relates to the close of business the day before. This is the book balance that resides in the account until the next demand deposit processing run. Generally, most investment decisions regarding overnight funds investments and temporary pay downs of loan amounts need to be made for the current day before noon eastern time. Because New York is the major money market and because there is a limited supply of investment instruments at any given time, most cash managers generally feel that short-term investments must be made before noon New York time. Time differences cause varying degrees of inconvenience to cash managers when viewed in conjunction with the noon investment cut off time. An east coast cash manager can obtain information in ample time from the east coast corporate banks. However, the west coast banks respond later because of the time difference.

Since the bank's demand deposit account processing provides yesterday's ledger balance* and the cash manager needs to mobilize funds before noon today, a forecast of individual account activity for today is necessary in order to forecast what the account balance will be at the end of today's demand deposit accounting run. After the forecast of account activity in each of the corporation's accounts, the cash manager can execute reasonable decisions concerning the allocation of funds for today. It is the forecast of account activity and the ending account balance for the close of business today that allows the cash manager decision-making options.

GENERAL TYPES OF CASH FORECASTING MODELS

Once convinced that forecasting the corporation's position early in the day is necessary to mobilize excess funds for profitable investment, it is incumbent upon the cash manager to develop a "model" that effectively serves short-term forecasting needs. Although forecasting requirements vary by industry and individual firms within industry, a general approach to forecasting can be outlined.

General Models Applicable to Cash Forecasting

The modeling approach to developing a cash forecast is recommended because it permits the cash manager to adjust basic values so that the model

---

*For banks using a proof of deposit system for dynamic float capture, the collected balance is using viable.

may reflect the effects of changing conditions. The types of quantitative models to be considered include:

- *Time series models*—These rely heavily on the past compendium of data to forecast a pattern into the future. The approach can be used successfully in short-term account forecasting if other discernable factors such as seasonal flutuations are taken into account.
- *Causal models*—This modeling category does not have significant applications for the immediate period time horizon in account balance forecasting because the related variables have lead time that cannot be accurately fitted to the narrow time frame required. For example, although sales volume and selling price affect the cash account position of the firm on a daily basis the time lag between the sale and the receipt of the accounts receivable payment cannot be accurately defined and related to the daily transaction level.
- *Statistical models*—These types do have application in account activity. Since they are based on the laws of statistical theory and probability, their degree of accuracy can be measured. The selection of this general model type should be mediated by the understanding of the data being forecast and the results to be achieved.
- *Mixed technique models*—These modeling types have wide application to cash forecasting because they do combine several techniques and approaches resulting in a customized and controllable approach to forecasting unknown variables in cash management. An advantage to using this type of model is that it is easily understood and translated from the cash manager's perspective of what needs to be done to a working model. The disadvantage is that the degree of confidence about the conclusion of the model cannot be stated statistically. However, since portions of this modeling type can be based on statistical measures some indication and ranges for forecasts can be established.

All of these modeling types are quantitative in nature because each makes some assumption about the time horizon of the variable to be forecast and the underlying pattern of the data. The most important consideration for the cash manager in considering and evaluating a modeling approach is an understanding of what is to be accomplished and an understanding of the methods being used. Confidence in the approach chosen is generated by an understanding of what is transpiring and the evaluation of results. If results are not satisfactory, modifications can be made to any of the techniques used in the models. However, this is difficult to do if the cash manager does not have a firm understanding of how elements are related in the modeling technique developed.

The previous two sections of this chapter discussed the general environment of forecasting and related the forecasting approach to cash management. In order to apply forecasting methods and techniques to cash forecasts, a review of the specific elements involved in cash forecasts is required.

CONTEXT FOR CASH FORECASTING

At first glance forecasting corporate bank account data may appear a simple task; however, when the number of different elements and transactions that affect the accounts during the business day are considered the complexity of the situation is soon apparent. Though many factors influencing the cash forecasts are considered, an overall view must be taken to achieve the proper balance toward cash forecasting as a control tool. The two factors that permeate all elements of cash forecasting are:

- The futurity of the elements and related decisions
- The definition of the certain and uncertain attributes of the elements and subelements to be forecast

The importance of the time horizon related to forecasting has already been emphasized. The futurity of the elements involved in the forecast here relates to the immediate budget or capital period time horizon for the forecast elements. Elements are defined as those identifiable transaction types (generally not individually) that affect the account balances for the corporation. The futurity of related decisions deals not with the elements forecast but with the time horizon committed as a result of the forecast. For example, an overnight repurchase agreement offers much less exposure and risk since the corporation extends itself only for a 24-hour period, than committing funds to a 90-day security. The security of government treasury bills, for example, are virtually assured, but economic disadvantages may be present if the corporation needs to use those funds before the maturity date. For securities not traded openly, this problem is significantly magnified.

The futurity of the time forecast also has implications on the degree of error allowable in many cases. For example, often a 1-year forecast needs to be more accurate than a five-year forecast because capital expenditures might be required to satisfy an 11-month construction lead time. Although some industries, like communications, require high accuracy for long-range forecasts, most corporations do not base current financial allocations based on longer-term plans. Recent government statistics indicate that capital expenditures lag the development commitment by approximately 16 months. The degree of knowledge and certainty about elements making up the forecast is also an essential philosophical overlay to the forecasting process. By degree of "certainty" and "uncertainty" is meant that each element and subelement (if appropriate) to be forecast has some degree of certainty or uncertainty associated with it.

The degree of certainty may only apply to a part of an element. For example, wire transfers is an element affecting the ending account balance. A corporation may have certain knowledge about all outgoing wire transfers because it has developed a control system to track outgoing wires. However, it may only have a limited knowledge of incoming wire transfers. This differentiation would cause the element of wire transfers to be broken into subelements of incoming and outgoing. It is the combination of these that comprises the element forecast. The degree of certainty about elements and their subelements affects the number of different variables that require forecasting. An element to be forecast consists of known (certain) and unknown (uncertain) properties.

ELEMENTS AND SUBELEMENTS—A DEFINITION

The term "element" is used in order to identify the parts that comprise a cash forecast of a daily bank account balance or future cash requirement. A cash management related forecast is composed of all the quantifiable elements known to affect it. These quantifiable elements are directly related to the forecast result. If one of the elements is significantly in error, the result is directly reflected in the forecast result. Elements have individual degrees of certainty and uncertainty. The properties of each element are known to the cash manager as controlled properties that have either a high degree of certainty associated with it or are uncontrolled, which suggests either a further examination of the subelements or a statement that the overall significance of this uncertain element has be handled at the element or macroforecasting level.

A macroforecasting level is defined as one where the element is forecast based on its total volume over a time period. The element is not broken into subelements where each subelement would be microforecasted to make-up a composite forecast for the element. A subelement is defined as part of an element where the sum of the subelements form the whole of the element. Not all elements in a cash forecast either need to be nor lend themselves to subelement definition. Subelements can exist because of a cross section of reasons including:

- *Logical definition*—An element in the cash manager's forecast may logically need to be broken with several subelements so that adequate certainty can be defined and data accumulated regarding the subelement. An example of the type of element breakdown is the forecast element of wire transfers, which has logical subelements of a) incoming wire transfers and b) outgoing wire transfers.

- *The time dimension of the element*—Elements that may not logically lend themselves to subelement identification may require this delineation because of the time span of the element. For example, lockbox deposits may be considered a discrete element because a forecast amount is deposited each day. However, since the availability of those funds varies based on the drawee banks involved, the lockbox element could be broken into the subelement of day 1 available funds, day 2 available funds, and day 3 available funds. With this subelement breakdown control can be exercised over each contributing portion of the element.
- *Degree of certainty versus uncertainty*—Elements, even if logically broken into subelements, may be best treated at the element level if there is a high degree of certainty involved about the element forecast. For example, if cash deposits as a forecast element always amounts to 40% of daily deposits with a variance of only 2% it may be more economical to use this historically certain forecast factor than to incur the cost required to break the element into subelements of location or sales product and increase the degree of certainty. If an element is significant in size in terms of its impact on the forecast, then a breakdown of the element in identifiable subelements is essential. In this manner, the subelement may be considered separately, and appropriate forecasting techniques may be applied to each element before composing the element level forecast.

The breakdown of elements into subelements becomes more meaningful as the degree of required accuracy increases. For every subelement identified, an analysis and collection of data must precede the development of the forecasting mode. The accuracy required should be based on the futurity of the decisions to be made by the forecast and the significance of the existing error in the current element forecast.

The more extended a forecast (capital period time horizon), the greater the advantage to consolidating subelement into elements and combining elements into marcoelements if they are closely related. For example, an auto manufacturer forecasting a 5-year capital budget program is not interested in using the same element/subelement breakdown that the corporate cash manager uses for the daily cash forecast. The 5-year forecast may actually combine six or more of the cash manager's elements and forecast them as one element in the capital period horizon forecast. This is possible because the micro(daily)forecasts contain variable detail information that are negated in the longer-term forecasts. Time span is

The Cash Forecasting Elements

The number of subelements required for a cash forecasting model vary based on the time horizon. However, the basic elements remain the same in most situations. In order to begin a methodology within which to approach a cash forecast, the cash manager should examine each of these elements and identify the level of subelements involved. Although we discuss several subelements, they are in relation to a specified time horizon, which is the daily cash forecast. In the remainder of this section, we relate specifically to daily cash forecasts as developed by cash managers. In those areas where other time horizons are discussed, this is identified.

In developing the cash forecast, the cash manager should bear in mind that the element forecast is the sum of the subelements or

$$EF_i = SE_1 + SE_2 + SE_3 + \cdots + SE_n$$

where

$$EF_i = \text{the element forecast for element } i$$
$$CF = EF_1 + EF_2 + EF_n$$

where

CF = cash forecast
EF_n = the sum of the individual subelement forecasts for element n.

Some of the major elements to be considered in a cash forecast include:

Deposits

The various sources of deposits already discussed originate from corporate remittance offices or depositing lockbox banks. For cash management purposes, many corporate cash managers use concentration accounts where all funds are systematically transferred daily to concentration banks. This is accomplished using depository transfer checks drawn on the deposit banks. While the local checks are clearing the bank system, the depository transfer checks are also clearing. Deposits as an element in the daily cash forecast need to be broken into subelements of days for availability purposes. The DTCs when written usually are accompanied with an availability listing. The subelement deposits by time for the daily forecast are: DTC_0, dollar amount of DTCs good today; DTC_1 dollar amount good in one day; DTC_2, dollar amount of deposit good in two days; and DTC_3, dollar amount good in three days. For daily cash forecasting, it is necessary to track the amount of DTCs available to up-date daily forecast records. In this manner, the cash manager can concentrate funds and forecast the amount of funds clearing in time to use the data. The subelement in the concentration environment described here has a high degree of certainty and as a result would not require the application of any other forecasting technique. The deposit element can be determined with a high degree of certainty because of the required check clearing times at local depositories. This current environment may be drastically altered in the future with the advent of widespread use of electronic funds transfer services.

Immediate Availability Deposits

This element has been separated out because of its uncertain properties. This is the dollar amount of concentration deposits that have immediate availability to the corporation at the concentration bank. It is significant because a cash manager at 8:00 A.M. knows that the DTC_1 amount from yesterday will be available at tonight's demand deposit account processing, but the dollar amount of the DTCs having immediate availability tonight is not known. It is the combination of the DTC_1 and today's DTC_0 that makeup the total concentration deposit available. Since a significant degree of uncertainty surrounds this variable, a forecasting technique is required.

It should be noted that we are not interested in the total amount of deposits anticipated for today but only that amount resulting in immediate availability to the corporation. The forecasting approach could be to forecast the total receipts for the day and, based on empirical experience, apportion an average percent as "immediately" available funds. A consideration in assembling this forecast data is recognition of seasonal fluctuation for the data. With the use of cash information services now provided by banks, it is possible to track deposits during the day. This provides the cash manager with a reality check prior to the end of business so that adjustments can be made.

Disbursements

Another major element in daily cash forecasting is disbursements. In this area, the cash manager is interested in the dollar amounts of disbursements to clear the account at the end of the day not necessarily the total dollar amount of disbursements made by corporate offices. This element can be broken into subelements of time so that dollars of disbursements made by location can be placed into a time matrix for anticipated clearings. To facilitate the tracking of disbursements, several banks offer disbursement analysis services. Essentially the service works in conjunction with an account reconciliation service and provides a report on the number of total days it takes a check from issuance to clearance. Through the judicious use of various disbursements points, a company can develop a highly reliable "days outstanding" factor for its issuing location. The degree of certainty in disbursement forecasting is invaluable. In some cases, quantitative forecasting methods may apply if disbursements are made by many local offices and no disbursement reporting service is available.

Maturing Investments

As an element in cash forecasting, it can be broken into subelements of time. This element has application to the budget and capital period time horizons as well as to the daily cash forecast. The common types affecting the daily forecast of funds include: repurchase agreements, certificates of deposit, and treasury bills. On a scheduled basis, sinking fund payments and bond maturities also affect this element. There is a high degree of certainty associated with this element because payment is by contract, and unless instrument delivery is delayed the cash manager can rely on these funds as another source of capital.

Wire Transfers

Another important element in the daily cash forecast is wire transfers and should be broken down into subelements for control. The subelements should be based on the type of wire transfer—Federal Reserve wire transfer or bank wire transfer—and also on whether the wire is incoming for credit or outgoing for debit. The certainty regarding the wire transfer of funds varies considerably by the corporation depending upon the level of controls exercised and the communication with wiring parties. An analysis of this forecast variable may indicate use of one of the quantitative techniques discussed later. The dollar amounts associated with wire transfers tend to be large and have substantial impact on the daily forecast.

Investments

Investment is an element in the daily cash forecast that is certain and controllable by the cash manager. Transfers out of the corporate account is reflected in that day's business activity.

Increased Borrowings

Another factor of some significance in the daily forecast is increased borrowings. Funds borrowed are deposited to the corporation deposit account with the bank. The corporate cash manager, if in close contact with the bank, knows when the transfers are being made and can take advantage of any delayed outflow of funds to invest in short term instruments.

Equity Sale Income

Although equity sale income is not usually significant in frequency, its size is large enough to warrant control. This element may be of more meaning to real estate investment trusts where large properties could be liquidated.

Scheduled Capital Payments

Another element with a high degree of certainty is scheduled capital payments. This element is usually known far in advance of its required due date. It could include such subelements as sinking fund payments and dividends.

Required Compensating Balance

The required compensating balance is important to maintaining a good banking relationship, as discussed in Chapter 2. The amount of the required compensating balance varies by day but can be reconciled with the bank at an agreed upon period. The amount can be computed daily based on outstanding loan amounts and estimated service charges. Since the loan amounts outstanding are available to the cash manager and these usually represent the bulk of the charges, the majority of the required balance is known. Additional balances for service charges are maintained on a 1-month lag time basis.

Effect of Varying Time Horizons on Cash Element Forecasting

The daily forecast of cash for corporate use contains many certain elements and subelements that can be controlled in the near term. Because of the high degree of controllability, quantitative techniques may not apply as extensively as they might in a longer-term forecast. The more extended the time horizon, the less certain knowledge a cash manager has of the contents of the elements and subelements in the forecast. Consequently, the greater the application of quantitative techniques to forecast a future position for an element or subelement.

The element/subelement concept has a direct effect on the accuracy of the forecast using quantitative measures. For example, at a macroforecasting level, the total account balance or ending position is forecast for the next 2-month period based on past experience. An alternative approach, used to increase accuracy, is to forecast each of the subelements based on past experience and the sum of the subelements.

The time horizon where a high degree of certainty exists is narrow. For time periods greater than a few days, or a week at the most, estimates must be based on more than lead and lag times for elements in the forecast. For example, the deposit breakout of clearing items is only known for parts of 3 days in the future since each day's deposits increment each time period's total dollar amount coming due. The idea is to be able to forecast the total number of receivable dollars coming due and, based on past experience, define availability. The forecast for next week or next month or the budget period could definitely be based on quantitative forecasting techniques. Deposits represent one obvious area where the larger the time frame involved the greater the possible application of quantitative forecasting techniques.

The following elements discussed in the daily cash forecast also lend themselves directly to quantitative forecasting techniques:

- Accounts receivable—by day, by availability, by product, and by location
- Disbursements—operational
- Wire transfers (unknown-incoming amounts)

As the forecast period is extended, the element definition related to time becomes negligible. By this I mean that individual availabilities become less important because the end point is the only one being forecast.

The quantitative techniques offer two advantages to the cash manager when forecasting for the budget term, and capital term.

First, these methods can be easily used year after year. The initial development is sometimes difficult because of the historical data required; however, since accounting is time oriented, the time series quantitative approaches have access to historical data at the element level. Additionally, quantitative measures can be used by the cash manager as a comparison of historical projections versus actual need. In many firms, the budget period is composed of accounting methods (discussed later in this section) of estimating required resources for the coming year. The actual performance is not always measured against planned results at year's end. This is natural since emphasis is appropriately placed on the future operating periods and not the past except to analyze whether targets were achieved and to evaluate the reasons for variances from plans. However, the cash manager is concerned with variances from plans because it affects the cash flow on a daily basis and the planning of capital requirements. To track variances, quantitative forecasting techniques can be used to compare the past accounting-based forecast with the results of quantitative forecasting techniques. This can provide two measures of future capital requirement analysis: one from the managerial forecast level and the other based on past actual experience developed through a forecast model. Of course, the output of the model can only indicate what occurs if no definite action is taken; however, it includes past managerial decisions and their subsequent effects.

The second advantage of quantitative techniques for budget and capital period forecasting is that degrees of statistical confidence can be developed based on the laws of probability, which indicate the degree of confidence the cash manager can place on the quantitative technique or model designed. Depending upon the model developed, it can provide a base for decision making. Although a similar approach may be taken in measuring the accounting-based variances of planned versus actual, the range of variances may not be caused by the same situation. Consequently, each accounting-based variance is discrete and its variability from the target does not necessarily indicate any pattern or continuity.

SUMMARY

In this section, we have reviewed an approach within which cash forecasting can be viewed—both generally and related to elements in the cash forecast. Time horizons were emphasized to underscore its impact on the approach chosen. The more immediate the time period the greater the certain or known aspects of the elements and subelements that comprise the total forecast. The nearer the forecast period, the greater the accuracy required and the more appropriate a microforecast model where each subelement is treated discretely. The longer the time frame, the more likely a macromodel may be developed encompassing several elements in a forecast treated jointly.

The individual elements of a cash forecast were discussed along with possible subelement distinctions so that the cash manager may begin to compose the individual elements which apply to their environment. Finally, emphasis was placed on the futurity of decisions based on the results of cash related forecast and the ability to modify direction during the implementation period through control techniques.

The specific methods chosen for forecasting cash and cash resource requirements vary significantly by company and industry. Defining the level of accuracy required determines to a large extent both the cost of developing the cash-forecasting model and the futurity of the decision based upon the model.

Although accounting approaches have been widely used, an alternative is quantitative forecasting techniques where reliability ranges can be established. Above all other considerations, the cash manager needs to understand the variables that go into the cash forecast and how the technique developed operates. Without this level of involvement, the cash manager will not feel comfortable with the forecasting method.

CHAPTER 7

ACCOUNTING APPROACHES TO CASH FLOW FORECASTING[1]

PERSPECTIVE

Accounting is essentially the recording of commercial events that affect the operations of a corporate structure. By its nature, accounting is historical in perspective. However, because current cash flows are recorded and evaluated on the basis of accounting information, any discussion of forecasting techniques and methods* would not be complete without a discussion of the accounting-based approaches to funds flow and cash flow analysis. The methods of funds flow statements and cash receipts and disbursements are actually not techniques of forecasting at all but rather reporting frameworks within which future related funds flow information is placed. The form of both of these accounting methods are based on the desire to report historical data, and in themselves provide only a guideline or format to be used to develop future elements. Neither approach has any relation to the *how* of developing or generating forecast data. When cash managers are asked how cash forecasts are made, they often reply with one or the other or both of these approaches. Rather than discussing the techniques of how forecasts are made, a review of the form (as it varies for the company) is offered.

This is not to say that there is any inherent error in using these approaches to recording forecast results, but it is important to realize that

---

[1] The author wishes to acknowledge Warren Solt for his assistance with portions of this chapter.

* A forecast technique is defined as the approach or mechanism used to develop the forecast value. A forecast method is defined as the organized approach and presentation of the forecast values.

they are only reporting vehicles. The time horizon applicable to each approach differs with subsequent emphasis on the element and subelement forecast level. Using accounting forecast approaches to the funds flow forecast has the advantage of providing consistency between historical reporting and forecasts. Additionally, if elements and subelements are accounted for historically, they provide the basis for selection of a forecasting modeling technique whose results can be reported in one of the accounting formats.

THE FUNDS FLOW STATEMENT

The primary purpose of the funds flow statement (sometimes referred to as the Sources and Uses of Funds Statement) is to measure changes in the working capital of a company. These changes relate to a budget and capital period time horizon. The overall objective of the funds flow statement is to define what inflow of funds (the life blood of the corporation) occurs in the forecast time period and to identify the required uses of those funds. Funds as referred to in this context can be viewed from three perspectives.

First, funds can be viewed as working capital. This is defined as current assets less current liabilities and is the most common perspective of funds for a corporation. Without forecasts of net working capital increases or decreases the company could find itself unable to meet its current obligations. Since a certain level of working capital is required to operate a firm, the change in the amount required should indicate a shift in the cash base of operation that enables the firm to operate. An example of such a shift in a budget period time horizon is presented here. As demonstrated, a decrease of $13,000 has occurred; this could indicate, through the use of a funds flow statement, that an increase in inventory has occurred or that sales were less than expected or that receivables outstanding had increased since the last reporting period. Regardless of the cause, it does indicate a detrimental shift in corporate liquidity that reduces its ability to meet current cash flow obligations.

	January 1	*January 31*	*Net Change*
Current Assets	$120,000	$126,000	+$6,000
Current Liabilities	80,000	99,000	−19,000
Working Capital	$40,000	$27,000	−$13,000

Funds as used here can also be defined as cash and include all inflow of cash and its uses. This concept of funds relates to the very immediate flow of cash and marketable securities through a firm and is more appropriately used to describe the reporting function associated with cash receipts and disbursements.

Finally, funds can also be viewed as pure resources and include all inflows of economic resources and the subsequent resource utilization. From this perspective, funds represent all purchasing power provided by external sources for use by management. Funds are more than immediate cash and working capital; they are the resource represented by its line of available borrowing.

The Funds Flow Statement is directed toward adjusting accounting statements to reflect a working capital environment. This approach permits the cash managers to adjust the company's earnings reported on an accrual basis to a working capital basis. This is important because capital investment items may be purchased at one point in time but not charged off as depreciated until used to produce income to the corporation. When the apportioned charges are accrued, there is an impact on the net earnings of the corporation. However, there may have been no cash outflow associated with that expense. Consequently, to determine funds available, we need to take the net earnings from operations and add to it the nonfund expenses such as depreciation. The actual out-of-pocket expense for the equipment could have actually occurred several years before. The focus, therefore, for the funds flow statement is the working capital position of the company not the reporting of net income adjusted for tax reporting considerations. In this regard, corporate cash managers need to keep a set of accounting records for tax and shareholder reporting and a separate set for management of the cash resources. Although the focus of the funds flow statement is working capital, there are situations where working capital does not change and the cash manager needs to be aware of these situations. Changes in working capital do not occur when transactions:

- *Result in an offsetting increase or decreases in both current assets and current liabilities*—This could occur if the cash manager borrowed cash from its bank on a short-term note. Although the working capital position is not altered in this case, the cash manager does enjoy the use of additional cash.

- *Result in an increase in one asset account and a decrease in another*—An example of this situation is the collection of an accounts receivables item. Cash is increased, and the accounts receivable decreased. This transaction does not change the complexion of the corporate working capital structure. However, a sale for cash increases the working capital situation of the firm by the amount of profit from the sale since the production expenses need to be paid from the sales price. The profit added to the working capital base provides a source of new funds to the cash manager.

- *A decrease in one current liability account can be offset by a corresponding increase in another current liability account*—An example of this situation is payment of a payable by issuing a short-term note. There is no net cash difference in working capital in this situation as related to cash management.

Although these areas do not directly affect the cash manager in the funds flow area, cognizance of these transactions is necessary because they represent *future* action that relates to the funds control function. For example, a note payable entry needs to be scheduled for future payment in the corporation's scheduling system.

The source of funds included in the forecast approach should be defined. Some of the unusual sources and uses of funds that require forecasting consideration are:

- *Liquidation of fixed assets*—This can be a source of funds that affects the cash position controlled by the cash manager. Prior knowledge of liquidations is required so that stated forecasts can be adjusted.
- *Redefinition of working capital*—The decision to use short-term borrowing as part of a more permanent debt structure must be "managed" by the cash manager to the extent that current obligations can be effectively satisfied without disproportionate interest expenses or unreasonable long-term reliance on loan refinancing.
- *Increased corporate stock issue*—This is a source of additional funds that can be used if an increase in working capital is required. This is another source of funds that is commonly considered in the capital period time horizon.
- *Increased long-term debt*—This is a source of additional funds that usually requires senior management approval and sufficient lead time to negotiate a banking agreement.

The use of these sources of funds provides the company with additional funds to increase working capital or for long-term capital expansion requirements. These elements in the forecast, however, are usually nonrecurring in nature; that is, they are used in reaction to an impending or projected future need. Consequently, these elements are not usually found in a typical funds flow statement but rather are reflected in the asset and equity accounts analyzed to construct the funds flow statement.

ASSEMBLING THE FUNDS FLOW STATEMENT

The basis for constructing the funds flow statement are the balances from asset and liability accounts since these reflect the effect of near cash transactions. Not all transactions that take place in a corporation involve the flow of funds. We are interested in only those cash and near cash-related transactions; consequently, the other accrued-type transactions must be reversed.

The types of nonfund transactions to be eliminated include:

- *Depreciation expense*—As described earlier, this is an allocation of a used resource to current production and has no relationship to dollar outlays. The funds were *used* when the equipment was originally purchased, not when it is expensed for production.
- *Amortization of intangible assets*—Although these may be written off as a business expense, they have no effect on the cash resources of the corporation. Consequently, they must be eliminated from cash related records.
- *Amortization of bond discount or premium*—This type of transaction affects the profits of the corporation but is, in effect, an accounting reduction of an asset that does not translate into a cash flow impact.
- *Declaration of a dividend*—Again, this is an accrued liability that does not immediately affect the corporate cash position.
- *Currency revaluations*—In terms of profitability currency revaluations are extremely important from a multinational corporation's viewpoint but have limited day-to-day impact on the immediate corporate cash position. This affects the cash flow position of multinational corporations because of resulting changes in working capital. It occurs because receivables and payables are stated in several currencies, thus making the firm vulnerable to currency shifts. The impact of international cash management is discussed in detail in Part IV of this book.

Once the asset and liability accounts are identified, the first step in developing the funds flow statement is to calculate the difference between the beginning and the end of the period. Exhibit 7-1 is an example of a comparative balance sheet for the Electra Corporation and is used to illustrate the development of the funds flow statement.

The Adjustment Procedure

In order to evaluate the funds flow effect of activity on a corporation, either in an historical perspective or as a projection, we begin by identifying

Exhibit 7.1 The Electra Corporation: comparative balance sheet (all figures in thousands).

ASSETS:	19 x 1	19 x 2	increase (decrease)
Current Assets:			
Cash and Short Term Investments	$ 500	$1,210	$ 710
Accounts Receivable	600	1,600	1,000
Inventories	500	1,500	1,000
Prepaid Expenses	100	400	300
Total Current Assets	1,700	4,710	3,010
Property at cost:			
Land and Building	500	1,000	500
Equipment	500	1,750	1,250
Less Accumulated Depreciation	(100)	(200)	(100)
Property - Net	900	2,550	1,650
TOTAL ASSETS	$2,600	$7,260	$4,660
LIABILITIES AND STOCKHOLDERS EQUITY			
Current Liabilities:			
Notes Payable to Banks	$ 100	$1,100	$1,000
Accounts Payable	400	800	400
Accrued Expenses	500	900	400
Total Current Liabilities	1,000	2,800	1,800
Bonds Payable (net of discount): 19 x 1, $100; 19 x 2, $90)	1,000	1,710	710
Deferred Income Taxes	50	300	250
TOTAL LIABILITIES	2,050	4,810	2,760
STOCKHOLDERS EQUITY			
Common Stock	500	2,000	1,500
Retained Earnings	50	450	400
Stockholders Equity	550	2,450	1,900
TOTAL LIABILITIES AND STOCKHOLDERS EQUITY	$2,600	$7,260	$4,660

changes in the balance sheet. Although many transactions occur during the accounting period, the items of direct interest are those involving a flow of funds and the elimination of those that did not involve cash-type transactions. The critical questions to ask of each transaction include:

- Did a change that occurred result in an increase (or inflow) of funds to the company?
- Did this transaction cause an outflow of funds?
- Did this transaction have any effect on the company's funds position?

These questions need to be asked of transactions that caused identifiable changes in the balance sheet in Exhibit 7-1. To accomplish this task, a funds flow work sheet is sometimes used. The steps include:

1. Identify changes from the previous period for each account on the balance sheet to be evaluated in terms of its affect on the flow of funds through the corporation.

2. Fund flows identified must then be tracked back to their original entry for evaluation. For example, the gain on sale of property is reflected in the income statement. This indicates that a source of funds—not explicitly identified in the balance sheet—has contributed to the flow of funds through the corporation during the year. Exhibit 7-2 is the income statement for the Electra Corporation for the corresponding period. The information regard-

Exhibit 7.2 Electra Corporation: income statement.
19x2 (in $000)

SALES		$9,000
Costs and Operating Expenses:		
Cost of Sales	$6,000	
General and Administrative Expense	700	
Selling and Delivery Expense	1,000	
Total costs and operating expenses*		7,700
Operating income		1,300
Other expenses (Income):		
Gain on Sale of Property	(50)	
Interest Expense**	300	
Interest Income	(100)	
Other expense - net		150
Income before Income Taxes		1,150
Income Taxes:		
Current	300	
Deferred	250	550
NET INCOME		$ 600

* Includes depreciation expense of $200
** Includes Amortization of Bond Discount of $10

ing changes in accounts dealing with the flow of funds from both the balance sheet and income statement is used to develop both the funds flow and cash flow statements.

3. Transactions that have been recorded but that do not involve the flow of funds are reversed out of consideration. Such is the case in the reduction of an intangible asset. Following the identification of nonfund transactions the funds flow statement can be assembled.

In evaluating the funds flow of the Electra Corporation based on entires from the balance sheet and income statements, we learn that:

- The net increase to retained earnings of $400 was affected by net income. However, since the increase in retained earnings for the period is less than the net income of $600, further examination is required.
- From the income statement, we learn that depreciation expense for this year was $200. This must be added back as a recorded transaction not affecting the flow of funds.
- The gain on the sale of property and equipment indicates that the proceeds added funds to operations during the year. To determine the facts of this transaction, we must go back to the original entries:

Cash	200	
Accumulated Depreciation	100	
Property and Equipment		250
Gain on Sale of Property		50

This transaction indicates that a fixed asset had a cost of $250 and $100 recorded against it as depreciation leaving a book value of $150. Since it was sold for cash of $200, we realized a $50 gain on the sale of the fixed asset.

The essential consideration in performing this analysis is identification of and adjustment for nonfund transactions so a clear "fund position" analysis can be performed. The common types of nonfund transactions include:

- Depreciation expense
- Amortization of intangible assets
- Disposition of fixed assets
- Amortization of bond discounts
- Deferred income taxes

Having reviewed the "evaluation" technique, the cash manager is ready to prepare the Funds Flow Statement using both the balance sheet and income statement as sources of information. Exhibit 7-3 is the funds flow statement for the Electra Corporation.

Examination of the funds flow statement of the Electra Corporation reveals a different picture than only reviewing the income statement or balance sheet. Though the firm is profitable based on operations, it did not

Exhibit 7.3 Electra Corporation: funds flow statement.

19x2 (in $000)

Sources of Funds:		
Operations:		
Net Income	$600	
Add expenses not using funds:		
Depreciation	200	
Deferred Income Taxes	250	
Armortization of Bond Discount	10	
Remove Gain from Sale of Property	(50)	
Funds Provided by Operations		$1,010
Sale of Bonds and Long Term Borrowing		900
Proceeds from Sale of Property		200
Sale of Common Stock		1,500
TOTAL SOURCES		$3,610
Uses of Funds:		
Purchase of Property and Equipment		$2,000
Cash Dividends		200
Repayment of Long Term Borrowings		200
TOTAL USES		$2,400
Increase (decrease) in Working Capital		$1,210
Increase (decrease) in Working Capital Components		
Cash and Short Term Investments		$ 710
Accounts Receivable		1,000
Inventories		1,000
Prepaid Expenses		300
TOTAL CURRENT ASSETS		3,010
Notes Payable		1,000
Accounts Payable		400
Accrued Expenses		400
TOTAL CURRENT LIABILITIES		$1,800
Increase (decrease) to working capital		$1,210

generate enough funds from operations to support itself. Rather it had to sell bonds and borrow against its bank lines for $900 and sell common stock for $1500 to generate sufficient funds to cover heavy but required investment in the purchase of property and equipment. Without this analysis, it might seem that the Electra Corporation generated an increase in available funds from operations alone when, in fact, without selling stock and borrowing the company could have been profitable but illiquid.

THE CASH FLOW STATEMENT

Cash flow statements are not the same as funds flow statements; although they are sometimes referred to in the same context, they have different objectives. The objective of the funds flow statement is to illustrate more than just cash-related activity.

The objective of the cash flow statement is to high-light all sources and uses of *cash* and near cash assets. It is a summary in many respects of the daily cash receipts and disbursement tracking method because it attempts to show where cash came from and what liabilities were created during the periods under comparison, whereas the funds flow works from the top down. Using the balance sheet and income statement, the cash flow statement can be viewed as a bottom up approach based on the detail of the cash receipts and disbursement approach to cash flow analysis. Exhibit 7-4 illustrates this concept. The cash flow statement shows the corporation's near term liquidity in managing income and satisfaction of cash obligations. Exhibit 7-5 is an example of a cash flow statement. It can be used by cash managers as a historical base on which to trace trends in accounts such as accounts receivables. If time horizons are consistent, it can serve as a basis for defining seasonal fluctuation in both accounts receivable and accounts payable.

Advantages and Disadvantages

The primary criticism of the cash flow statement is that it does not record all significant transactions in working capital accounts. The cash manager can, however, use this report to his advantage on a weekly basis to evaluate cash-related activity. It can be developed from the cash receipts and disbursement control method. In contrast, the funds flow statement is limited because it only illustrates changes in working capital and does not high-light trends in individual accounts.

As the cash flow statement illustrates, a quite different perspective is achieved of the Electra Corporation's liquidity position. Although the firm

Exhibit 7.4 Forecasting format, structural development

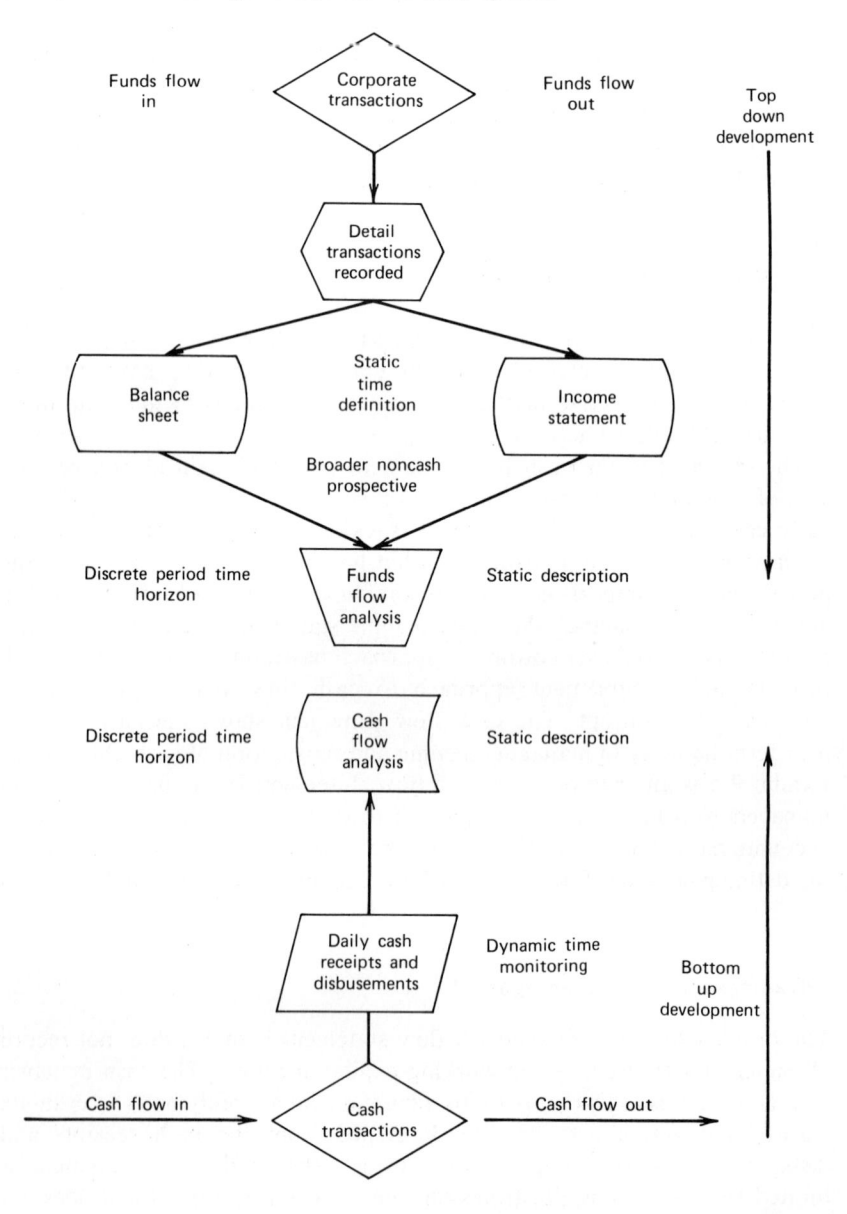

Exhibit 7.5 Electra Corporation: cash flow statement

19x2

Sources of Cash:

Operations:			
Sales		$9,000	
Add decrease (deduct increase) in Accounts Receivable		(1,000)	$8,000
Interest Income			100
Costs and Expenses:			
Costs and Operating Expenses		7,700	
Interest expense		300	
Income taxes		550	
Add increase (deduce decrease) in Inventories		1,000	
Add increase (deduce decrease) in Prepaid Expense		300	
Add decrease (deduct increase) in Accounts Payable		(400)	
Add decrease (deduce increase) in Accrued Expenses		(400)	
Add decrease (deduce increase) in Deferred Income taxes		(250)	
Deduct Non Cash Expenses:			
Depreciation		(200)	
Amortization of Bond Discount		(10)	
		8,590	(8,590)
Cash provided by (used by) operations			(490)
Increase in Notes Payable to Bank			1,000
Sale of Bonds and other long term borrowings			900
Proceeds from sale of fixed assets			200
Sale of Common stock			1,500
Total Sources of Cash			3,110

Uses of Cash:

Purchases of property and equipment	2,000
Cash Dividends	200
Repayment of Long Term Borrowing	200
Total Uses of Cash	2,400

Increase in Cash and Short Term Investments $ 710

generated $600 profit from operation, based on the income statement, and looks to be in liquid position, we find from the cash flow statement that operations actually used $490 of net cash. Even though the income statement and the funds flow statements do not indicate it, if Electra Corporation had not borrowed funds of $1000 from the bank and sold additional common stock for $1500, the firm could have found itself unable to meet current financial obligations. While there was a net increase in the firm's liquidity, it rose not from operations but the increase in liability and stockholders equity. Although the funds flow statement shows an increase to working capital of $1210, the increase in available cash for the Electra Corporation is only $710. This example illustrates the importance of using several approaches to evaluate the liquidity-related position of a company.

SUMMARY—FUNDS FLOW AND CASH FLOW STATEMENTS

There are two principal reasons for the cash manager to use the funds flow and cash flow statements:

- As an analysis of what has happened
- As a planning tool for future periods

The historical components of both methods can be used by the cash manager as a basis for using quantitative forecasting methods (described in Chapter 8) to accurately predict trends in individual elements. The planning aspect relates to the use of the format to describe what may happen based on past results. For the cash manager, these cash-forecasting methods indicate the degree of internal financing that has historically occurred and the extent that required funds have been derived from debt issues as opposed to equity offerings. Since corporate policies change over time, these approaches can be helpful, not only in identifying basic shifts in operational factors, but also shifts in internal policies that affect the cash manager's functions.

A funds flow statement shows the sources of funds used by the corporation and how the funds were used. The funds flow statement centers on the change in working capital in total and as such does not deal with *detail* shifts in receivables, payables, or inventory. Funds provided by operations as net income are adjusted for depreciation expense and other noncash-related transactions. For quarterly, semiannual, and annual projections, the funds flow method provides a useful measure of corporate direction. However, to be relevant to the cash manager, important changes in the working capital accounts should be continually monitored from a bottom up perspective.

Neither the funds flow approach nor the cash flow statement provides a daily control mechanism for the cash manager. This daily control vehicle takes the form of the cash receipts and disbursements methods.

CASH RECEIPTS AND DISBURSEMENTS METHODS

In the previous section, we discussed the funds flow approach to cash forecasting for the cash manager. While the basic funds flow and cash flow approaches focus on the changes in working capital accounts for the firm over an accounting-based period, the cash manager involved in an aggressive cash management program requires a firm control on the daily activity of the corporation's cash resources. This daily control is not provided by the funds flow or cash flow methods. The approach most commonly used today to provide this microlevel of control is the cash receipts and disbursements accounting method.

Purpose

On a daily basis, it is essential that appropriate amounts of cash are available to cover operating expenses. If enough cash is not available, the corporation needs to borrow short-term funds to cover its obligations. To effectively accomplish this, the cash manager must trace daily activities through each cash-related account. The purpose of the cash receipts and disbursements method is to track specific entries in the companies cash-related accounts. Although the overall *structure* of working capital is important to the corporation, it does not have a direct impact on the daily need for cash funds. The time horizon related to the cash receipts and disbursements forecasting method is usually daily, weekly, and monthly forecasts of transactions affecting cash accounts. To this extent, this method is more control oriented than long range–planning oriented.

In order to track cash items, it is convenient to consider cash and marketable securities alike and to envision that they are recorded in one account. It is the changes to this account that interest the cash manager on a daily basis. To the beginning balance of cash are added all sources of cash for the next day based on the forecast of each element in the format. From this is subtracted all anticipated use of cash for the period being forecast. One approach to control the process is to construct a "T" account reflecting the probable forecast elements for the period. By making summary entries to the cash account, the projected balance may be obtained. The debits to the cash account represent sources of cash, and the credits represent uses of cash. The method used to track items is not as important as the inclusion of all input sources and the breakdown of elements to the appropriate tracking level.

Elements in the Cash Receipts and Disbursements Approach

In order to construct a cash receipts and disbursements forecast, the cash manager must first list the major elements that apply to the daily *input and output* of cash related elements for his particular company. These elements, and subelements, can be generically described as:

Accounting Approaches to Cash Flow Forecasting

Inputs to the Cash Receipts and Disbursements Forecast

Cash Sales. For companies operating from decentralized locations, the cash sales need to be identified by location. The forecast for cash sales is made for each day of the planning period. This enables the cash manager to estimate the total cash contribution made to the company cash position. Each location can be forecast based on the overall ratio of cash sales to total sales by day or through use of a quantitative forecast methods that is discussed in Chapter 8. An example of the ratio approach follows:

Electra Corporation. Daily Sales Forecast

Division "A" Total Weekly Sales = $100,000

Day	Total Sales	Percent Cash Sales	Forecasted Cash Sales
Monday	15,000	5	750
Tuesday	25,000	10	2500
Wednesday	25,000	4	1000
Thursday	20,000	7	1400
Friday	15,000	2	300

The daily cash receipts from operations for the Electra Company would be entered on a cash receipts and disbursements worksheet as one of the required daily cash-related elements. In lieu of a straight ratio forecast, a moving average of the percent distributions of cash to sales on a daily basis could be maintained so that changes in the daily percentages could be detected and included in the daily forecast.

Collection of Accounts Receivable. Although, the most important contributor to the daily cash position for most firms, it is also the most difficult element to forecast because it depends on the accuracy of the sales forecast as well as the paying habits of customers. One approach to determining daily collection patterns is to project the collection of receivables for the month for the company and then, based on historical experiences, deduce the estimated daily receivables. Of course, such factors as seasonal patterns of sales and paying habits of customers must be considered. Additionally, the pattern of receipts from receivables is influenced by the mail service from various areas of division locations. An example of a method of forecasting sales for a company and relating it to daily receipts is:

Forecast of July Accounts Receivables Receipts

Historical payment patterns indicate that of sales made receipts will be:

- 60% in the month of the sale
- 35% in the month following the sale
- 3% in the third month following the sale
- 2% bad debts

Sales forecast by the Sales Department are:

March	$110,000
April	120,000
May	150,000
June	140,000
July	110,000

Expected Forecast of July Accounts Receivable Receipts

60% of 110,000 = $66,000
35% of 140,000 = 49,000
3% of 150,000 = 4,500
Element Forecast $119,500

Having determined the forecast amount for the month, it is the task of the cash manager to refine this data into weekly and then daily forecasts for cash receipts. Using past experiences and taking into consideration such factors as seasonal effects on customer payments, the distribution of weekly receipts can be forecast. For Electra Corporation, the following distribution was defined:

Weekly Receipts Forecast Distribution of Total Monthly Accounts Receivable

Receipts for July of $119,500

First week = 20% = $23,800
Second week = 40% = $47,800
Third week = 10% = $11,950
Fourth week = 30% = $35,850

Since forecasting is not an exact science, there will be some variance from week to week. However, studying the patterns of daily payments and using moving averages (illustrated in Chapter 8) for the weekly forecast, the percentage distributions can be dynamically up-dated during the forecasting process. The last step for the cash manager is to develop daily receipts for the collection of the corporation's accounts receivable. The same approach can be used for the daily forecast as was used to develop the weekly distributions. The cash manager needs to chart the dollar receipts daily for a test period to determine percentage distributions for daily deposits of receivables. For the Electra Corporation, the following distributions were derived by plotting daily distributions percentages for a 1-year period.

Daily Percentage Distribution for Receivables

	Week 1	Week 2	Week 3	Week 4
Monday = 30% =	$7,140	14,340	3,585	10,755
Tuesday = 25% =	$5,950	11,950	2,988	8,963
Wednesday = 15% =	$3,570	7,170	1,792	5,377
Thursday = 10% =	$2,380	4,780	1,195	3,585
Friday = 20% =	$4,760	9,560	2,390	7,170

In using this forecasting approach, the cash manager must make allowances for gradual modifications in the percentages used for each of the time horizons. The specific methods available to facilitate this are discussed later under quantitative methods of forecasting.

Forecasting the daily receivables is difficult not only because conditions outside business control affect the accuracy of the forecast (such as strikes and weather conditions) causing slower mail deliveries, but also because the payments scheduled for receipt must clear the banking collection process and be centralized. The clearance process has been covered in Chapter 2. The important consideration in this area is that deposits made by divisions of a company are not available to the cash manager until they are "collected" through the banking system. The method of using depository transfer checks has already been discussed. Under this concentration method, the cash manager needs to distinguish between the dollar of deposits that are available immediately, in 1 day or in 2 days or more. The cash manager needs to forecast the amount of funds that will be deposited today for the corporation from accounts receivable payments that will be immediately available for use. The funds that have 1-day availability are placed in tomorrow's summary columns. The cash manager receives the information of deposits daily from either deposit-reporting services or from division and sales corporate locations direct daily reporting.

Since forecasts of daily funds must be made early in the day, the cash manager does not know the total funds deposited during the day that have immediate availability. It is this amount that is forecasted daily. The accuracy of the forecast is known by the end of the day when deposit reports for the day are produced. At that time, the total dollar deposits are also known so that subsequent days' forecasts may be modified if significant variances have occurred. The degree that subsequent forecasts are modified depends to a great extent on the judgment of the cash manager and his confidence in the overall accuracy of the weekly forecast.

The collection of accounts receivable is at the same time the most important item in most daily cash forecasts and the most difficult to estimate. These examples have summarized a common approach to the forecast problem. The basic source of information regarding the sales amounts for a period and for obtaining up-dates is the annual sales projections. These may need modification by the cash manager based on empirical experiences. For example, if the actual sales have been only 85% of projections, then receivable projections should be scaled down to be in concert with past experience.

Sales of Investments. Another contributing element in the daily cash forecast is the dollar amount of short- and long-term investments maturing. Based on the daily cash receipts and disbursements worksheet presented in Exhibit 7-6, investments can be made to mature on days when it is known that expenditures are greater than projected receipts. When investments are initially made, their due amount should be logged on the worksheet so the maturing funds are counted in the day's total receipts. Since this element possesses a high degree of certainty, there is no need for sophisticated forecasting techniques. When investments are made, the due amount and due date are known factors that can be entered into the system well in advance of their impact on the cash position of the corporation.

Sale of Fixed Assets. This element can have a significant effect on the daily forecast of funds. Although it does not occur with any regularity, a reporting mechanism needs to be established so that major influx of funds are reported. In some firms, there is a standard procedure requiring divisions to report to the cash manager any transactions that will affect the cash position over a defined dollar amount a specified number of days in advance of the transaction so plans can include the impending transaction.

Interest and Dividend Collections. During the quarterly forecast, this element requires input from subsidiaries owned by the company or projections of earnings of stock held by the company. Interest may be collected from

Exhibit 7.6 The Electra Corporation: cash receipts and disbursements forecasts

JULY - WEEK #1

ELEMENT ID	MONDAY Projected	MONDAY Actual	TUESDAY Projected	TUESDAY Actual	WEDNESDAY Projected	WEDNESDAY Actual	THURSDAY Projected	THURSDAY Actual	FRIDAY Projected	FRIDAY Actual
INPUT:										
Cash Sales	750		2,500		1,000		1,400		300	
Receivable Receipts	7,140		5,950		3,570		2,380		4,760	
Investments Maturing	300,000		1,500,000		750,000		2,500,000		1,250,000	
Sales of Fixed Assets	-0-		-0-		-0-		500,000		-0-	
Interest/Dividends Collections	-0-		-0-		-0-		-0-		20,000	
Short Term Bank Loans	-0-		300,000		-0-		-0-		100,000	
Stock/Bond Issued	-0-		-0-		-0-		-0-		-0-	
Other Sources										
TOTAL INFLOW	307,890		1,808,450		754,570		3,003,780		1,375,060	
OUTPUT:										
Clearances										
Payables	100,000		40,000		15,000		60,000		240,000	
Payroll	-0-		-0-		-0-		-0-		1,100,000	
Insurance	-0-		-0-		70,000		-0-		-0-	
Drafts Presented	200,000		140,000		70,000		90,000		60,000	
Special Purchases	-0-		-0-		-0-		100,000		100,000	
Scheduled Loan Payments	-0-		-0-		-0-		500,000		-0-	
Other Disbursements	-0-		-0-		9,000		-0-		-0-	
TOTAL OUTFLOW	300,000		180,000		164,000		650,000		1,410,000	
NET CASH POSITION	7,890		1,628,450		590,570		2,353,780		- 34,940	

long-term investments made in other firms, as part of a longer-term investment policy. On a daily basis, this element does not have a major bearing on the activities of the cash manager.

Bank Loans. Since short-term borrowing is common for most businesses to help them over temporary shortages in working capital, the element of bank loans becomes both a source of daily cash and a possible investment media for short-term placement of excess funds. Usually, as the corporation notifies the bank of its desire to draw on its line of credit, the bank lending officer effects a deposit of the funds to the demand deposit (checking) account of the corporation. Since several financial executives in a company may have the authority to borrow funds, it is essential for the cash manager to be notified of loan drawdowns because it may be possible to use all or part of these funds before they are cleared through the bank system. This basic communication problem becomes more complicated when several decentralized corporate locations have the autonomy to drawdown for operational requirements. The control of cash movement in using borrowed funds is facilitated by consolidated dealings with a few major banks. However, decentralized corporate locations sometimes have authority to negotiate credit lines locally because of indigenous local requirements or community concerns.

Even though most corporations do not have funds transferred to their account until the money is needed, in some cases there are unanticipated delays in the disbursement of the funds or float in the actual payment of the funds. For this reason, the cash manager may be able to temporarily use these funds to balance his daily cash management program. An example of this situation occurred when a vendor released pipeline supplies to a customer on the verification—by the customer's bank—that the $5 million required for the sale was on deposit. The vendor was paid by check and the cash manager notified. Because of inclement weather (place of payment was in Alaska) and attending transportation problems, it was 9 days before this large item was cleared against the issuing company's bank account. The cash manager was involved in the initial transfer of funds, because he was to be notified of company transfers of $1 million or more, thus he was able to use the $5 million for 9 days at a money utilization rate of 8%, earning $9863. Even if the funds could not be withdrawn from the bank, the corporation still receives credit for the funds on deposit that apply to satisfying loan-related compensating balances or support transaction charges for depository, wire transfers, or similar services.

Issuance of Stocks or Bonds. As a daily consideration, this element is significant only occasionally. However, when new funds are being generated by the sale of stock or the issuance of bonds, the planned schedule of receipts from subscription should be followed closely because of the large amounts of cash generated from this element. The cash manager in conjunction with the parties responsible for issuing the stocks or bonds should develop a cash flow forecast for the period within which the offering is planned. Since the funds may not be required immediately, the cash manager may acquire large amounts of funds, which are unrelated to the operational aspects of the corporation.

Although these elements represent the major sources of cash to the cash manager involved in daily cash forecasting, the following elements describe the major uses of cash on a daily basis.

Outputs Affecting the Cash Receipts and Disbursements Forecast

Payment of Current Liabilities. The most common elements in this generic cash-utilization category include: operational material suppliers, payroll expenses, supplies, taxes, freight, insurance expense, dividend payments, and rent. Although these in no way exhaust the list of normal short-term disbursements, they represent many of the elements likely to cause daily expenditure of funds. Next to forecasting the daily amount of accounts receivable, the forecast of the disbursements to clear the corporation's account in a given day is the most difficult element to forecast. Since the cash manager is only concerned with the amount of funds being presented against the account on a daily basis, tracking the total funds issued by location may not appear important. Usually each check-disbursing (major) location of the corporation reports daily the amount of check disbursements issued that day. If a central disbursement account is used by the corporation, control is improved; otherwise many local banks may result in varying clearance schedules and compound the float factors that the cash manager must monitor.

Many cash managers using centralized disbursement accounts are able to purchase a disbursement tracking service from their support bank to reconcile their corporate checks and to provide a comprehensive float factor for check clearance based on when and where checks are issued. Basically, this service is available by major cash management banks and operates as follows: The company sends a list (manual listing or magnetic tape) of checks issued on the bank. When checks are presented for payment, the bank matches the issue location and the check number to produce reports that summarize how long it took for the check to be presented for payment from the date it was written.

Cash managers can make significant use of this type of service to forecast how long checks written in a specific location of the company will take to clear as opposed to any other corporate location. Consequently, when a reporting location calls in its disbursement amount daily it can be "spread" based on the percentage distributions known to exist for that location. Exhibit 7-7 is an example of the type of analysis report produced by the disbursement float service. By continual review of the percentage distributions produced by the service, the cash manager can detect changes in disbursement patterns before they distort the daily disbursement forecast. This relatively new computer-based service provides a significant degree of certainty to the cash manager in the daily forecast of disbursement funds. Basic changes in the clearance patterns are caused by modification of postal services and changes in the Federal Reserve's methods of clearances.

Large dollar payments also affect the clearance pattern because they are separately handled. An additional level of disbursement-forecasting sophistication is available for daily dynamic input of corporate disbursements. Through a time-sharing terminal, the cash manager enters the amount being disbursed, bank locations, and receiving points. A series of interpretive programs based on historical experience then predict the presentment amounts by day for a specific period.

Recently, a cash manager in Los Angeles found that these normally accurate daily forecasts were significantly overdrawn. After some analysis, the company discovered that the Federal Reserve had initiated a regional check-processing center in their area of operation. As a direct result, payment clearances were accelerated leaving the corporation overdrawn with their concentration bank. Had this firm been using one of the two disbursement tracking systems described it could have known the effect on each location of the firm resulting from the improved check processing approach.

Draft Payments. Draft payments are another element in the daily use of funds. They have been separated from the payment of current liabilities because they are usually handled centrally for control purposes and are payable to the presenting bank. Drafts have been described earlier in Chapter 3. Since the cash manager must complete his daily forecast in the day he must estimate the amount of drafts that are presented for payment by the payable through bank or banks. This information is available to the cash manager using a cash management control bank. The drafts are processed through the bank as checks but are handled as exception items since they must be presented directly to the corporation for payment. From the daily direct deposit account computer run, the cash manager control bank can extract the total dollar amount of drafts due for presentation to the firm. The cash manager can use this information to estimate the end-of-day balance early enough to invest excess funds or move funds to cover

Exhibit 7.7 Float report

DATE 04/07/78
ACCOUNT NO. 000 05555555 NAME PNB FLOAT ACCT 5 - VARIABLE PERIOD ENDING 03-31-78
CHECKS EXCEEDING $25.00

DAYS	COUNT	PCT	AMOUNT	PCT	DEPOSIT GENERATION
0		.00	.00	.00	.00
1	68	18.78	12,400.40	22.82	688.91
2	58	16.02	10,837.66	19.94	1,204.18
3	22	6.07	4,369.48	8.04	728.24
4	4	1.10	834.22	1.53	185.38
5		.00	.00	.00	.00
6	4	1.10	512.02	.94	170.67
7	8	2.20	1,321.67	2.43	543.98
8		.00	.00	.00	.00
9	2	.55	392.37	.72	196.18
10	2	.55	395.86	.72	219.92
11	2	.55	247.34	.45	151.15
12	1	.27	181.53	.33	121.02
13	78	21.54	9,674.99	17.80	6,987.49
14	50	13.81	5,744.48	10.57	4,467.92
15	9	2.48	1,092.72	2.01	910.60
16	14	3.86	1,556.65	2.86	1,383.68
17	9	2.48	1,313.75	2.41	1,240.76
18	9	2.48	876.85	1.61	876.85
19	10	2.76	1,000.45	1.84	1,056.03
20	1	.27	121.45	.22	134.94
20-40	10	2.76	1,318.41	2.42	
OVER-40	1	.27	137.59	.25	
TOTAL	362	100.00	54,329.89	100.00	21,237.90

WEIGHTED AVERAGE DAYS OUT 7.03

PD-NO-ISS   26   4,783.10
DROPPED   0   .00
BALANCE   388   59,112.99

FLOAT REPORT

DAYS	COUNT	PCT	AMOUNT	PCT	DEPOSIT GENERATION
0		.00	.00	.00	.00
1		.00	.00	.00	.00
2		.00	.00	.00	.00
3	68	18.78	12,400.40	22.82	1,430.81
4	58	16.02	10,837.66	19.94	1,667.33
5	22	6.07	4,369.48	8.04	840.23
6		.00	.00	.00	.00
7	4	1.10	834.22	1.53	224.59
8		.00	.00	.00	.00
9		.00	.00	.00	.00
10		.00	.00	.00	.00
11	4	1.10	512.02	.94	216.62
12	8	2.20	1,321.67	2.43	610.00
13		.00	.00	.00	.00
14	2	.55	392.37	.72	211.27
15		.00	.00	.00	.00
16		.00	.00	.00	.00
17	79	21.82	9,895.92	18.21	6,470.40
18	2	.55	247.34	.45	171.23
19	50	13.81	5,720.57	10.52	4,180.41
20	1	.27	174.93	.32	134.56
20-40	60	16.57	6,973.65	12.83	
OVER-40	4	1.10	649.66	1.19	
TOTAL	362	100.00	54,329.89	100.00	21,237.90

WEIGHTED AVERAGE DAYS OUT 7.73

PD-NO-ISS   26   4,783.10
DROPPED   0   .00
BALANCE   388   59,112.99

deficit positions. For banks unable to provide this service, the cash manager must estimate the amounts being presented. This can be accomplished by using historical experience of clearance times from issuing locations (since drafts are not included in the tracking system previously described) or develop a quantitative model based on an appropriate combination of techniques described later.

Purchase of Long-lived Assets. The elements included in this generic category are planned purchases of capital equipment, land, or special security equipment and are written off over a period of time. Since these expenditures are large, the cash manager must be included in the scheduling of payments so that funds may be used to the point of collection by the payee. This is an area where the cash receipts and disbursements approach differs from the funds flow method. The purchase of long-lived assets results in a reduction of funds when issued and no further concern with the transaction. The funds flow statement, on the other hand, in each succeeding period adds back to the net income figure the amount of depreciation charged against the income. It is this approach that has led to so much confusion about the nature of depreciation as a source of income as described previously. Suffice it to say, in the purchase of a long-lived asset, the day the funds are issued represents when the actual cost borne by the corporation. As the cash receipts and disbursements work sheet demonstrates, the firm's account balances are immediately affected by the purchase of a long-lived asset, and there is no entry for depreciation of that asset as a real source of funds. Its only purpose is accounting based for tax purposes and is not reflected in the real daily disposition of corporate funds.

Loan Payments. Another set of elements that the cash manager uses as a use of funds is the scheduled or unscheduled payment of bank loans. Scheduled loan payments are defined in the original borrowing agreement made between the bank and the corporation. Unscheduled loan payments are short-term paydowns of loans by a corporation to reduce its overall interest expense. This unscheduled paydown is an investment of excess corporate funds on a temporary basis in the reduction of its own liabilities. The short-term investment approach is often used by cash managers whose firms operate in a net borrowed position with its banks. This type of firm is typically aggressive in its expansionary policies and would rather place working profits back into the expansion of the business rather than permanently pay off its loans outstanding. Interest payment paydowns rather than short-term investments are more appropriate in this situation because the company utilizes a policy of heavy permanent debt structure.

Other Disbursements. Even though the disbursement elements already described represent most of the common areas of daily cash outflow, other areas indigenous to the company exist. Two of these—the payment of bond interest and scheduled sinking fund payments—affect the daily forecast in major proportions, but they are not regular in nature. As described, the cash manager must develop an internal method of communication so that major expenditures do not occur without his cognizance.

OUTPUTS OF THE CASH RECEIPTS AND DISBURSEMENT FORECAST

The cash receipts and disbursements method can be used for varying short-term time periods with good results. The basic output form is demonstrated in Exhibit 7-8. This must be modified to account for the needs of each company using this approach to monitor their daily, weekly, monthly, or quarterly position. A modified format is presented in Exhibit 7-6. It is advisable to include a forecast and actual column for each element and each day. By placing the cash-related data in the appropriate element when known, a component picture of future funds begins to appear days before the forecast day. This forward posting includes items of receipts and disbursements. Additionally, if forecasts vary significantly from actual, the cash manager may want to adjust subsequent forecasts. The amount of the adjustment is dependent upon the degree of confidence placed in the original forecast.

FACTORS AFFECTING ACCURACY

While physical factors affect the accuracy of this short-term forecast method, there are other factors that influence the use of this method including:

- *Pattern recognition*—Since each element discussed must be forecast each day, the known pattern of the elements has a direct effect of the reliability. This is especially important for elements such as receivables and disbursement clearances.
- *Degree of central control*—The greater the number of locations, the greater the difficulty for the cash manager to receive, modify, and analyze the data related to various disbursed bank relations maintained by the corporation. If central management of deposit accounts and disbursement accounts can be effected, the cash managers job is greatly simplified. Otherwise, extensive worksheets must be maintained for the various locations.

Exhibit 7.8 General cash receipts and disbursement format

	LAST YEAR'S DAILY ACTUAL	THIS YEAR'S DAILY FORECAST	THIS YEAR'S DAILY ACTUAL	INCREASE OR DECREASE
CASH RECEIPTS				
Collection on receivables by divisions				
Total collection on receivables				
Dividend Income				
Sale of Assets				
Other				
Total Cash Receipts				
CASH DISBURSEMENTS				
Operating expenses by division				
Total operating Expenses				
Income Taxes				
Capital Expenditures				
Payroll				
Advertising				
Insurance				
Repayment of Debt				
Interest Expense				
Dividends				
Other				
Total Cash Disbursements				
Excess cash disbursements				
Excess receipts over disburesements				
Cash and Short-term Investments Period beginning				
Increase (decrease) in bank loan				
Cash and Short-term Investments Peroids ending				

- *Business disruptions*—Such disruptions as strikes and adverse weather conditions result in delays in receipts of cash and presentation of disbursements. When this occurs the daily accuracy of the cash receipts and disbursements method requires significant short-term adjustment.
- *Insensitivity to trend changes*—Because this method works with the daily flow of items through accounts, it cannot distinguish between random changes in data and gradual trend shifts in the individual accounts. Consequently, longer-range inaccuracies are likely to occur if this approach is used for any but the immediate period time horizon.
- *Undrawn funds*—Undrawn funds occur when disbursements are ordered by the cash manager but when the order is not executed. Securities that are purchased but that the securities agent does not collect the funds on the same day as agreed is an example. Here the cash manager has use of the uncollected funds to cover required compensating balances at the bank while enjoying the interest income from the securities purchased. The amounts involved in this area of unanticipated balances varies significantly, but if the corporation is in an investing position, it is possible to forecast the percentage amounts of investments placed that are not collected the same day. In addition to uncollected funds, corporations may also want to forecast the "variable" or "random" distortion in their forecast. This can be accomplished using quantitative techniques or developing simple ratios of historical variances to total cash projected.

ELEMENT FORECASTING TECHNIQUES

The cash receipts and disbursements forecasting method provides a format within which elements of a daily, weekly, or monthly forecast may be placed. However, it does not indicate how to forecast the elements. The cash receipts and disbursements method elements may not be forecast either by ratios, direct estimating, or quantitative methods. The appropriate method varies by company because of the diversity of different elements from one corporate environment to another. Any element can be forecast using ratios or direct estimating, although the results may be questionable. However, because of possible patterns and historical basis, the following elements used to derive the daily cash forecast can use quantitative methods:

- Miscellaneous disbursements
- Draft payments currently due

- Daily check clearances (variances)
- Zero day deposits from accounts receivable
- Cash sales
- Undrawn funds

The methods that can be used for quantitative forecast of these elements are covered in the next chapter. The essential characteristics of using a quantitative method is that there is a reasonably high degree of uncertainty about the element in the forecast and that direct information is not available early enough to be useful.

SUMMARY

The funds flow method is beneficial for quarterly, annual, and longer-term cash forecasting. This method is useful because it:

- Examines changes in working capital accounts from one period to another
- Monitors projected changes not only in daily cash accounts but in other accounts, such as inventory and accounts receivable, which affect working capital
- Identifies trends over a period of time and thus provides a planning capability

This method adds back noncash operational expenses (e.g., depreciation) to develop the total operating income for a period for the corporation. This approach to a forecasting form is used more as a planning tool than a control approach. Although it does identify trends within the corporation, it does not assist in the daily management of cash control.

The cash flow statement is similar to the funds flow statement, except it does not lump together all current assets and current liabilities as working capital. Changes in individual asset and liability accounts are treated separately so tracing of the transactions of the corporation is possible.

The cash receipts and disbursements forecasting method is used because it:

- Provides a short term tracking of individual elements in the forecast array

- Is accurate in a daily and weekly forecasting environment
- Provides daily control on inputs and outputs of cash-related elements

This method is for control at a microlevel. Because it deals with the specifics of day-to-day forecasting, it is limited in providing visibility into developing trends. Additionally, major shifts in element trends or direction cannot be identified with this approach.

The choice of the forecasting method is important because it establishes reporting levels within the company's communication link to the cash manager. However, of far greater importance is the individual forecast of each element by the cash manager. The three general techniques to forecasting individual elements are:

- *Ratio forecasts*—This is based on establishing ratios or fixed relationships of one element to another element or to the total forecast.
- *Direct forecast*—This is the direct estimating of an element value based on "expert" input from various corporate sources.
- *Quantitative forecasts*—These are based on statistical or nonstatistical approaches to forecasting individual elements.

Although most cash managers use the ratio or direct approach to forecasting, there is a growing interest in the application of quantitative methods to all time horizons of forecasting. Before examining some of the specific models of these quantitative methods, it is appropriate to review the basic techniques commonly used.

CHAPTER 8

QUANTITATIVE FORECASTING TECHNIQUES

In the previous, chapter we reviewed the accounting approaches to formatting cash-forecasting information. These do not describe how individual elements should be forecast but rather in what form they should be presented. The purpose of this chapter is to identify reasons why cash managers may want to use quantitative forecasting techniques and to describe the common techniques available.

MOTIVATING FACTORS FOR CHOOSING QUANTITATIVE METHODS

Historically, the short-term penalty for inaccurate forecasts has been minimal because of low interest rates. To cover the short-term position, funds could be easily moved without major disruptions. Long-term forecast errors, such as working capital availability for the 2-year time horizon, could usually be covered without significant borrowing exposure. During the past 10 years, the acceleration in interest rates and wide fluctuations have placed ever increasing penalties on the cash manager. Additionally, if working capital funds are projected incorrectly, the company may have difficulty raising required capital because of tight national monetary constraints. Because of these factors, cash managers and other business executives are viewing quantitative forecasting techniques to:

- Obtain more accurate estimates
- Develop statistical measures to determine the accuracy of the forecast
- Develop models that can adapt to changes over time

- Use techniques to develop models that apply to different time horizons (e.g., daily, weekly, monthly)
- Provide a mechanically simple approach to making forecasts
- Eliminate or reduce direct estimating costs

More accurate estimates often result from the use of quantitative forecasting techniques because historical data can be used as a basis to predict future results. Additionally, some of the techniques such as simple regression and correlation analysis are statistical in nature and consequently allow for estimates of the probable degrees of error in the forecast developed.

Understanding the nature and pattern of the elements being forecast is essential as discussed in a previous section. This knowledge can be applied using quantitative methods through the construction of models that combine several techniques to account for factors indigenous to a particular company. Thus a firm that experiences seasonal fluctuations in sales can build this factor into a model rather than by observing and estimating these swings subjectively. Additionally, the techniques described can be selected so that they build a model that is best suited for the time horizon being forecast. For example, exponential smoothing might be applicable to an element in a daily forecast rather than a regression formula because exponential smoothing adjusts quickly to changes caused by trend, whereas the regression equation needs to be computed daily at some expense to provide a daily up-date of the trend line.

For some companies, quantitative approaches to forecasts are attractive because they can reduce the expenses associated with direct estimating. Consider a company with many dispersed physical locations. The cost to assemble estimates from the profit center managers can be prohibitive if intermediate- and long-range forecasts are performed with any regularity. The expense lies not only in information gathering of these direct estimates but also in the time required to make the estimates by the profit center managers. Quantitative forecasting techniques offer an alternative to this sometimes costly direct estimating approach by providing a mechanically simple manner of projecting future values based on past experiences.

FORECASTING TECHNIQUES APPLICABLE TO CASH MANAGEMENT

Even though there are a number of complex techniques that may have some application to forecasting cash management-related elements, the three generic approaches which are straightforward but useful are:

- Smoothing techniques
- Statistical techniques
- The decomposition time series technique

Smoothing Techniques

The purpose of smoothing techniques is to provide a forecasting method which can be applied to cash forecast elements that require daily or weekly forecasts but whose values change only slightly from one period to another even though there are occasions when significant fluctuations occur. An example of an element that may fit this classification is daily cash sales for a division. Although daily cash sales vary depending on the day of the week (seasonally), the amount of dollar sales from one Monday to another Monday might not vary significantly.

The objective of smoothing techniques is to account for the random fluctuation in data by "smoothing" or averaging historical data over time. By doing this, the random fluctuations for extremes are eliminated so that estimates can be based on more "expected" values.

Smoothing forecast techniques are nonstatistical in nature. This means that probability-type statements cannot be made regarding the results of the forecast produced. However, they are useful and popular because of their intuitive appeal to managers. The use of smoothing techniques are based on a time series model. Consequently, to use them, it is necessary to have historical data available in order develop a smoothed starting value.

An example of cash management elements to which smoothing techniques apply are:

- Daily division location cash sales for many product lines
- Deposits to low-activity bank accounts (zero day amounts) not justifying daily reporting
- Drafts due and payable

Of course, the application of smoothing techniques varies by company but generally is useful when there are a number of items to be tracked and where individually they do not justify a separate analysis (such as daily cash sales by product line for each corporate division). The smoothing methods most often used are simple moving averages and exponential smoothing.

Advantages/Disadvantages

The advantages of forecasting with smoothing techniques include:

- Provides reasonable forecasts for many items that individually would not justify a forecast

172 Quantitative Forecasting Techniques

- Provides ease of use and understandability
- Provides a forecast based on historical data

The principal disadvantages are that it:

- Requires storage and up-dating of historical data
- Requires additional computation for each new time period
- Can only be used for one forecast period in advance

Types of Smoothing Techniques

Simple Moving Average. The purpose of the simple moving average forecasting techniques is to eliminate random fluctuations by averaging a number of past observations to predict the next periods value. The number of observations used in the moving average is initially chosen by the cash manager and then remains constant for future forecasts. As each new observation occurs, a new average is developed by adding the last value to the series and dropping the first value.

Exhibit 8-1 illustrates a 3- and 5-week moving average for weekly cash sales for a corporate division.

Exhibit 8.1 Nova Corporation
Cash Sales—Division A—Per Products

			Actual Cash Sales (thousands)	Forecast with 3-Week Moving Average	Forecast with 5-Week Moving Average
January	Week	1	$5000	—	—
		2	5800	—	—
		3	4600	—	—
		4	5200	$5133	—
February	Week	1	5800	5200	—
		2	6100	5200	$5280
		3	5700	5700	5500
		4	5900	5867	5480
March	Week	1	6200	5900	5740
		2	6000	5934	5940
		3	5600	6033	5980
		4	5800	5933	5880
April	Week	1		5800	5900

The 3-week moving average in Exhibit 8-1 is derived by computing the mean for the first 3 weeks as the forecast for week 4. Hence $5000 + 5800 + 4600 = $15,400. Divided by 3, the average is $5133, which is the forecast for week 4. The same approach applies to the 5-week moving forecast. The sum of the first 5 weeks' actual values $5000 + 5800 + 4600 + 5200 + 5800 results in $26,400 and an average of $5280, which is used as the forecast for the second week in February. As each actual value is known, the next week's forecast can be made by dropping the first value and adding the most recent. For example, in the 3-week forecast—February Week 1 is developed by summing $4600 + 5200 + 5800, resulting in a total sales of $15,600 and an up-dated mean of $5200, which is used as the forecast for February Week 2.

Determining the optimal time period for forecasting an element related to cash control varies. However, an evaluation of varying time periods can be made by comparing the forecasting errors that have occurred using each method. The mean-squared error is used as a comparison of which moving average time produces better results. Exhibit 8-2 illustrates that the mean-squared error of the 5-week moving average is greater than the 3-week average. This indicates that better forecast accuracy is obtained by using a 3-week moving average as opposed to a 5-week moving average. Additionally, the longer forecast period does require significantly more data for storage and computation. Additional time periods could be evaluated to determine the optimal time frame for the application.

Limitations

There are three basic limitations to using simple moving averages:

- The element being forecast must generally change only slightly from one period to the next—This assumes a horizontal growth rate.
- The basic lack of adaptability to changing trends
- The need to maintain historical data

Because it is based on an average or smoothing of values, wide variances, on a discrete basis, are not handled in a timely manner by this method. In particular, changes in the basic trends of data, up or down, are only reflected slowly in the moving average forecasting technique. This is further emphasized by the fact that since we are averaging over several periods equal weight is given to all occurrences even though the most recent observation may contain more meaningful information on trend movements. Consequently, if a large number of occurrences were used in order to

Exhibit 8.2 Moving Average Forecasting Errors*

Time		Actual cash sales ($)	Three-week average			Five-week average		
			Forecast ($)	Error ($)	Squared error ($)	Forecast ($)	Error ($)	Squared error ($)
February	Week 2	6100	5200	900	810,000	5280	820	672,400
	3	5700	5700	–0–	–0–	5500	200	40,000
	4	5900	5867	33	1,089	5480	420	176,400
March	Week 1	6200	5900	300	90,000	5740	460	211,600
	2	5000	5934	66	4,356	5940	60	3,600
	3	5600	6033	–433	187,000	5980	–380	144,400
	4	5800	5933	–133	17,689	5880	–80	6,400
Total-squared error					$1,110,623			$1,254,800
Mean-squared error					$ 158,660			$ 179,257

*The time period begins with Week 2 of February so that the total number of observations are the same.

obtain better accuracy (although this is not necessarily the case), the adaptability of the technique to changing trends is reduced because of the greater number of occurrences being averaged.

Depending on the number of items being forecast, the amount of data required to utilize this method can be costly. Additionally, each new period to be forecast requires a new computation of the average. The gathering as well as the storage and manipulation of the data are important aspects in selecting this forecasting method.

Exponential Smoothing. The purpose of exponential smoothing is to overcome the major disadvantages of the moving average forecasting method and to provide emphasis on the more recent observations that often contain more current information about the environment than previous observations.

Exponential smoothing operates in a fashion similar to moving averages in that it smooths historical observations to eliminate randomness. The method used is different, however; rather than requiring large amounts of historical data, this technique only needs the last actual value and the forecast for the same period. The exponential method uses a weighting factor α to apply to the variance between the forecast value and actual value. The basic formula is $ST_{(T2)} = ST_{(T1)} + \alpha XT_{(T1)} - ST_{(T1)}$ where:

$ST_{(T2)}$ = the forecast value for the next period
$ST_{(T1)}$ = the forecast value for this period
α = the weight factor—between 0 and 1 (e.g., 0.8)
$XT_{(T1)}$ = the actual value for the current period

Technically, to forecast week 3 of March using a 0.8 α factor, the cash manager would use his known experience from week 2 of March, which would consist of the actual results and the forecast amounts. Applying the 0.8 α factor to the week 2 actual results state that we feel it has more truth contained in it concerning what will happen next week in the forecast. The 1 - α or 0.2 is applied to the forecast that was made for week 2. The combined values of both constitute the forecast for week 3.

$$(0.8)(\$6000) = \$4800$$
$$(0.2)(\$6135) = \$1227$$
$$\text{Forecast week 3} = \$6027$$

The same results can be achieved by taking the α factor times the actual sales and adding "1 - α" times the forecast amount for the same period. This can be expressed as:

$$ST + 1 = \alpha XT + (1 - \alpha)ST$$

To determine an optimal value of α, it is necessary to vary α for the same data and examine the mean-error squared. As is shown in Exhibit 8-3, the lower value of α seems to produce overall better forecasting results in this example. The optimal value for α is determined by selecting the analogous problem to selecting the number of periods to use in moving averages.

In order to use exponential smoothing, a manager needs only the most recent observed value of a recent period forecast and a selected value for α. The small amount of data required to construct a forecast is one of the major advantages of this forecasting technique. Another advantage of exponential smoothing is that the manager can choose the degree of responsiveness desired in the forecast; that is, by varying the value of α the manager can place greater or lesser emphasis on the most recent observations.

The limitations of using exponential smoothing includes:

- *Relying on managerial judgement for factors required to adjust for trend changes, step changes or other complex patterns*—Exponential smoothing does not provide an adjusting method.
- *Developing an appropriate value for the weighting factor*—This can sometimes be a long process if optimal results are to be achieved. The only way to obtain the weights is through trial and error.

Exhibit 8.3 Exponential Smoothing Forecast

Time			Actual cash sales ($)	$\alpha = 0.5$ Forecast ($)	Error	$\alpha = 0.8$ Forecast ($)	Error	0.5 error squared	0.8 error squared
February	Week	1	5800	—	—	—	—		
		2	6100	5800	300	5800	300	90,000	90,000
		3	5700	5950	−250	6040	−340	62,500	115,600
		4	5900	5825	75	5768	132	5,625	17,424
March	Week	1	6200	5863	337	5874	326	113,569	106,276
		2	6000	6032	−32	135	−135	1,024	18,225
		3	5600	6016	−416	6027	−427	173,056	182,329
		4	5800	5808	−8	5685	115	64	13,225
April	Week	1		5800		5777			
	Total-Error Squared							445,838	543,079
	Average Error							63,691	77,583

- *Reevaluating and resetting the factor α,* if the pattern of the data changes.
- *Assuring that no basic changes have occurred*—The user must check the accuracy of the selected α factor periodically or when the forecast error changes noticeably.

Statistical Techniques

The purpose of statistical forecasting techniques is to develop formulas where results can be described in relation to probable degrees of certainty. The nature of the statistical technique probabilities can be associated with the applicability of the model and with the results it produces. Statistical models have not been used widely because they tend to be difficult to understand, even though their accuracy is generally greater than nonstatistical models. The simple regression and correlation technique is described in this section as having application to cash management forecasting. The time horizon associated with regression and correlation analysis related to cash management is monthly, quarterly, and annual as opposed to daily forecasting application. The reason is that the underlying assumption of this technique is that the pattern of the data is linear in nature; that is, over time a straight line relationship exists between the two variables.

An example of cash forecasting elements to which this method may apply are:

- Annual company sales
- Inventory levels
- Sales of fixed assets
- Accounts receivable
- Accounts payable
- Purchase of capital assets

The principal advantage of using statistical models is that statements can be made regarding:

- The applicability of the derived equation to the problem at hand; that is, Does the equation represent a chance occurrence or is it significant?
- The percent of confidence that the resulting forecast will be within a narrow range
- The resulting equation which accounts for the trend that is in the data and provides a range of confidence that estimates the randomness

The principal disadvantages of statistical-forecasting techniques are:

- The mathematics get involved so use of computer programs are usually required
- The greater the number of observations the more accurate the model
- Development expense tends to be high

Simple Regression and Correlation

The underlying assumption of this forecasting technique is that a straight line pattern exists for the variables being examined. The purpose of the regression and correlation forecasting technique is to define an algorithm that can be used to forecast future periods. For example, What will the accounts receivable balances be three years from now? Based on historical data, an equation is to fit an annual straight line growth pattern. By entering the number of years, 3, from the starting point, the forecast figure results. Exhibit 8-4 is an example of fitting a straight line projection to data.

The regression and correlation forecast technique is a causal model and assumes a relationship between the two variables—in this case, time and accounts receivable. Whatever the variables are, the manager needs to be assured that there is a relationship between the two.

The general form for the regression equation is:

$$Y = a + bX$$

a—This is the point where the regression line intersects the *Y*-axis. In Exhibit 8-4, it is approximately 205. This means conceptually that with no business activity outstanding accounts receivable are $205,000. Of course, this may not always be the case.

b—This is the regression coefficient and represents the slope of the line. Another way of viewing it is as the trend of the element being forecast over time. In Exhibit 8-4, the *b* regression coefficient is an upward sloping line.

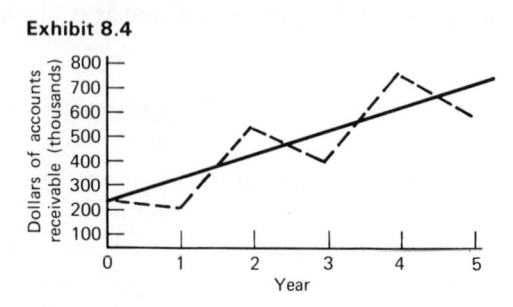

Exhibit 8.4

X—This represents the number of periods for which this forecast is desired. In our example, if X is zero then a equals 205. If X is 5 the Y-value, total accounts receivable, equals $600,000.

In order to use the regression and correlation technique, the manager must first determine the applicability of the straight line assumptions to his forecast. There are two methods for accomplishing this:

- Direct method
- Least-squares method

The direct method is simply plotting the historical observations and drawing a line that seems to fit these points. Although this method may be satisfactory for a few observations for samples requiring several hundred observations, it is almost impossible to get reliable results. For this purpose, the method of the least squares is recommended.

The method of the least squares states that the distance between the actual observation and corresponding points on the regression line should be minimized. In order to apply this method, several iterations are sometimes necessary. Most commonly, computer programs are used to perform the mathematics. The concept is that the best line fit results in the lowest sum of the squared deviations. The trend line with the least amount of deviation is the best suited for the b slope line (regression coefficient). Following the slope down in a straight line, it intersects the Y-axis, and the value at which it intersects is the a or fixed value of the regression equation.

By using the method of the least squares, it insures that actual occurrences are just as likely to be above the forecast as below it, and that most of the values tend to be close to the line rather than widely dispersed from it.

Reliability.* The reliability of the regression equation is authenticated through the use of statistical measurements. In evaluating the regression coefficient b, we would like to know whether it is significantly different from zero, or if we assume that the regression coefficient b is zero, What is the chance that we could derive a value for b? This is determined by employing the standard error of the coefficient. The specific method for determining the standard error of the coefficient is beyond the scope of this book. However, once the standard error is developed, we can determine how many standard errors away from zero our value of b is. Once we know how many

---

* See Wheelwright, Steven, and Makrivakis, Spyros, *Forecasting Methods for Management*, Wiley, New York, 1973.

standard errors away from zero our value is, we use a table of normal probability values to determine what chance there is that our h value is a result of a random occurrence.

A second test of significance determines the confidence interval for the regression coefficient. The 95% confidence range would be one where the manager would be 95% certain that the b regression coefficient lies between two values. The exact method of determining this is beyond the scope of this book, but it would be plus or minus two times the standard error of the estimate. To apply this measure, assume b = $500,000 (in Exhibit 8-4) and the standard error of the estimate is $24,000, then we can say that the value of b is, with 95% confidence, between $50,000 and $550,000—that is, plus or minus two standard errors.

A third measure of reliability is to determine the confidence interval for a specific forecast value. This is called the standard error of the forecast. The specific mathematics are again beyond the scope of this book. Its purpose, however, is to determine a standard deviation for the sample data. This is used in relation to individual forecasts to establish a range confidence that is usually at the 95% level. Using the simple example in Exhibit 8-4, the regression equation is:

$$\begin{align} Y &= A + bX \\ &= 105 + 500X \\ &= 105 + 500(2) \\ &= 1105 \end{align}$$

Given a standard deviation of ±20, we can be 95% sure that the actual accounts receivable outstanding for 2 years hence will be between $1,085,000 and $1,125,000.

The final measure of statistical statement is to what extent the two variables (b and X) are related. This is accomplished through correlation analysis. Simply stated, the coefficient of correlation that measures the degree the two variables are related is the square root of the explained variation from Y over the total variation. This can be stated:

$$R^2 = \frac{\text{Explained Variation}}{\text{Total Variation}}$$

$$= \frac{E(Y - \bar{Y}^2)}{E(Y - \bar{Y})^2}$$

Y-Axis. The explained variation is simply the amount of the total variation explained by the regression line. The key point of misinterpretation regarding correlation analysis is based on the number of observations. For example, if five observations were used and a coefficient of correlation value of 0.825, which indicates that 82.5% of the variance from the mean value of Y was explained by the regression formula, could lead to incorrect assumptions because of the limited observations; consequently, a high degree of confidence in that correlation statistic is unrealistic. The greater the number of observations used the better the confidence expressed in the correlation coefficient.

Multiple Regression Analysis

The simple regression and correlation technique is called simple only because it relates to the interaction of two variables. As often happens in life there are many other variables which a manager needs to consider concurrently. To this extent multiple regression and correlation analysis is useful. In its simplest form, it is:

$$Y = a + b_1 X_1 + b_2 X_2 \ldots + b_n X_n$$

For detailed information on multiple regression and correlation, see the reference reading list.

Decomposition Technique

These methods of quantitative forecasting techniques have attempted to define and separate patterns from randomness in observations but not break the forecast down into elements. The decomposition technique decomposes a forecast into identifiable elements. The elements are seasonal, trend, and cyclical. This approach to forecasting is particularly helpful when a manager needs to separate a seasonal pattern from data being forecast. This helps a manager distinguish between real rises and those caused by seasonal fluctuations. For example, the forecast of accounts receivable outstanding or sales can easily vary by season for the retail industry.

The trend described in decomposition forecasts is the long-range slope of the variable as discussed in regression analysis. The cyclical element is the long-term wavelike movement of the forecast. For example, some industries experience cyclical patterns in 10-year intervals. The methods discussed previously do not take into account these cyclical movements in forecasts.

Decomposition can be expressed as:

$$S = T \times I \times C + u$$

This simply states that the forecast (S) equals a trend value (T) times a seasonal index value (I) times a cyclical value (C) plus some degree of

182 Quantitative Forecasting Techniques

random occurrence (u). The decomposition method of forecasting must be developed individually for each application and some elements, such as cyclical values, may not always apply.

Developing the Decomposition Forecast

There are three steps in constructing the decomposition forecast:

- Developing a seasonal index
- Determining trend
- Defining cyclical value (if any)

    The seasonal factor can be computed by using a moving average based on the period to be forecast daily, weekly, or monthly. Exhibit 8-5 is an example of this technique. In the example, a 10-week period by day is used to develop an individual day of the week index (ratio of actual to moving average) to form the basis for developing a seasonal index. The seasonal index calculations are illustrated in Exhibit 8-6. *Column 3 is the ratio of actual to moving averages. This forms the basis for the seasonal estimate.* In order to more accurately define the seasonal index, we then take and list all the monthly seasonal values. The medial average in Exhibit 8-6 simply eliminates this high and low value and uses the average of the monthly data as the seasonal index. Sometimes it is necessary to adjust the medial average so that the total index will equal 1200 for the year.

    The second step in using the decomposition technique is to develop the trend data for the model. This can be accomplished by either plotting the data available as described in the previous section and free fitting a "best" trend estimate or by using regression analysis. As previously described, this regression equation should be developed using available computer programs. This greatly reduces the data manipulation. Once the trend equation is developed and the seasonal index defined, the manager could construct a forecast. Often this is the situation with short- or intermediate-term forecasts since cyclical variations tend to have negligible effects. The effects of cyclical variations is more meaningful for longer term forecasts of 3 to 5 years, depending upon the industry. However, if identification of a cyclical pattern is desired it can be derived after the trend equation is defined and the seasonal index is determined.

    The seasonal fluctuations have been eliminated through the use of the moving average. The moving average developed represents:

$$\text{Moving Average} = \text{Cycle} \times \text{Trend}$$

Exhibit 8.5 Development of 5-day Moving Average for Daily Cash Receipts for 10-Week Period

Week	Day*	(1) Actual cash Receipts ($)	(2) 5-Day Moving average	(3) Ratio of actual to moving Average [(1)/(2)]	(4) Cyclial Factor† [(3)/Trend × 100]
1	M	3140			
	T	2855			
	W	3089			
	Th	3597			
	F	3797			
2	M	3199	3296	97.1	64
	T	3115	3307	94.2	63
	W	3499	3359	104.2	69
	Th	3222	3441	93.6	62
	F	4165	3366	123.7	82
3	M	3339	3440	97.1	65
	T	2979	3468	85.9	57
	W	3244	3441	94.3	63
	Th	2653	3389	78.3	52
	F	2993	3276	91.3	61
4	M	2336	3041	76.8	51
	T	2042	2782	73.4	49
	W	2340	2594	90.2	60
	Th	3259	2414	135.0	90
	F	3995	2535	157.6	105
5	M	2707	2735	99.0	67
	T	2356	2809	83.9	56
	W	2497	2872	86.9	58
	Th	3286	2904	113.2	75
	F	3233	2909	111.1	74
6	M	2417	2757	87.7	58
	T	2124	2699	78.7	53
	W	2327	2652	87.7	58
	Th	2563	2618	97.9	65
	F	2955	2474	119.4	80
7	M	3266	2418	135.1	90
	T	3405	2588	131.6	88
	W	3393	2844	119.3	80
	Th	2387	3057	78.1	52
	F	3342	3022	110.5	74

Quantitative Forecasting Techniques

Exhibit 8.5 (Continued)

Week	Day*	(1) Actual cash Receipts ($)	(2) 5-Day Moving average	(3) Ratio of actual to moving Average [(1)/(2)]	(4) Cyclial Factor† [(3)/Trend × 100]
8	M	3334	3099	107.5	72
	T	3689	3113	118.5	79
	W	3821	3055	125.1	83
	Th	3820	3140	211.7	81
	F	3655	3427	106.7	71
9	M	3500	3489	100.3	67
	T	3479	3523	98.9	66
	W	3466	3481	99.6	66
	Th	2409	3410	70.6	47
	F	2635	3127	84.2	56
10	M	2378	2923	81.3	54
	T	2318	2699	85.8	57
	W	2432	2467	98.6	66
	Th	3088	2260	136.6	91
	F	2604	2396	108.7	72

* Saturday and Sunday omitted.
† The trend is assumed as a constant 150 for this illustration.

If the moving average is divided by the trend what remains is the cyclical factor.

$$\text{Cyclical} = \frac{\text{Moving Average}}{\text{Trend}}$$

Using Exhibit 8-5, the 12-month moving average is divided by the trend, which has been determined as a constant (horizontal) of 150.

In analyzing the most recent cyclical value, the manager would forecast a value close to the last cyclical value because wide variations, especially in a short time frame, are unlikely for cyclical elements. Using this, the forecast for the next period is

$$S = \text{Seasonal} \times \text{Trend} \times \text{Cycle}$$

To determine the accuracy of this forecasting technique, we compute the mean-squared error or the mean absolute deviation. If we want to determine a range for the forecast similar to that performed in regression analysis, we could estimate the standard deviation of the forecast to be 1.25 times the mean absolute deviation. This is not statistically accurate but does provide a confidence range. Therefore, if we calculate the mean absolute deviation trend 1.25 and use two deviations, we are approximating (not precisely) a 95% confidence interval for our forecast.

Summary

The decomposition method of forecasting has intuitive appeal in the cash management area because it does breakdown the forecast into elements that can be individually examined and forecast. In the next chapter, an example combining the decomposition forecasting technique with exponential smoothing is developed. Because the decomposition technique does breakdown elements of a forecast, it does permit the cash manager greater control over account activity, while lending itself to modification to meet an individual company's need.

There are several disadvantages associated with this method, however. The most noted is that it is nonstatistical in nature, which means that its accuracy can be approximated only by examining the forecast errors rather than using statistical statements. A second limitation of this model is that it assumes a time series pattern that means only two variables are considered in the forecast.

Exhibit 8.6 Seasonal Index Factors for Daily Cash Receipts

Week	Monday	Tuesday	Wednesday	Thursday	Friday	Total
1	—	—	—	—	—	
2	97.1	94.2	104.2	93.6	123.7	
3	97.1	85.9	94.3	78.3	91.3	
4	76.8	73.4	90.2	135.0	157.6	
5	99.0	83.9	86.9	113.2	111.1	
6	87.7	78.7	87.7	97.9	119.4	
7	135.1	131.6	119.3	78.1	110.5	
8	107.5	118.5	121.1	121.7	106.7	
9	100.3	98.9	99.6	70.6	84.2	
10	81.3	85.8	98.6	136.6	108.7	
Medial average*	95.7	92.2	99.1	102.5	110.2	499.7
Seasonal index†	95.8	92.2	99.1	102.6	110.3	500.0

* Average after eliminating the high and low value.
† Based on adjustment of 500.0/499.7 = 1.0006.

The time horizons applicable for use of the decomposition forecasting method is one of short or intermediate durations, although it can be used in longer-term situations. Most often it is used when the value of the forecast is substantial because the development expenses can be significant. Additionally, when basic trends or elements change, the values need to be recomputed. Its best application is for short- to medium-term cash forecasts, especially when seasonal factors are present. Some of the shortcomings of this method have been overcome through the development of more sophisticated versions of the decomposition technique. The reader is advised to review the reference reading list for further information.

APPLICATION OF QUANTITATIVE METHODS TO CASH MANAGEMENT FORECASTS

The selection of the method of forecasting elements for which the cash manager is responsible is governed by the *value* of the forecast made and the frequency required. Development of a regression formula, for example, is not warranted for a daily forecast of zero day receipts from one bank's lockbox processing because the dollar value probably would not justify the expense to develop the model. Therefore, the cash manager needs to define the tradeoff between the cost of error, the model developed, and the associated expenses for developing more accurate models. The type of model chosen for cash management forecasting purposes varies from company to company. Exhibit 8-7 represents a chart of methods that are generally applicable for various time horizons. Additionally, sample cash management elements are listed to provide an example of what may be forecast with this method.

CURRENT USE OF CASH MANAGEMENT FORECASTING TECHNIQUES

For a majority of the cases, most corporate cash managers today base forecasts on accounting-based measures. The format of forecasts are described in cash receipts and disbursement for short-term time horizons funds flow for longer-term periods. The forecasting techniques most often used today are directly estimated by various company "experts" or by the use of ratio analysis. Of course, the longer the forecast under each of these methods the less reliable the results because the more uncertain are circumstances surrounding the time horizon. A major limitation to the direct method is that the forecast is dependent on the company expert in the area. For example, if the sales manager develops an estimate for a future time period, the cash manager is dependent on the sales manager's objective

Exhibit 8.7 Matrix of Time Horizon and Applicable Cash Management Forecasts

Time Horizon	Quantitative Methods Applicable	Sample Cash Forecast Elements
Daily	Moving average deseasonalized values Exponential smoothing Modified decomposition (no cycle)	• Daily zero day branch deposits • Zero day lockbox deposits • Drafts presented • Checks to clear
Weekly	Same as daily	Same as daily
Monthly	Moving average, deseasonalized Values, modified decomposition (no cycle) Regression and correlation analysis Exponential smoothing	• Deposits to concentration A/Cs • Presentment drafts • Checks clearing • Increase in borrowing
Quarterly	Modified decomposition (seasonal but no cycle), Regression, and correlation analysis	Same as monthly
Annual	Regression and correlation analysis Modified decomposition (no seasonality)	• Cash bank balance • Accounts receivable • Accounts payable • Inventory

appraisal to estimate sales for some future period. As often and naturally occurs, the sales manager may desire to be optimistic or pessimistic about sales forecast to support his current position.

Based on the estimates provided by the company, conclusions must be made about future account balances that indicate whether the company will be in a borrowing or investment position. In order to minimize the effects of biased forecasts, the cash manager may prudently seek direct estimates from several sources within the corporation. This only provides a basis of measurement for other direct estimates and opinions about future activity. To solve the problem of multiple direct estimates from various areas, the ratio method is commonly used. As previously outlined, the cash manager uses a sales projection often directly estimated and applies a historical ratio for each of the accounts involved to determine the forecast amounts. This

Exhibit 8.8 The cash flow forecasting family tree.

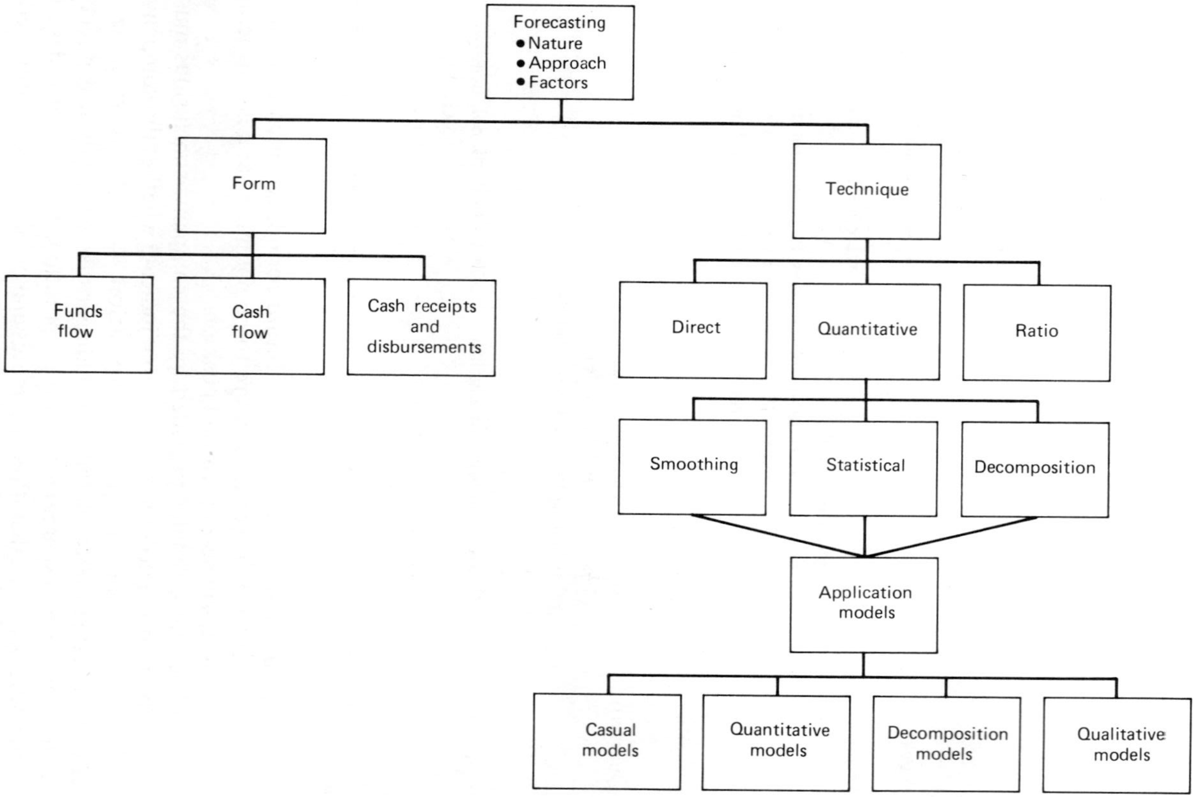

method is limited in that it assumes that the relationship of one account with another stays constant over time.

This method does account for a growth trend through use of sales projections that should increase in growth periods. However, it does not allow for proportional changes in individual accounts. Consequently, it cannot isolate and emphasize a growth trend in inventory accumulation or an increase in accounts receivable over a time period. Similarly, any efficiencies that a company has introduced could not be reflected in the forecast because decreasing trends would not be high-lighted. Although the direct estimating method (used extensively for short-term forecasts) and the ratio method (used for longer term forecasts) are the most widely used, they often are not as accurate or useful as the quantitative method described in this section.

CURRENT TRENDS

While the direct estimating and ratio techniques are still the most commonly used today, there is a gradual trend toward application of quantitative methods to short-, intermediate-, and long-range cash management forecasts. The trend is slow but deliberate. It is slow because cash managers are reluctant to change forecasting techniques unless they can be assured that better results are forthcoming and that the techniques are understandable. The implementation of quantitative techniques to cash forecasts has also lagged because the need for greater precision has not widely existed. Resulting from the increasing long-term capital cost, the need now clearly exists and cash managers are now becoming more actively concerned with performing regular cash forecasts with increasing accuracy.

The future of forecasting for the cash manager encompasses the use of quantitative models in an interactive time-sharing mode. These automated forecasting services are offered by banks as packages to the corporate cash managers at nominal costs. The cash manager needs in turn to carefully evaluate what the characteristics are of the elements to be forecast so that appropriate techniques are selected.

This chapter has reviewed the techniques that are available to aid the cash manager in forecasting. The relationship of the forecasting techniques is described diagramically in Exhibit 8-8—the Forecasting Family Tree. The selection of techniques is determined based on perceived value, availability of technical expertise, and need for accuracy. Having discussed the various techniques available to the cash manager, it is now appropriate to form forecasting models customized to the corporation's requirements.

CHAPTER 9

CASH FORECASTING MODELS

INTRODUCTIONS

In previous sections we reviewed various quantitative methods that can be applied to managing cash balances and forecasting for elements within the forecast. The purpose of this section is to provide an overview of current cash forecasting models. Since the discussion of various models is intended to be a survey in nature, specific discussion of the mechanics of the models are not within the scope of this book. For the reader who is interested in detailed formulation of the model, a reference reading list is provided.

In this section three major types of models are discussed: the inventory model, the linear programming model, and other nonstatistical modeling methods. The basic characteristics of each model are discussed so that its practical application to the firm may be determined.

INVENTORY MODEL APPROACHES

The Baumol model approaches to cash forecasting models represents the oldest attempt to optimize cash flow control. The father of the inventory approach to cash forecasting is W. J. Baumol. He approached cash balances as an inventory item. This model approach assumes that a corporation disburses funds in a steady stream. Furthermore, the model assumes that cash is obtained by borrowing it or withdrawing it from an investment. In either case, when funds are needed they are obtained at an interest cost of dollars per day. When withdrawals of funds are made, a fee b is charged, representing the cost to convert a security into usable cash.

The objective of the model is to determine how much cash should be borrowed so as to minimize the "brokerage" fees while still providing adequate cash. The pattern of activity experienced under this approach is depicted in the following graph:

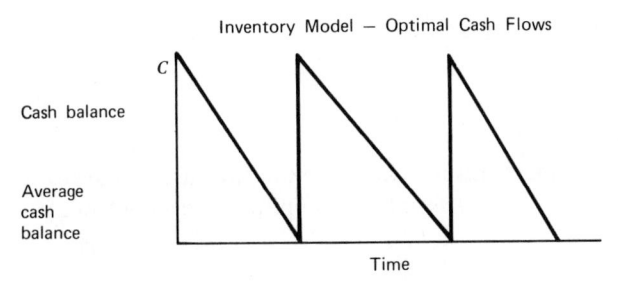

Inventory Model — Optimal Cash Flows

The simple inventory-based equation to determine the amount of cash required is:

$$C = \sqrt{\frac{2bT}{i}}$$

b = fixed cost per transaction
T = amount of cash outflow
i = the interest rate

As illustrated, the optimal average cash balance is $C/2$. This method assumes that payment schedules are known and disbursements approximate a constant rate. One of the major limitations of this approach is that it does not consider the interrelationships between subsequent time periods. The model is limited to the time period between the receipt of funds, and since this occurs daily for most firms, the actual application of this model is not very practical. Although this model has not been used widely because of the limitations mentioned, it has provided the catalyst for several other inventory based models.

An extension of Baumol's model was developed by Sastry. Baumol in his model did not take into account the costs incurred by a cash manager if he was overdrawn and needed to borrow funds. The cost of inaccurate estimating in Sastry's model is the cost of temporary borrowing. Incorporating this into Baumol's basic approach the model becomes:

$$C = \sqrt{\frac{2bT}{i}} \sqrt{\frac{R}{i+R}}$$

where

R = the cost of temporary borrowing

Because the Sastry version takes into consideration the costs associated with overdrawn cash positions, it is more sensitive to interest rates than the

Baumol model. To illustrate the differences between the two models, assume:

Expenditures for the year = $9 million
b = $100
i = 5%
R = 6%

The Baumol model results in optimum average balances of $95,000, whereas the Sastry model results in an optimum level of $70,250.

Limitations

Although both the Baumol and Sastry approaches represent pioneer approaches to optimizing balances, neither has enjoyed widespread use. Their basic limitations include:

- *Assumed constant disbursement rate*—This, of course, is not true if we only examine the disbursement patterns of corporations. Even though payables can be managed, due dates vary and constant pay out rates cannot be reasonably assured.
- *The assumption that there is no cash receipt during the projected period*—Based on daily experience, most corporations experience both cash sales and receipts of accounts receivable items daily. These are not accounted for in these inventory approaches.
- *No consideration of the interrelationship between time periods*
- *Both methods are limited to the time period between cash receipts*—Since most companies have receipts daily, it lessens the applicability of this method.

The Miller–Orr Model

The purpose of the Miller–Orr model is to forecast the optimum cash level assuming that net cash flows fluctuate in a random (stochastic) rather than a deterministic manner. That is, instead of assuming that cash flows are at a constant known rate as the Baumol model suggests, assume that they really occur more in a random pattern. The Miller–Orr model assumes two working assets—cash and a securities portfolio into which excess funds can be invested. The model requires the user to establish maximum cash balances and minimal acceptable levels. When the cash balance reaches the upper boundary of the range, funds are transferred to the securities portfolio. Conversely, when the balances drop to the low end (zero), securities are sold to bring the balance up to the minimal range. An illustration of this cash control technique is:

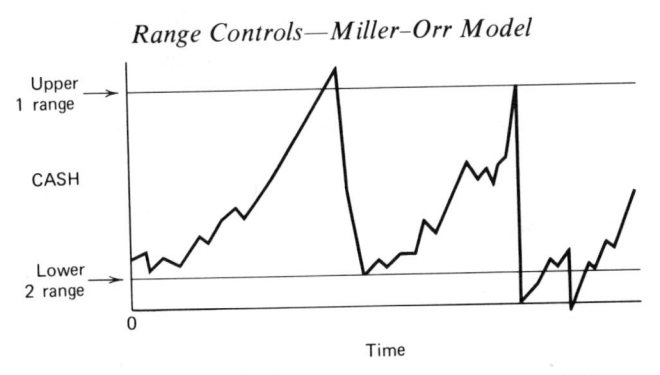

Range Controls—Miller–Orr Model

[Chart showing cash levels fluctuating between an Upper 1 range and Lower 2 range over Time]

In the execution of their model, the authors derive quantitatively the optimum levels of the upper range (1) and the lower range value (2). The basic oversight of this approach is that the assumption that all cash flows are stochastic overlooks the control that the cash manager exercises over disbursements, and the high degree of predictability that short-term cash flows possess.

These three basic models of forecasting cash are all representative of the approaches using an inventory approach and suffer from the same basic limitations:

- The payment schedule and receipts are both assumed to be uncontrollable by the cash managers. As discussed in the first four chapters, there are many techniques available to the cash manager to exercise some degree of control over the disbursements and receipts function.
- The only decision covered by the inventory models is the size and timing of transfers between cash accounts and a securities portfolio.

Because of these basic limitations, we conclude that the current inventory models for cash management do not provide a viable approach for most companies.

Linear Programming Models

Linear programming is used to solve a wide range of business problems. It was first applied to finance by Charnes, Cooper, and Miller[*] in the area of

[*] Charnes, A., Cooper, W., and Miller, M., "Application of Linear Programming to Financial Budgeting and Costing of Funds," *Journal of Business*, January 1959.

operating and financial planning. The model developed was designed to optimize operating decisions subject to various financial constraints including the opportunity cost of long term funds. A later extension of the model incorporated marketable securities transactions but limited only to a single period. The advantage of linear programming techniques when applied to cash management is that a large number of variables and constraints can be included and manipulated using existing computer programs.

The Robicek et al. Model*

The first use of linear programming to short-term financial decision making was by Robicek et al. in attempting to define minimal levels of "total relevant costs."

Given a set of constraints, this approach defines levels of the variable that provide the best overall results for the cash manager. The "total relevant" costs consists of explicit costs that are defined as interest on loans and discounts lost less any interest derived from investment of surplus funds. Implicit costs consist of illwill to creditors when payments are stretched and cost associated with the terms of a loan. The types of cash management constraints included in the model include:

- Amount of unsecured line of credit a firm can use (e.g., a standing line of $2,000,000)
- Required compensating balance required by the bank (e.g., 10% of the unused balance and 5% of the used funds)
- Percent of pledged accounts receivable on which the bank lends money
- Time that accounts payable may be lengthened and the corresponding loss of discount
- Short-term securities used for investment of excess cash

This model encompasses more cash management decisions than the other models already discussed. However, it should be noted that this model does not account for two way transfers between cash and marketable securities. Another limitation of this modeling approach is that it does not provide sufficient daily information for cash management because the time horizon is divided into monthly periods.

* Robicek, A. A., Teichroew, and Jones, J., "Optimal Short Term Financing Decision," *Management Science,* September 1965.

The Orgler Linear Programming Model

The Orgler model is the most comprehensive of the linear programming models because of the number of constraints it takes into consideration and the ability to forecast using uneven periods. Uneven periods occur where the forecast for X periods in the future can be of varying lengths (e.g., the first three periods can be 1 day; the fourth period, 10 days; etc.). The types of constraints included in Orgler's model are:

- *Payments*—This refers to accounts payable primarily and states that payments must be scheduled within the time span and subject to the credit terms specified by the creditors. Any controllable payment—not just payables—can be incorporated into the model.
- *Short-term financing*—This constraint includes all sources of funds except securities sales, which are treated separately. Requirements of short-term financing may affect *other* constraints and must be taken into consideration. For example, a required 10 + 10 compensating balance does not affect the short-term financing constraint but does affect the minimal cash balance and cash flow constraint.
- *Securities sales*—This constraint relates to the sales of securities from the company's portfolio. It is assumed that securities are sold at the beginning of the day.
- *Minimal cash balance*—The model assumes that a minimum cash balance must be maintained by the company to support services rendered by the bank and to support required loan balances. This constraint is not established to balance cash balances over several periods but rather to use an average daily minimum to control the minimal cash balance.
- *Cash flows*—This essential constraint equates net cash flows with the change in the cash balance. Each period has its own derived cash flow constraint and includes cash inflows and outflows that result from past and present cash management decisions and fixed flows (other constraints) that are beyond the cash manager's control. These are illustrated in the model as "other receipts" and "other payment" constraints.

Even though these elements represent the major areas included in Orgler's model, they by no means limit the number of constraints that can be included. The number of constraints used for a model for any corporation depends entirely on the needs of that company. To illustrate the extensive possibilities of this approach, consider that a medium-sized corporation can easily have 200 constraints and 500 variables built into its model.

The Orgler model is a very complete and general approach for determining optimal levels of cash for a short or longer time frame. Another advantage of using the Orgler model is that linear programming techiques provide a measure of marginal importance for each of the constraints, so a manager can determine how much slack exists in the manipulation of the variable before optimization is diminished.

The fact that the Orgler model is so comprehensive is also one of its major disadvantages. For a larger firm, the number of constraints that need to be defined are so large that it might be impossible from a practical viewpoint to achieve a realistic definition. For the model to be useful, it must be up-dated frequently. This means that the maintenance expense is high. Another limitation of this approach is that it assumes that cash flows and future interest rates are known with certainty. Based on the volatility in the interest rates over recent years, this can produce reliability problems. The inventory models discussed earlier assumed a lack of control over payments and receipts, but this model does apply that level of control as well as considering many decision variables. The most significant disadvantages of this method are:

- *The amount of time required to establish the model*—The development of the constraints can involve a significant investment of a cash manager's time in order to initially define the values and relationships.
- *The level of user sophistication*—the corporation would require data processing specialists who can operate the model and possesses a thorough knowledge of the meaning of the output so that meaningful conclusions can be drawn by the cash manager.
- *Frequent up-dates with the consequent increase in operational costs.*

In addition to these disadvantages, the greatest barrier is to achieve a level of general management understanding about the way in which the model operates so that confidence can be generated about the results of the model.

Other Model Types

In addition to the inventory and linear programming approaches to modeling for cash management, other less structured and sophisticated models have been developed. The source of these models often arises out of the internal need of the company; that is, the cash manager decides that an internal tracking system will aid his management performance and, consequently, develops a model that fits his particular set of circumstances. Models similar to this have been developed by large retailers and governmental agencies. The models developed for daily forecasting usually take the form of cash receipts and disbursements tracking methods. The forecasting techniques used for the individual element and subelement forecast usually tend to be either direct or a form of exponential smoothing in nature (this includes averaging and weighted averaging).

The techniques chosen and models developed tend to be simple but effective in their approach. This fortifies the tenant that the method and technique of forecasting employed must be understandable by its users so that a broad level of intercompany confidence can be generated for its use.

Most of the company-based methods used for either daily, weekly, or monthly forecasting are based almost exclusively on averaging, and little use has been made generally of techniques that cause the model to adjust to changing trend patterns or isolate seasonality. Longer-term forecast models used for quarterly and annual forecasts generally employ the same techniques as the short-term models. It is infrequent that techniques such as regression analysis are used to forecast either the aggregate future cash level of requirements or elements within the forecast.

A DECOMPOSITION MODEL

Many of the models developed that have not been based on inventory or linear programming approached by companies have included basic techniques that apply specifically to this corporate environment, and, consequently, it sometimes is difficult to apply the approach to a broader set of circumstances. There are a few models, however, that are general enough in nature to provide the factors of understandability, ease of use, and applicability to a wide range of environments. The Beehler Cash Forecast Model is a representative model of a general application type. The model was originally designed for use by a large data processing service bureau that was planning a national expansion program. Because this service bureau worked in conjunction with a bank, the method of charging for the service included both fee charges and float realized by immediate account charges for payable and payroll items. The market was basically the smaller and medium-sized firms that traditionally did not enjoy cash concentration of disbursement techniques. Since float utilization created by the services was considered in pricing the payables and payroll services, it was imperative that a comprehensive cash management package be developed. In addition to the uncertainty of cash accounts receivable receipts, the volatility of the daily float generated by the issuance of payroll and payable checks to many disbursed payrolls significantly complicated the disbursement float control problem.

Additionally, seasonality in the balances existed because higher end-of-week disbursements were experienced and because seasons of the year affected the sales of the service bureau subscribers. Consequently, the seasonality trend and randomness were major factors affecting model development. The service bureau planned to concentrate disbursement funds in three locations. To control national float, a model was needed to forecast an ending account balance in order to facilitate daily investments. It was also desirable to define the extent to which funds could be committed in relation to the long-term placement of investments versus, short-term daily investments. The importance of float management in this situation dictated daily management reporting that the company's financial management could review. This was special significance because the income generated by the investment of outstanding float was part of the profit that the service bureau relied upon.

The model described in the next section is representative of a "modular" approach to modeling, which attempts to fit the techniques to the situation and to adjust the approach to achieve practical results. Models of this nature tend to be nonstatistical in nature but intuitively appealing to management because they can identify how different situations are being handled by the approach. The model is described in detail so that the reader can place the approach in perspective to techniques previously described and relate them to personal experience.

THE BEEHLER CASH FORECAST MODEL

Purpose

One of the major impediments to the widespread acceptance of mathematical models, such as the Orgler or Miller–Orr, is the degree of sophisticated mathematical knowledge required. Simply stated, if it cannot be understood by those responsible for results, it will not be used. It is difficult—and impractical—to be reliant on something that we cannot be understood. The Beehler Cash Forecasting Model* is based on the decomposition of data associated with individual elements or groups of elements with which a cash manager is involved. The model can be applicable to a wide range of forecast applications. The time horizon for which it is designed is limited to the short (daily or weekly) to intermediate range (less than 1 year). The basic approach to developed decomposition models has been discussed in Chapter 7. The purpose of this nonstatistical model is to

---

* The author recognizes Don Erbel for his essential contributions in development of the model.

combine the appeal of decomposition, with other quantitative methods, to produce an easily understood, reliable, and inexpensive modeling approach that can be used by intermediate-size firms, as well as large corporations.

Another objective of this model is to provide the cash manager with a modeling approach that can be executed in a manual mode, although maximum benefit is more easily derived when computer modeling is used.

Functions

The features that the model provides are:

- Identification and analysis of seasonal patterns in data
- Adaptation to changing conditions through the use of exponential smoothing
- Identification of trend affecting the balance levels
- Use of exponential smoothing techniques to filter randomness from current observations
- Continual analysis of the forecast error and the use of Mean Absolute Deviation (MAD) to develop a statistical estimate.
- Development of statistical estimates to provide forecasts with probable ranges of results

This model can be applicable to a wide range of cash flow-forecasting environments. It can be used to forecast ending account balances at the microlevel if desired. More often it is applicable to forecasting elements and subelements with a high degree of uncertainty for daily forecasts such as dollars of zero day deposits, receivables for the current day, or projected daily cash sales. These elements usually display a high degree of uncertainty in forecasting the ending balance in daily monitoring accounts.

The certain elements are reported by the responsible areas and combined with model results to produce the daily cash balance forecast for the company.

Elements of the Model

Seasonality

The first step to developing the basis for this decomposition-based model is identification of the seasonal patterns, if any, in the data being analyzed. The method used to identify patterns is usually graphic display of historical data for the purpose of visual analysis. Through this approach, a visual identification can be made of periodic peaks and valleys in the series under examination. If the elements fluctuate in a reasonably consistent pattern, it is appropriate to establish indices to convert actual data to a common denominator. The frequency within which the fluctuations take place are not as important as the reasonable consistency of the pattern. Depending upon the elements being forecast, the period may be weekly, 10-day, or monthly, or some other cycle basis. A significant sample of the data should be graphically displayed so that random occurrences can be eliminated. For example, if a daily element is used in this forecast model, 1 year by days would be plotted by day to define the pattern of fluctuation for the element.

Exhibit 9-1 is an example of daily data plotted for a 6-week period. As the graph illustrates, a weekly pattern seems to exist where lower cash sales are recorded on Mondays and a gradual building in volume during this week with high balances occurring on Friday.

After identifying the seasonal pattern in the data, the starting daily indices for the model should be developed. Since each new week provides more information about the index number for each day, we need to define only the starting values and subsequently adjust them for changes. In this manner, the indices are modified for changes in the pattern over time. In order to develop representative starting indices, a significant time span should be chosen perhaps as extensive as that used to develop the seasonal graph. For purposes of illustration, 6 weeks of data has been used to develop the initial indices in Exhibit 9-2. The index was developed by summing each of the week's actual amounts then developing the average daily amount for the element. If the time span were different from the 5 days used in this example, then that period would be used to determine a starting average. The index is really a comparison of the actual experience for the individual day compared to (divided by) the average for the period under examination. This process really states that for the period under considera-

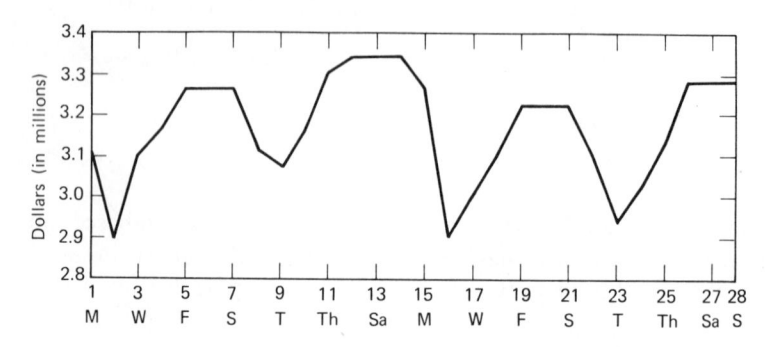

Exhibit 9.1   Historical cash balances.

Exhibit 9.2 Daily cash forecasting worksheet (all figures in thousands).

EXHIBIT 9-2

DAILY CASH FORECASTING WORKSHEET

ALL FIGURES IN THOUSANDS

	1	2	3	4	5	6	7	8	9	10	11	12	13
DATE	ACTUAL CASH BALANCE	SEASONAL INDEX (EXHIBIT 8-6)	DESEASONALIZED ACTUAL CASH BALANCE	AVERAGE ACTUAL CASH BALANCE	CHANGE IN AVERAGE ACTUAL CASH BALANCE	TREND (F) ESTIMATE	NEW FORECAST DESEASONALIZED	NEW FORECAST SEASONALIZED	FORECAST ERROR	MEAN (E) ABSOLUTE DEVIATION	ESTIMATED STANDARD DEVIATION	INVESTMENT RECOMMENDATION (G)	NET INVESTMENT ERROR
October 18	3,140	.9580	3,278	3,368	-18	00	3,346	3,085	230	0	---	3,085	---
October 19	2,855	.9220	3,097	3,350	-51	-04	3,257	3,228	139	46	58	3,170	-230
October 20	3,089	.9910	3,117	3,299	-36	-42	3,222	3,306	291	65	81	3,225	-081
October 21	3,597	1.0260	3,506	3,263	+49	-41	3,289	3,628	169	110	138	3,490	+372
October 22	3,797	1.1030	3,442	3,312	+26	-23	3,325	3,182		122	153	3,029	+307
October 23				3,338		-13		SATURDAY					SATURDAY
October 24								SUNDAY					SUNDAY
October 25	3,199	.9569*	3,343	3,339	+01	-10	3,329	3,032	17	101	126	2,906	+170
October 26	3,115	.9108	3,420	3,355	+16	-05	3,350	3,284	83	97	121	3,163	+209
October 27	3,298	.9802	3,365	3,357	+02	-04	3,350	3,436	14	80	100	3,336	+135
October 28	3,422	1.0247	3,340	3,354	-03	-04	3,350	3,728	14	67	84	3,644	+086
October 29	4,165	1.1128	3,743	3,432	-78	-19	3,413	3,247	437	141	176	3,071	+521
October 30								SATURDAY					
October 31								SUNDAY					
November 01		.9515											

E – Exponential Smoothing Factors Applied 80% of Historical Plus 20% of Current Data.
F – In This Example the entire trend is used to forecast the next days value. Exponential smoothing could be used to mediate the daily Trend Volatility.
G – The investment recommendation (COL. 12) is the New Forecast Seasonalized (COL. 8) minus yesterday's Estimated Standard Deviation (COL. 11).
* – The New Index Factors are computed as the 20% of the Actual Weekly Index plus 80% of the Historical Index for each day. For Example:

	ACTUAL DAILY BALANCE	ACTUAL DAILY INDEX	HISTORICAL INDEX	NEXT WEEKS INDEX
MONDAY	3,140	.9527	.9580	.9569
TUESDAY	2,855	.8662	.9220	.9108
WEDNESDAY	3,089	.9372	.9910	.9802
THURSDAY	3,597	1.0193	1.0260	1.0247
FRIDAY	3,797	1.1520	1.1030	1.1128

tion the individual day of the week is some percent of the actual experience if seasonal fluctuations were removed. Related to Exhibit 9-2, this could be expressed by stating that every Friday is more than 100% of the average daily experience because the index is always greater than 1.0000.

After developing the individual weekly index factor for each of the 6 weeks, the development of a starting index for each day of the week must be initiated. This is simply the average of each day of the week. For example, the starting Monday index is the average of each of the six Mondays used to develop the seasonal starting index. As previously illustrated in Exhibit 8-6, the sum of the medial average starting index developed in this manner does not equal 100. Consequently, an adjustment factor is applied which is computed as $500/499.7 = 1.0006$. This is used to adjust the medial average into the starting seasonal index by multiplying the adjustment by the medial average.

In the model, additional seasonal index information is available to up-date the next week's indices. Using this approach, we can be assured that the index values change over time because of generally changing economic conditions (e.g., the effects of a recession or an inflationary period can cause shifts in the seasonal patterns). To account for the trend changes that can exist in the seasonal index, we apply an exponential smoothing factor. The basis used for illustration in this model is that heavier emphasis is placed on past experience. To this end, we use 80% of the past observations and 20% of the current experience to forecast the next periods value. As the last index number in column 2 indicates, the index number was derived for Monday 11/01 by developing the actual weekly index of the last full week (as previously described) then using 0.8 of 0.9569 and 0.2 of the actual computed index for Monday.

Trend Identification

As discussed in the decomposition approach to forecasting, the elements to be considered are seasonal, trend, cycle, and randomness. In this model, we use a deseasonalized amount (column 3) as the basis to develop the average element value. Since the cycle of the data occurs over a long time span, it is not included in this model since it is intended for short time horizons. The trend is estimated as being the difference in the average balance from one period to the next. As illustrated in Exhibit 9-2 on 10/20, the change in the average balance from the previous day (column 5) represents trend in the data, randomness, and cycle. To develop the trend, the model uses exponential smoothing by stating that the trend value for any given day is 0.8 of the previous day's trend value plus 0.2 of the current change in the average actual expense (Column 3). This approach states that the trend is modified gradually for basic shifts. The trend could be determined alternately by developing a regression analysis that would state the slope of the trend line. If this approach were chosen, the developmental expense would be increased, but it would provide a method of forecasting this trend several periods in advance. In using exponential smoothing to determine the trend line in this model, we are filtering our estimate of the randomness and cyclical fluctuations out of current experience.

Analysis of the Forecast Error

In this model, we are using an average as the basis for adjustments and forecast amounts. In order to track the accuracy of the forecasts made, it is necessary to develop a mean average deviation on a daily basis. This is the difference between the forecast amount and the actual results for the period. We are not interested in whether the forecast was over or under actual experience; we are just interested in the total amount of variance. Over time we expect the differences to almost completely cancel out and come close to zero. The mean absolute deviation is developed as a measurement of the error so that some adjustment or safety factor can be applied to the next period's forecast. Again, a simple average of the last MAD and current forecast error can be used or exponential smoothing can be used. In this case, exponential smoothing has been used to provide greater emphasis on past experience. Based on this approach, we can develop an average seasonalized forecast for the next period, adjust it by the amount of the mean absolute deviation, and have a better than average chance of being correct.

Establishing a Statistical Estimate and Forecast Safeguard

Since the MAD has been set up in the model, it is possible to "estimate" a standard deviation based on a value of the MAD. The standard deviation is estimated to be 1.25 times the MAD developed. The standard deviation can be used as a safeguard in this model to increase the chance that we under-forecast amounts rather than over-forecast. Since this model is based on developing an average amount for the forecast element, any given forecast has a 50% chance of under-forecasting or over-forecasting on any given day. The costs associated with one variance or another must be measured by the cash manager to determine to what degree the risk of under-forecasting should be insured against so that overdrafts do not occur. Therefore, as a safety valve, the model can take the best average estimate for the next period, which includes trend and seasonality, and use the standard deviation to account for randomness and cycles (which are insignificant in the short term) to increase the probability that a forecast for the next period will under- or over-forecast. For example, by taking the average forecast for the next period and reducing it by one standard deviation, we decrease the chances of over-forecasting (and hence over-investing). We can then state that there is a greater than 50% chance that the forecast figure for the next period is less than the actual element value. The use of the estimated standard deviation in the model is not statistical in nature because it is not based on the strict statistical requirements. Therefore, the model is really estimating the variances in a relatively simple and straightforward manner. Fine tuning the individual elements in the model is essential, and to this extent the use of exponential smoothing factors in the elements provide for various emphases on different elements depended on the cash manager's needs. The elements the model applies exponential smoothing to are:

- Seasonal index
- Average actual balance
- Trend estimate
- Next period forecast
- Mean Absolute Deviation

Since the factors used in each of the elements can vary considerably by company, this becomes the largest factor in establishing the starting point for the model. The correct balance in establishing the smoothing factor determines the overall effectiveness of the model. As suggested, the cash manager can protect from over- or under-forecasting through the application of an estimated standard deviation.

Investment Strategy

Since the purpose of this model is to establish a period-by-period forecast of available funds for investment, a basic definition of long- versus short-term funds availability must be made by the cash manager in order to determine the short-term investment amounts.

The basis of determining long- versus short-term investment can be based on the graph developed to chart historical daily cash balances. The graph indicates a level below which funds must not drop. This level represents the amount of long-term investment available to the corporation. This long-term investment may be increased depending upon management philosophy regarding the frequency with which a corporation borrows to increase its long-term investment amount. For example, if borrowing five times a month would increase the amount of long-term funds invested by 20%, the associated costs of borrowing should be weighed against the total revenue gained from those funds during the monthly investment period. The amount of long-term investment significantly affects the optimization of the cash management program.

Model Walkthrough

Basically, the forecasting model uses the average actual cash balance to project the element value for the following day. The model used for the walkthrough is forecasting the ending daily account balance. The model can be used to forecast any of the elements that comprises the total such as zero day deposits or daily cash sales. The average actual cash balance forecast is modifed to account for identifiable trends and seasonal fluctuations. To reduce the probability of over-investing on a given day, the projected average actual cash balance is reduced by the amount of historical variance in the forecast as expressed by the standard deviation. The resulting recommended investment funds are then committed to long- and short-term, revenue-producing securities.

Exhibit 9-2 represents a daily worksheet for using the model. The level of long-term investment and adaptability via exponential smoothing factors have been defined by management. The starting weekly indices have been developed by averaging the prior 10-week actual indices by day as illustrated in Exhibit 8-6. Consequently, the initial index for Monday is a composite of actual experience for the past 10 Mondays. Since each daily index is developed in relation to its respective weekly total, the daily index average should provide a representative starting point for the model.

Future weekly indices are developed by computing the actual index daily values for the past week and applying 20% (0.2) of the actual experience, plus 80% (0.8) of the last index to form the next week's daily index value. In this way, each new week's experiences are reflected in the following week's index values. This method is used in this model walkthrough for purposes of illustration. However, over time seasonal distortion in the indices can occur. To avoid this tendency, either new indices can be computed periodically or using computer modeling a weekly up-date of the seasonal indices can be obtained. The size of the initial sample for determining indices directly affects the cost of a weekly recomputation. However, depending on the value of the forecast element and the availability of computer models, this method provides optimal development of weekly index values.

The actual daily cash balance, entered in column 1, must be deseasonalized by dividing it by the seasonal index to measure the deseasonalized value (column 3) against the average actual cash balance (column 4). Exponential smoothing is used in developing the average actual cash balance (column 4). *The model uses 80% of the previous day's average actual cash balance plus 20% of the deseasonalized actual cash balance for the current day.* This places greater emphasis on past experience while allowing the model to adapt to a changing environment. The actual values chosen may vary for each factor, and the weights used must reflect management objectives and experiences.

Since the forecasted cash balance for the next day is based on the deseasonalized average actual cash balance, changes in the balance must be examined to evaluate the trend affecting it. In order to determine *the trend, we first calculate the change in the average actual cash balance (column 5) by subtracting the current average actual cash balance from the previous day's result. The resulting positive or negative amount is used to estimate the trend affecting the average actual cash balance.* The trend is developed by applying a weighted factor to our current experience. The trend line may start at zero as indicated and adapt to existing experiences. The factors may differ from one column to another to account for various degrees of flexibility desired within the model. If desired, no adjustment need be made to the trend, rather its entire value can be applied to the average cash balance. In this example, the same weighted factors used previously are applied in calculating the trend line. Consequently, the up-dated trend is 80% of the trend from the previous period plus 20% of the current change in the average actual cash balance (column 5). The result (column 6) indicates the current trend for this period. The new forecasted deseasonalized cash balance (column 7) is simply the average actual cash balance for the current day adjusted by 80% of the trend. This is the projected deseasonalized value of tomorrow's cash balances.

The deseasonalized forecast (column 7) is then seasonalized by multiplying it by the seasonal index factor (column 2) for the appropriate day. The new forecast corrected for seasonality becomes the projected cash balance for the following day (column 8). Without any further adjustments, this result can be used for short- and long-term investing for the following day. Depending upon management constraints, it may be desirable to build a margin of error into the model to account for irregular fluctuations in cash patterns and to provide for required reserves to support a line of credit.

The standard deviation can be used to reduce the possibility of overinvesting. For example, the chances of the *average* cash balance being correct for any given day are approximately 50%. To reduce the probability that the average cash balance forecasted will exceed actual experience, standard deviations are applied to the basic average. If the seasonalized forecast (column 8) is reduced one standard deviation, we increase our confidence in the model from 50% to approximately 84%. Consequently, we expect the investment recommendation to be less than the actual cash balance approximately 84% of the time.

Examination of historical forecast is the first step in developing a standard deviation. The forecast error (column 9) is the difference between the seasonalized forecast (column 8) and the actual cash balance (column 1). It is unimportant to note whether the forecast error itself is over or under the actual cash balance since the result is used to develop a range value.

The Mean Absolute Deviation (column 10) is up-dated each period to account for the degrees of error that are experienced in the model. Heavier emphasis is again placed on past experience in this model; consequently, 80% of the old MAD plus 20% of the new forecast error (column 9) comprises the up-dated MAD.* One standard deviation (column 11) is simply estimated to be 1.25 times the mean absolute deviation. In the model under discussion, one standard deviation is used as the safety margin. In other words, the investment recommendation for the next day (column 12) is the seasonalized forecast (column 8) minus one standard deviation (column 11). As the model illustrates, the previous day's standard deviation is applied against the current seasonalized forecast (column 8). The acceptable margin of error varies by company depending upon the fluctuation in the actual cash balances or other elements forecast and the risk philosophy of management. For example, if cash balances fluctuate little, perhaps only one-half of one standard deviation would be necessary to provide a safety margin. Conversely, if extreme fluctuations take place, perhaps two standard deviations are necessary to insure investment policies consistent with the corporation's goals.

The Management Summary

Although forecasting is critical to the cash management program, the financial manager is interested in evaluating the daily *results*. Consequently, daily management summary is recommended regardless of the elements or subelements being forecast. The purpose of the summary is to illustrate daily results. In this case, the actual performance of the model is measured in terms of profit generated from invested funds.

Exhibit 9-3 is an example of the daily summary resulting from the calculation of the model. The projected funds (column 2) represent the recommended investment amount. The projected balance in excess of committed long-term funds represents the short-term or overnight investment amount (column 6). If the long-term funds committed are greater than the investment recommendation, no short-term investment is possible. Consequently, funds are borrowed against the line of credit in order to maintain long-term investment. The amount of long-term funds invested and the resulting

---

* The MAD is initiated at zero since it is based on forecast results. As used in this model the MAD is really a modified absolute deviation rather than an average.

Exhibit 9.3 Daily forecast management summary (all figures in thousands).

FIGURES IN THOUSANDS

	1	2	3	4	5	6	7	8	9	10	11	12
DATE	ACTUAL CASH BALANCE	INVESTMENT RECOMMENDATION	VARIANCE	LONG TERM INVESTMENT	LONG TERM INVESTMENT REVENUE (1)	SHORT TERM INVESTMENT	SHORT TERM INVESTMENT REVENUE (2)	GROSS INVESTMENT INCOME	OVERDRAFTS DOLLARS COST (3)		NET INVESTMENT INCOME	OPERATING COST (2)
October 18	3,140	3,085	----	----	----	----	----	----	----	----	----	----
October 19	2,855	3,170	-230	2,500	$451.25	355	$ 32.06	483.31	230	$76.66	$ 406.65	----
October 20	3,089	3,225	-081	2,500	$451.25	589	$ 53.19	504.44	81	$27.00	$ 477.44	----
October 21	3,597	3,490	+372	2,500	$451.25	1,097	$ 99.06	550.31			$ 550.31	$ 33.59
October 22	3,797	3,490	+307	2,500	$451.25	1,297	$117.12	568.37			$ 568.37	$ 27.72
October 23	3,797	3,490	+307	2,500	$451.25	1,297	$117.12	568.37			$ 568.37	$ 27.72
October 24	3,199	3,029	+170	2,500	$451.25	699	$ 63.12	514.37			$ 514.37	$ 15.35
October 25	3,115	2,906	+209	2,500	$451.25	615	$ 55.53	506.78			$ 506.78	$ 18.87
October 26	3,298	3,163	+135	2,500	$451.25	798	$ 72.06	523.31			$ 523.31	$ 12.19
October 27	3,422	3,336	+086	2,500	$451.25	922	$ 83.26	534.51			$ 534.51	$ 7.77
October 28	4,165	3,644	+521	2,500	$451.25	1,665	$150.35	601.60			$ 601.60	$ 47.04
October 30	4,165	3,644	+521	2,500	$451.25	1,665	$150.35	601.60			$ 601.60	$ 47.04
October 31	4,165	3,644	+521	2,500	$451.25	1,665	$150.35	601.60			$ 601.60	$ 47.04
November 01		3,071		2,500	$451.25	571	$ 51.56	502.81				

(1) Based on a long term annual rate of 6.5%. The daily factor of .0001805 is applied to determine daily revenue.

(2) An annual short term rate (e.g. repurchase agreements) of 3.25% is used. This equates to a daily factor of .0000903 to determine daily short term revenue.

(3) Cost of borrowing computed at 12% or a daily factor of .003333.

revenue is assumed to remain constant between periods of adjustment. The daily long-term revenue is developed by multiplying the *daily* factor for the long-term rate by the amount of the long-term investment. As indicated in Exhibit 9-3, $2,500,000 is extended by the daily long-term rate to develop revenue of $451.25 per day. Similarly, the short-term daily rate is applied to the varying amount of short-term funds invested to develop actual income. Funds in excess of the invested amount may be used to cover compensating balances for lines of credit. The overdraft dollars (column 9) represents the over-invested funds occurring on any given day. The appropriate borrowing rate is applied to develop the cost of borrowing (column 10) the funds from the line of credit. Net investment income (column 11) is derived by subtracting the cost of borrowed funds from the daily gross investment income. The opportunity cost (column 12) is based on the overnight investment rate and represents the additional income that could be earned had the forecast been completely accurate.

The financial director uses the daily recap to determine:

- *the performance of the model over a period of time*—Daily analysis of the variance is easily obtained through the management summary. The cost of over-projecting is represented by the cost of overdrafts. Similarly, lost opportunity costs are reported daily.
- *Profitability of the model*—The net investment income demonstrates the daily earnings directly attributable to cash management.
- *The level of long-term investment*—The management summary can indicate the trend of outstanding funds while providing the informational base to increase the amount of long-term funds to earn higher yields.

CASH FORECASTING—OBSERVATIONS AND TRENDS

The previous chapters have been specifically directed toward the current aspects and environment of cash forecasting. The purpose of these chapters has been to:

- Define the environment and suggest various approaches to evaluating corporate cash forecasting
- Examine and evaluate the accounting-based approach to cash management placing them in a working perspective.
- Define quantitative techniques applicable to cash forecasting related to various time horizons
- Review the types of cash management models currently available

These sections have provided a comprehensive scope of what approaches and methods are available in establishing a cash-forecasting system for a corporation. The methods discussed do not apply to every firm. In fact, a combination of approaches are often the most reasonable approach to satisfying a company's forecasting requirement. The selection of the forecasting technique must be based on the company's individual needs. To this extent "custom" modeling is always necessary. In addition to customizing the forecasting model to the company, the techniques chosen to develop the model are largely influenced by:

- *The nature of the company's business*—this factor influences the type of model and related techniques because of the degree of disbursement and receipt control that exists in various industries. For example, a large southeast construction firm receives contract payments every two weeks from a government agency based on percentage of completion. The receipts are known as well as the timing of the payment. This known environment can be contrasted with more random receipts from retail charge sales.
- *The time horizon*—A company needs little sophisitcation in forecasting if the daily cash receipts and disbursements have a high degree of controlability. The model constructed, however, should take into account trend patterns for long-term forecasts cyclical factors.
- *Managerial understanding and acceptance*—This is the most critical item influencing the development of corporate cash-forecasting models. Without managerial understanding of the purpose of the model and the factors that influence the forecast, the model cannot have practical application. The purpose of modeling is to reasonably represent in abstract terms what is occurring in the corporate operating environment.
- *Degree of required accuracy*—This influences the model both in the development expense incurred and in the operation and maintenance of the model assumptions. For capital intensive firms, such as public utilities, the accuracy of long-term capital requirements is essential to future company viability. Accordingly, a significant investment in model development can be justified. Conversely, a firm with modest capital needs, much of which may be internally provided, has no need to incur the costs for an extremely reliable model.
- *Development and operational costs*—This final major modeling consideration need not be directly related to the accuracy of the model. At times, a simple approach (e.g., forecasting the total account balance as opposed to total debit and credit activity) may produce adequate results at significantly less cost in both development and operation. Use

of computer systems in development and operational expenses must be weighed against manual-modeling approaches, which offer initial simplicity with the potential of eventual computerization.

CURRENT CASH FORECASTING APPLICATION

Short-Term Forecasts

In the majority of cases today, corporate short-term forecasting is based on the cash receipts and disbursement accounting method. The individual values for the elements comprising the forecast are derived from direct estimates made by responsible divisions within the corporation. Often projected sales are used as a base to apply ratios to determine daily, weekly, or monthly element values. The purpose of the cash receipts and disbursements approach is to both manage and lead bank balances and to better use excess funds through investments or loan repayments. Many firms use prior years' data adjusted for industry-related economic projections for daily, weekly, or monthly forecasts. Additionally, firms in seasonally affected industries adjust prior years' data based on current conditions. For example, a large midwest retail corporation cash manager's forecasts are modified if the temperature goes above 90° for three days or more because his past data indicates that sales of air conditioners significantly increase causing a temporary swell in this cash position.

Currently, forecast modeling by corporations has been limited to automating the tracking of balances and deposits related to short-term cash forecasting. Forecasts per se have not been addressed but rather increasing balance control through reporting systems. To date, little application of quantitative techniques have been applied to short-term cash-forecasting functions. The models developed (Orgler, Sastray, etc.) have not been widely accepted because they are often difficult to understand in theory and more difficult in application because of the number of variables and constraints that require definition.

Intermediate-Term Forecasts

For most intermediate-term forecasts, firms today use the funds flow approach. The techniques used to develop this element's values are based on future sales and activity projections from various corporate areas. Often ratios are commonly used to relate future activity to current experience. This use of ratios can lead to forecasting problems because trends in inventory accumulation or increasing receivables are not recognized. Generally, there is to date little application of quantitative methods to intermediate-term cash forecasting.

Trends in Cash Forecasting

Current developments indicate that cash forecasting today is an evolutionary period between "indigenous" corporate internal forecasting methods and gradual adoption of more model-oriented methods. The basic movement in cash forecasting is in two areas: the media used to develop and control forecasts and the techniques that are used in making forecasts. These two factors are interrelated and affect the large corporations as well as intermediate-sized firms.

The delivery systems available to provide cash forecasts are now accelerating in development through time-sharing vendors. These services provide basic short-term forecasts (daily) for the corporation by duplicating a cash receipts and disbursements approach automatically for the corporation. This modus operandi is more advantageous than manual methods because it has the ability to extract data from other services such as automated deposit reporting services that are currently offered. Although there are quantitative techniques available through automated services, the potential use is only embryonic in its current manifestation. However, as a practical matter, short-term use of quantitative techniques are limited because most firms have not experienced a demonstrated need for these techniques. There is a diminished trend within corporations to develop internal forecasting models as flexible package forecasting models become available. Very large corporations, however, still develop internal models specifically to meet indigenous operating requirements.

Within the next few years longer term forecasts will also be increasingly provided by general purpose forecasting services offered by banks and time-sharing vendors. In this area, a wider use of quantitative modeling will occur because of user operational ease. Liaison personnel from the supplier will work with the corporate cash manager to define forecast requirements and implement appropriate techniques for the corporation. Results will not always be optimal to the corporation, however, under this approach, but development and operational expenses will be minimal. Direct estimating of elements in the forecast will continue to be input by the corporation; however, the forecast of many elements will be based on techniques illustrated in Exhibit 8-7.

Specific applications will focus on dynamic forecasting of disbursements using time sharing models. This use will be extended to forecasting of collections using daily inputs from corporate cash managers utilizing office resident computer terminals. Following a period of experimentation the outputs of both models will be merged into dynamic daily cash receipts and disbursement forecasting services.

CONCLUSION

For the near term, corporations are beginning an evolutionary movement in the application of quantitative techniques to cash forecasting. The evolution is on a selective basis and primarily relates to intermediate time horizons not short-term forecasts. The evolutionary process is aided by automated cash-forecasting services that are now being developed and introduced in the market. They will remove the cumbersome mechanical apsects of cash forecasting and expand use of preprogrammed quantitative techniques. Although corporations continue to develop models internally, the development and operational economics of cash forecasting services attract many firms away from internal development. The determining factor affecting cash forecasting continues to be the marginal accuracy of results as compared to the marginal value derived from the results achieved. To this extent, corporations invest in more accurate cash forecasting only if the value (internal or external to the company) of funds concerned continues in an upward trend.

BIBLIOGRAPHY

Anthony, Robert, *Management Accounting,* Richard Irwin, Homewood, Ill., 1970.

Baer, Wilmer, "A Cash Flow Model," *Managerial Planning,* March–April 1972.

Bedford, Norton, *Introduction to Modern Accounting.*

Beehler, Paul J., "Cash Management: Forecasting for Profit," *Management Advisor,* July–August 1973.

Miller, M., and Orr, D., "The Demand for Money by Firms: Extensions of Analytic Results," *Journal of Finance,* December 1967.

Orgler, Yair, *Cash Management,* Wadsworth, Belmont, Calif., 1970.

Orr, David, *Cash Management and the Demand for Money,* Praeger, New York, 1971.

Sekhar, Sethu, Cash Management Models and Practices, A thesis, University of California, June 2, 1972.

Slater, S. D., *The Strategy of Cash: a Liquidity Approach to Maximizing the Company's Profits,* Wiley, New York, 1974.

Wheelwright, Steven, and Makrivakis, Spyros, *Forecasting Methods for Management,* Wiley, New York, 1973.

PART 4

INTERNATIONAL CASH MANAGEMENT

CHAPTER 10

CHARACTERISTICS OF INTERNATIONAL CASH MANAGEMENT[1]

INTRODUCTION

The previous sections of this book cover the domestic techniques associated with cash management and forecasting as it relates to cash management functions. Because of the growing importance of international business to corporations, cash management would be inadequately covered without examining the elements comprising the management of international corporate assets.

Many companies today are becoming more dependent on international business as a major source of net profit. This results from the penetration of domestic markets and the simultaneous expansion in demand and sophistication of foreign markets. For example, Bank of America, the world's largest bank, realizes over 50% of its net profit contribution from its world banking division, which concentrates financing outside the United States, as a profit source. Similar situations are being experienced by other national corporations. Often foreign involvement begins through establishing sales agencies. Eventually as economic situations indicate, this leads to a full manufacturing plant. Usually, the initial capital investment is low and often consists of antiquated equipment that is serviceable, but because of domestic productivity pressures, is not economically viable. Often this type of equipment can be used in foreign countries where product demand is high and the cost of labor low. This combination leads to the initial involvement of American corporations abroad. As post World War II economic development accelerated, the small production and service facilities in foreign countries grew.

---

[1] The author wishes to acknowledge Edwin Protiva for his contributions to this section.

Loosely structured control was typical of international subsidiaries for most foreign corporations. This is still a prevalent pattern today, with a high concentration of foreign nationals actually operating as profit center managers. Even though foreign nationals act as profit center managers for production and distribution facilities, the financial aspects of international subsidiaries is often controlled by corporate headquarters. To this extent, international growth is placing increasing pressures on corporate cash managers, treasurers, and financial officers and the functions they perform because the techniques, financial instruments, and approach to financial optimization is significantly different from customary domestic applications. The purpose of this section is to outline the differences in techniques in international cash management, to define the most commonly used instruments in international financing for short- and medium-term working capital financing, to isolate the major cash management problems and available solutions, and to discuss the considerations in optimizing the management of international funds for the overall benefit of the parent American company.

It is estimated that foreign-owned assets of American corporations are growing by more than 10% per year. However, the growth trend in the international area, coupled with the involvement of medium-sized firms indicates increased involvement of the domestic cash manager in the financial affairs of foreign subsidiaries. The primary objectives of the cash manager in international areas are to:

- Establish and control a common cash pool for overall corporate use
- Establish a global money management strategy
- Optimize global cash and near cash utilization
- Minimize borrowing costs
- Minimize foreign exchange costs

ESSENTIAL INTERNATIONAL CONSIDERATIONS

The number of foreign subsidiaries the international cash manager controls disproportionately increases the complexity of his functions. This occurs because the number of rule variations that exist from one country to another. However, the basic or essential areas to be considered include differences in:

- Basic economic philosophy
- Methods of financing available

- Exchange rate vulnerability
- Cultural-related differences in terms of business customs
- Governmental involvement

These factors must be considered in terms of the conventional approach of inflows and outflows of funds that provide a familiar base for cash management; however, this approach is not practical in evaluating the international implications because the five major factors defined here permeate and affect all areas of international cash management. Rather than reviewing from the bottom up the various effects that international differences have on cash management functions these two chapters suggest a top down perspective to provide a working framework for the effective planning and control of cash management in an international environment.

Chapter 10 approaches the subject from the perspective of financial control and funds flow control since these two generic functions comprise the source of financing and the control over the flow of funds into and out of the multinational company. Exhibit 10-1 illustrates the general structure of these two chapters.

Financial Control

Financial control is defined as those functions of the international cash manager that deal with acquisition and control over the assets of foreign subsidiaries. In the effective management of the overall financial health of the multinational corporation, the cash manager is concerned with how to finance the international subsidiary, both initially and on an on-going basis so that company-wide financial optimization may be attained.

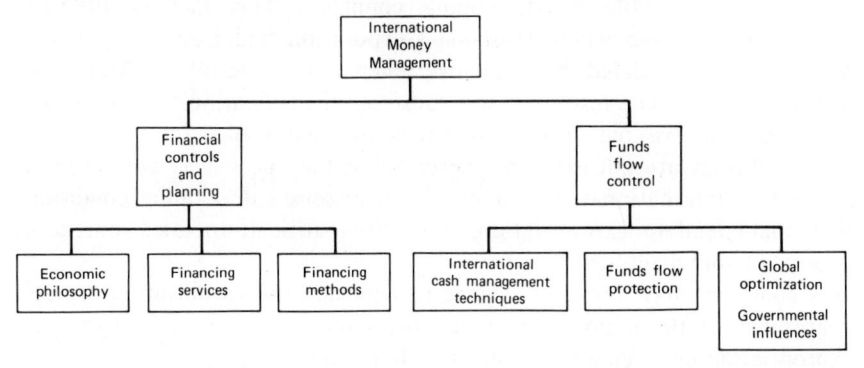

Exhibit 10.1   Overview structure of international cash management.

```
                        International
                           Money
                         Management
          ┌─────────────────┴─────────────────┐
      Financial                             Funds
      controls                              flow
        and                                control
      planning
   ┌──────┬───────┐              ┌────────────┬────────────┐
Economic Financing Financing  International  Funds flow   Global
philosophy services methods   cash management protection optimization
                              techniques
                                                         Governmental
                                                         influences
```

To analyze the major elements for consideration in financial control, the international cash manager includes identification of:

- Economic differences in philosophy in foreign subsidiaries
- Alternative financing techniques in dealing with foreign subsidiaries
- Sources of funds for the international subsidiary
- Governmental regulatory constraints

Economic Differences

The variety of various cultural practices and the evolution of economic philosophies is a fundamental consideration in international financial management. In accounting for underlying economic differences, four basic areas of concern emerge:

- Risks of asset loss
- Inflation policies
- Special foreign taxation
- Capital controls

In marked contrast to domestic money management, there is an ever present risk to the international cash manager that the foreign corporate asset base will be suddenly lost to the corporation. The principal source of fear for asset loss occurs from potential foreign asset expropriation, foreign exchange currency losses, and gradual currency devaluation.

Foreign expropriation is the partial or full confiscation of corporate assets in a foreign country with or without compensation to the parent company. Expropriation usually results in the permanent loss of assets to a corporation with significant attending losses. Expropriation is not uncommon in politically volatile or developing countries. This fact of life was emphasized in 1975 when Marcona Corporation had iron ore mines in Venezuela expropriated by the government. As a result of Marcona's dependence on this resource and lack of diversification, the company experienced a 75% reduction in revenues and finally filed for bankruptcy. Expropriations are not expected; nevertheless they persist as an important element of international risk. Even if a firm senses developing conditions that could lead to expropriation, it is often difficult to take short-term action to avoid asset loss.

A company may, however, reduce its exposure to expropriation through cognizance of the major factors and perceptions that often lead to asset expropriation by foreign governments. They include:

- *Unfair competition by American corporations in a foreign country by supporting lower prices to eliminate foreign national competition*—This occurs because the American multinational firms may have far greater resources available than local competition.
- *Fear by the foreign country that the American firm will ignore local customs making the competitive environment impossible for local firms and workers.*—This cultural ignorance can be overcome to some extent through employment of foreign managers and adherence to local customs.
- *Significant capital resource drained from the host country to the United States.*—This concern arises from the frequency and amount of dividend payments, management fees, and royalties remitted to the parent company. Many foreign countries see this as damaging to the overall balance of payments position and a threat to their current stability.
- *Fear arising from instable governments that significant concentration in one industry by an American multinational corporation leads to governmental pressures from the United States government on the foreign political environment.*

While these concerns may not be warranted, it is the perception of the host government that provides an economic indicator. While direct expropriation may take place to correct what is viewed as a politically undesirable situation, it is usually considered a serious move at best because it discourages further investment by multinational firms until assurances can be obtained regarding the security of future investments.

An alternative to direct expropriation is "asset freezing," which results in loss of asset control. This occurs when a foreign government places controls on the use and movement of assets. Common examples of asset control includes: a temporary limit on the amount of funds that can be remitted to the parent company, limitations on imported raw materials, export limitations on finished goods, and discriminatory taxation. The object of this type of asset control is usually to coerce the foreign owner to sell the firm to the host government or local investor. The major advantage to the host government is that business initiation risks and required technical expertise have been defined. Asset control has been widely used in countries such as Mexico and India.

Foreign Exchange Asset Loss

As the sun in the morning sky is taken for granted, similarily the solid financial economic base that the United States enjoys is taken for granted by domestic cash managers. Not so for the international financial managers who are concerned with every possibility of potential devaluations or shifting relationship with other currencies. Indeed, if the corporation is doing business entirely within the United States, there is little concern that the value of corporate assets will diminish because of an unstable economic environment. But this is not the case for the international cash manager. The volatility of economic philosophies in foreign countries fosters an everpresent concern over the safety of corporate assets. The principal sources for concern lie in:

- Expropriation of assets
- Currency devaluation
- Governmental restrictions on funds availability

Expropriation of Assets

The most dramatic risk to assets in the international environment is foreign government expropriation. Though expropriation often seems swift and unpredictable, an objective assessment by the international financial manager reveals guideposts to possible future government actions related to expropriation. The key questions and issues to be examined include:

- What is the current stability of the government?
- What is the official government attitude toward private property?
- What is the probable future of the existing government?
- What is the long-range economic climate?
- To what extent does the foreign government need the business or technology represented?
- Is required technology easily available within the country?

Even though political stability and government rapport are extremely important, the essential consideration is the *need* perceived by the host government for the product or service produced. The government may value the foreign investment in the industry because it provides basic required products within its borders or provides a source of increasing exports to other countries that can strengthen its balance of payments position. Another essential consideration is the extent to which the foreign business adds to the local economy through employment. Even if the industry is required by the host government, expropriation is still possible under volatile economic conditions. The final major consideration is the degree of technical ability required in the production and management of the foreign facility. Perhaps more important than the actual ability required is the ability perceived by the host government. The host government is less inclined to expropriate a firm whose output is deemed essential if it does not possess required technical expertise to control operations. The use of technical expertise as a strategic planning factor, however, must be tempered by the knowledge that host governments view foreign corporations unfavorably when production facilities are established and local employees are not skill trained. While creating the need for technical expertise, the corporation needs to demonstrate its willingness to be a "good neighbor" in order to avoid expropriation. Some approaches to demonstrating this constructive attitude include:

- Training local labor in technical development areas based on the requirements of the industry
- Training local labor for managerial positions so the "emphasis" on American control is mitigated
- Locating physical plant to accommodate geographical preferences of the host government
- Establishing specific managerial and training objectives
- Using indigenous raw materials to support the local economy
- Providing equity investment to the host country's investors

Through a balanced approach and continued evaluation of the local environment, the firm doing business in a foreign country can minimize the risks of expropriation. If expropriation is feared, the corporation may wish to increase borrowings in the country by pledging the local corporate assets as collateral. Subsequent conversion of the currency to a secure currency shelters it from any currency fluctuations that may accompany expropriation actions. Repayment of the loans to the countries central bank can act as a negotiating base if the corporate assets are taken over.

Currency Devaluation

Even though expropriation is a periodic threat in the international environment, inflation and the eventuality of currency devaluation is a permanent concern of most international financial managers. Countries cannot indefinitely run a balance of payments deficit position because the sources to finance the deficit diminish and its own reserves of foreign currencies (and in prior years, gold) do not stimulate confidence on the part of foreign governments to lend funds to support deficits. The major factors that create balance of payments deficits include:

- Inflation that results in local goods being less competitive globally while increasing the demand for less expensive imports
- Business cycles that occur within the country or other parts of the national market place but that can have direct results in the host country
- Structural economic conditions such as excessive reliance on imports (e.g. England) or over-dependence on one or two major export items (e.g., sugar exportation from Cuba and coffee from Brazil)

In order to correct the external effects of inflation (a lessening of international competitive ability), countries may:

- Devalue currency in relation to the rest of the world
- Impose controls on capital movement
- Control domestic price levels

Of the three primary actions that can be taken by host governments, the first two result in a dilution of corporate asset value. The devaluation of currency results in lowered American value for all assets held in that country. The net effect is measured by subtracting total debt and other liabilities from total assets. The result is the "exposure" the corporation experiences. Currency devaluation is reflected in two types of exposure:

- Translation exposure relates to the equivalence of foreign assets into American dollars for statements in consolidated accounting statements
- Transaction exposure that relates to current business exposure resulting from a promise to pay or receive funds at a future date when there exists a chance for currency devaluation

The specific strategies available to combat currency devaluation are discussed in Chapter 11.

Governmental Restrictions

Governmental controls on capital movement affect asset value because assets do not earn an appropriate return if movement is constrained. Consequently, real asset value defined in terms of return on assets is greatly diminished. Additionally, governmental restrictions can result in a reduction of the assets as earning power by limiting the corporation's ability to produce. This can be accomplished by various controls, including:

- *Input surcharges*—Here the cost of raw materials is raised, and the firm's competitive position is reduced.

- *Advance deposit requirements*—A substantial amount of funds are required on deposit before an import or export transaction can be executed.
- *Multiple exchange rates*—These rates are government controlled and biased against imports. This singular action severely limits the sale of many foreign subsidies.

Although currency devaluation and expropriation are significant differences in the operating environment for the corporate financial manager, their effects can be predicted with some accuracy and actions can be taken within the existing foreign political framework to reduce or minimize the effects on both corporate earnings and asset value. Cognizance of the major differences in economic philosophy provide an evaluation basis for the international cash manager.

SOURCES OF INTERNATIONAL FINANCING

Controlling the financial environment of an international firm mandates cognizance of the sources of financial support available to the various subsidiaries of the multinational firm. The contemporary international money manager must be aware of the internal corporate sources of funds available and the types of loans available from:

- Government financial services
- The World Bank
- Development banks
- Private investment companies
- Commercial banks
- Multinational corporate poolings

Governmental Financial Support

The motivation for governments to provide support to alien firms is to manipulate local economic development, expand undeveloped areas, or stimulate a favorable balance of payments environment through industrial development, which uses abundant raw materials in the production of export products. Although many countries deal through nationally established development banks whose purpose is to underwrite and support specific areas of desired development, it is not uncommon for governments to provide direct loans to corporations at reduced rates to stimulate specific industry or geographic area development. Another form of financing is government guarantees of loans at specified rates to third parties. This provides corporations with access to required funds for high-risk projects with the host government's backing. Consequently, the government has a vested interest in the success of the project. Other forms of financial support can include:

- *Cash grants*—This can be provided as a stimulus to develop an underdeveloped geographic area with desired new industry.
- *Labor supply support*—Assistance in this area includes the transfer of labor to other areas at government expense, as well as economic incentives to stimulate labor force mobility. Additionally, special government-supported training, specified by the corporation, can sometimes be provided as a form of financial support.
- *Reduced taxation or tax forgiveness for a specified time period*—The reduced taxes can apply to income or real estate and are usually for a specified term period (e.g., 10 years). Reduced real estate taxes are manifest through lower tax rates or assessments. Lower real estate tax rates stimulate movement of industry to specific geographic locations.
- *Government creation of support utilities*—Another form of government financial support is the building of major roads, dams, and power supply stations in order to provide required resources to stimulate development. Without this type of support, the costs associated with establishing an environment conducive to industrial development would be magnified significantly.
- *Guarantees of government control*—Assurances of stipulated levels of government controls over the remission of funds to the parent corporation is another form of financial support to the corporation because it provides some assurance that earnings on the investment can be moved to other subsidiaries or can be remitted to the parent company. The types of controls and methods for remission of funds are discussed in Chapter 11.

The types of financial assistance and the terms vary from country to country depending upon the social policies and objectives of each country. Exhibit 10-2 is a matrix for selected countries establishing a guideline to the basic financial support provided. It is not intended to be a full delineation of all government-supplied financial sources but a specific example for the selected countries.

World Bank Financing

The World Bank group is another source of major project financing available to the multinational corporation. Though it was initially established for reconstruction after World War II, its current philosophy is to assist in the development of economically disadvantaged countries. In order to meet its goals, the World Bank is broken down into three main agencies:

- The International Finance Corporation (IFC)
- The International Bank for Reconstruction and Development
- International Development Corporation

Perhaps the most important agency to the international financial manager is the International Finance Corporation. Its purpose is to supply loans and equity capital for development of underdeveloped countries where reasonable loans are not otherwise available. The IFC has two principal departments. The first is designed to assist in establishing, expanding, or modernizing in geographic areas where capital is not available from the country but where the population can support the industry proposed for development. A separate section is devoted to major project developments such as electrical plants. The major projects area provides corporate capital to initiate, modernize, or expand operations. Any business area may be eligible for financial support under this department's charter. The selection criteria is the degree of demonstrated need within the company. In addition to providing loan and equity support, the IFC may also provide underwriting support. The agency may also assist multinational firms locate other sources of funds needed for development.

The second major section of the World Bank Group is the International Bank of Reconstruction and Development. The agency provides funds at reasonable rates to governments or corporations. If a corporation borrows, it is required to have the host government guarantee the loan. The last member of the World Bank group is the International Development Association. Its primary purpose is to raise the standard of living in the less-developed areas of the world. It provides project financing that, because of its nature and risk, requires longer periods of amortization and lower interest charges than would be provided by the other World Bank groups. It provides development funds specifically to less-developed countries. Although it has concentrated on the less-developed countries, it can provide development assistance to more developed countries. As a source of financing, the International Development Association is not a true source of financing for the international cash manager. However, the availability of this type of low cost development funds to underdeveloped countries does permit them to provide financial support in major road construction and electrical facilities as inducement to prospective industry.

Exhibit 10.2 Governmental Financial Support Matrix

Country	Supporting Institutions	Term	Maturity	Justifiable Reason	Provided	Special Development Conditions
Italy	• Instituted mobilize Italiano • Banco di Credito Finanziario Ente Finanziario • Interbankcario • Societa Finanziario Eanesto Breda	Medium- and long-term	5 to 20 20 years	New development, modernization, expansion	• First Mortgage • Other Guarantees • Bond underwriting	• Cash grants • Low interest for development in southern Italy or central and northern mountain areas
France	• Credit National • Credit Hotelier	Medium- and long-term	8 to 20 20 years	Hotel construction, industrial development	First Mortgage secured	• Cash grants • Worker training available for defined undeveloped areas or to help decentralize industries

Country	Institution	Term	Duration	Purpose	Security	Notes
Belgium	• Caisse Generale d' Epargne et de retraite • Societre Nationale de Credit á l'Industrie • Societé Nationale d'Investissement	Medium- and short-term	5 to 15 years, some 20 years	Industrial development	• State guarantees • First Mortgage	• Extra incentives for coal mining area development • Cash grants, tax free
Germany	Kredit anstalt fur Weideraufahr	Medium-term	usually 10 to 12 years	• Automation • Reconversion • Industrialization • New industry	First Mortgage	• Extra incentives for East German border development and West Berlin • Ruhr region development • Special water offer
The Netherlands	Nationale Investerings Bank	Medium- and long-term	5 to 15 up to 25 years	New industry to improve industrial distribution	• Mortgages • Guarantees	Special incentives for eastern regions

Development Banks

In some cases, multinational firms seeking financing in foreign countries find themselves faced with a supply of willing but diffused capital investors. Providing a concentration point for investment funds and an investment focal point is the objective of development banks, which are private development financial institutions. The use of development banks can be viewed as an alternative to commercial bank funds. The development banks (over 350 internationally) in addition to providing long-term capital may also perform private placements and supply management advisory services to developing industries. Although it is usually designed to be profitable, most are not. The motivations for participants in a development bank, however, does not find its origin strictly in the profit motive. Participating countries and banks view it as a vehicle to establishing good relationships and improving their international image, as well as an opportunity to assist the development of lesser-developed countries through financing of high-prospect projects. The object of a successful development bank is to locate and interest capable experienced managers. Once competent management is located, the development bank must find a variety of projects worth evaluating. This is essential so that available resources are constantly used. From the international money manager's perspective, if projects are desirable in an underdeveloped country and experienced project management is provided, the development banks may be a potential source of external financing.

Private Investment Companies

The primary mission of private investment companies is to provide captial for economic development in underdeveloped countries. Basic to most of the agencies is the philosophical interest to raise the standard of living in these countries. To this extent some of the firms may be approached for financial assistance if it can be demonstrated that the industry or business being developed will be fact lead directly to an improved standard of living. The major private investment companies are:

- International Basic Economy Corporation (IBEC)
- Adela Investment Company, S.A
- Private Investment Corporation for Asia (PICA)

All three investment companies have as a general goal the development of less-developed countries through the satisfaction of solid basic consumer demands. The differentiating fact is how each goes about achieving their objectives. The oldest member of the group is IBEC. It has concentrated in the Latin American countries and has developed support in terms of project financing and managerial expertise in basic agricultural areas and housing. The expertise gained since 1947 has enabled it to become a profitable entity.

The Adela and PICA groups are similar in as much as PICA is the Asian extension of Adela. The basic premise of the Adela group is that a project must be marketable, have a reasonable return on investment, and have competent management. When these criteria are satisfied, Adela attempts to get local governments, commercial banks, and investors to participate in the project funding. Both Adela and PICA take an active role in the monitoring of the project and the on-going operation. Unique to Adela (the Latin American group) and PICA is that once a demand for a product or service in a country has been identified, this group actually seeks out a developer rather than taking a passive supportive role. The international cash manager may approach these firms as sources of development funds for less-developed countries; however, he needs to realize that their inducement and interest could be an encumbrance on the company's management style and restrict strategically desired corporate policies.

Commercial Banks

Commercial Banks internationally represent the most frequently used sources of capital for short-, medium- and long-term arrangements. The purpose of the financing—that of plant construction versus short-term borrowing for self-liquidating seasonal inventory financing—plays a major role in the international money manager's choice of loan types. The array of different types of loans available to the international cash manager is discussed in the next section because of the variety of loan types available and their applications.

Corporate Pooling

Internal corporate financing for development projects may be a viable alternative if international money pools can be established by the cash manager. This occurs where a subsidiary in one country cannot earn a substantial income on excess cash reserves. The adroit cash manager can determine the length of funds required and work out an equitable loan arrangement between the subsidiaries so that the lender receives a higher rate than available in the market and the borrower obtains a lower rate than provided through a commercial loan arrangement.

This section of the chapter has identified the major sources of capital available to the international cash manager to satisfy the medium- and long-term capital needs. Transactional sources of funds as well as a description of the variety of international borrowing methods are now examined. Careful evaluation of the corporation's developed goals and the merging of these with available sources of funds can provide significantly lower development costs. Evaluating the benefits and disadvantages is a complex but financially important aspect of the international money manager.

METHODS OF INTERNATIONAL FINANCING

Essential to the international money manager's involvement is not only a familiarization with the basic philosophical differences in economics and specific knowledge of the sources of financing available but also an understanding of the various forms of financing options available. It is in this area that the complexity of international as opposed to domestic cash management becomes obvious. In the domestic sphere, the traditional bank-supplied and investor-provided avenues for funds are familiar and limited in number. They include: line of credit, revolving lines of credit, bank notes, long-term bank loans, and stock and bond issuance. Development of financing methods in other countries evolved from a different cultural background and philosophy, and this has resulted in a wide variety of financing methods with which the domestic cash manager may lack familiarity. The purpose of this section is to identify these major financing methods, which have evolved because of a lack of capital market development. The methods described are generally applicable in Europe and the Latin American countries and to a lesser extent in Asia.

Overdraft Banking

Within the United States, overdrawing of corporate accounts is usually considered anathema by banks. The reason is that the temporary overdraft is viewed by the Federal Reserve Bank as a loan, and the bank consequently must maintain higher reserve requirements with the Fed to cover these loans. An overdraft is defined as a negative ledger (book) balance with the bank. As discussed earlier, the corporation can have a positive ledger balance and a negative collected balance. Internationally, the use of what is sometimes referred to as a "standard overdraft system" is common as a short-term capital source. Overdraft banking is used extensively in Europe. Mechanically, the corporation negotiates a line of credit with the bank. To draw on the line of credit, the corporation simply overdraws its account. This overdraft approach is beginning to be used in the United States in the retail market but has not been directly applied to the corporate market.

Currently in the United States, the corporate cash manager traditionally contacts the bank when desiring a draw down on the line of credit. If an overdraft occurs, there is usually a penalty charge associated with it. The overdraft banking approach is essentially a one-day automatic demand loan. More often, however, the amount borrowed is covered for short- to medium-term periods. The amount of overdraft limits are usually negotiated annually. The costs included for use of overdraft privileges include interest in the loan amount, service charges, and turnover fees. The use of overdraft banking can greatly aid the international cash manager by permitting greater flexibility in forecasting cash flows and involvement in aggressive investment policies. The forecasting models described in Chapter 9 can be used in relation to the overdraft facilities. Even though the basic overdraft process usually stipulates repayment within a 1-year period, renewable overdrafts are not uncommon. The purpose of renewable overdrafts is to provide for a medium-term financing method where other techniques are not available.

Discounted Bills and Promissory Notes

Discounting is the technique whereby a transaction or interest amount is deducted from the face value of an instrument. This technique is often used in relation to both trade bills and promissory notes internationally. The essential distinction between trade bills and promissory notes that trade bills are an order to a bank to pay funds to a third party and a promissory note is a promise by the originator to pay a stimulated amount to a second party on a specific date. While both are used for transaction financing, basically the promissory note can also be used for short-term financing. The availability of discounting varies from country to country and is, to some extent, dependent on the willingness of the central bank to "rediscount" the notes. Custom varies regarding who pays the discount—the seller or the buyer. The cash manager can use the discounted trade bill or promissory note to collect funds immediately if the capital can be put to work at a higher return internally or wait until the complete amount is due and payable. Of course, the future exchange rate risk must be considered and this is discussed in the next chapter.

Secured/Unsecured Loans

A common supply of short-term funds from commercial banks is the unsecured loan. This loan method is similar to the American system by bank policies defining the characteristics of a secured lender versus an unsecured lender vary by country. Secured loans (those backed by collateral) are granted to those customers who lack sufficient credit ability or where bank management deems the amount to be in excess of that indicated by the project. Secured and unsecured loans are sometimes rediscountable to central banks. Secured and unsecured loans are solid traditional sources of funds available to the cash manager for purchase of seasonally required inventory fluctuations and medium-term project needs.

International Interest Arbitrage Financing

When the international cash manager finds the cost of short-term capital prohibitive in the host country, he may wish to search for financing in other money markets. To satisfy this desire, international arbitrage financing (ARBI loans) are available. The purpose of these loans is to tap sources of capital in another country where capital is less scarce and convert it to local currency for use. In this situation, there is an exchange risk involved regarding the future repayment of borrowings in the second currency. The prudent cash manager usually purchases a forward exchange contract to cover this exposure. The cost of the forward contract must be included in the interest expense, nevertheless, it does not significantly diminish the profitability of this transaction type.

Factoring

Though factoring is a source of funds to the firms domiciled in the United States, it is also worthy of mention as an international source of short-term funds. Factoring—the selling of discounted receivables—is more common internationally than within the United States. Factoring can be used with or without recourse. In either case, it represents the most expensive source of funds to the international cash manager because of the amount of investigation that must be performed by the company purchasing the receivables. The popularity of factoring in the international environment arises from the ability to free an American-domiciled management from the problems indigenous with a number of countries and cultures regarding bill payment customs.

Bridge Loans

Because long-term interest rates may be unattractive or funds are just not available for long-term projects, the international cash manager may need to use a bridge loan. The bridge loan is designed to span the gap between short/medium-term financing and the location of long-term funds. Usually the borrower signs promissory notes renewable at specified times until suitable financing is obtained. When final long-term loans have been secured the bridge loan is repaid. The interest rates paid for bridge loans are short-term based and are usually renegotiated each time they are renewed. While bridge loans are usually supplied by commercial banks, outside capital is sometimes employed.

Link Financing

The international cash manager faced with a scarce capital market within the host country should evaluate the feasibility of borrowing medium-term (1 to 7 years) funds from other countries. Link financing provides the international cash manager with this opportunity. The term "link financing" arises from the environment where the second country's supplier of liquid funds is linked to the borrower. After suitable arrangements have been negotiated (including additional fees and special considerations), the lender deposits funds in the borrower's bank specifically identified for use by the borrower. This arrangement is advantageous for the lender because he realizes a higher interest rate than available within his country and he may also receive other "bonus" incentives. Since the lender is often located in a country other than where funds are borrowed, he must prudently purchase a forward contract for the repayment of funds in order to be immune to the exchange rate fluctuations that could significantly reduce his return.

The borrower normally pays interest to a local bank and, in addition, pays a broker or finder's fee for the capital employed. Because of the exchange risk potential that exists between a low-interest country and a high-interest country, the application of successful link financing depends upon a high degree of currency stability in the high-interest rate country or a well-developed forward exchange market.

Equity Financing

In securing financing internationally, the cash manager may be faced with the possibility of equity financing as a viable alternative. Sources of equity financing can be local commercial banks or Edge act banks. In equity financing, the host country's commercial bank takes an ownership position and agrees to provide long-term funds for development. This entitles the bank to share in the dividends and profits of the company, as well as to share in the risks of losses. Equity participation by local commercial banks can be both advantageous and disadvantageous depending upon the distribution of control. The advantage of equity participation is that principals within the country are actively involved and interested in the business operation. Because of this interest, they provide support in terms of business contacts locally and internationally to assist the firm in achieving its profit objectives. Of equal importance, local banks can intercede for the firm with local and national governmental agencies to convince them of the participating attitude of a foreign firm. To this extent, equity participation can provide some shelter from the political vagaries discussed earlier in this chapter. A second major benefit to the bank equity position is the sense of specific knowledge regarding local customs and habits, as well as access to financial and statistical marketing data that might otherwise be difficult to isolate. The major disadvantage to equity participation lies in the extent to which the commercial bank becomes involved in the management of the company. Agreements should be clearly stated regarding management participation so that the borrowing firm does not find itself restricted in its marketing efforts. Edge act companies provide a source of capital—sometimes equity based—to the multinational corporation. Edge act companies are affiliates of American banks that are chartered to conduct international business transactions. Capital can be provided to start up operations for expansion, modernization, or automation. Edge act loans usually contain extra inducements for the lender such as convertability of loans outstanding to start holdings or options to purchase stock at a future time. In this way, the edge act lender participates in the growth of the firm if it is successful. Edge act companies may sell their equity interests after a company has matured so it may refocus funds in other venture capital areas. The interest rate and terms of loans vary in accordance with money market conditions and the risk environment of the project.

Eurocurrency Financing

The final major type of financing available to the international money manager is Eurocurrency financing. Eurocurrency refers to any freely convertible currency that is domiciled outside its native country. An example of this is John Doe, Inc., opening an American dollar account with a major French bank. The dollars on deposit outside the United States in the French bank are refered to as Eurodollars and are available to be lent out just as French francs. A major reason for an American company to open an American dollar account overseas is the current Federal Reserve restriction that prohibits the payment of interest on demand deposit accounts in the United States. Although banks provide services based on earnings credit rates to corporations, the rates are generally significantly lower than savings or foreign rates. Additionally, most banks deduct required Federal Reserve requirements before calculating the amount of service credit. Also corporations may only have savings accounts to $100,000. London is the focal point for Eurocurrency transactions, and most loans are sizeable in nature ranging from $5 million upward. Generally, the stated rate for Eurodollar borrowing is higher than stated domestic rates; however, the overall costs are lower. This occurs because a firm borrowing Eurodollars does not pay compensating balances to the lending institution. Consequently, the overall "real" cost of borrowing is lower.

Eurocurrency markets may be used by the international cash manager for short- medium- or long-term sources of capital. Careful use of the Eurocurrency market by the international cash manager can insure reasonably priced funds when required.

This chapter has focused on the elements involved in overall financial planning and control for the international cash manager. Identification of major considerations in economic philosophy and specific areas of concern have been reviewed. Second, we evaluated the various sources of capital, long-term and short-term, available to the multinational corporation. Finally, we reviewed the major financial instruments available to international cash managers to use in arranging for investment or short-term working capital needs. Cognizance of each of these areas is necessary in order to cope with the variations that occur within each country.

Having reviewed the financial control area of the international cash manager, we must now specifically review the techniques used in the international environment, protection strategies, and the cash manager's role of global optimization.

CHAPTER 11

INTERNATIONAL FUNDS FLOW CONTROL

Chapter 10 discussed various aspects of financial control from an international perspective. This includes the basic economic differences, the sources of funds available to the international cash manager, and the various credit instruments available. Having examined how and where working capital and longer-term capital are located, it is now appropriate to turn toward the daily transactional aspects of the international cash manager's position and how it differs from domestic cash management. In this chapter, we evaluate the various cash management techniques used in the international arena and evaluate what forms of protection are available to protect from currency fluctuations, while suggesting specific strategy actions. Finally, we identify perhaps the most difficult areas of the international money manager's job, that of optimizing profits in a multinational environment, and the problems associated with the remission of funds to the parent company.

INTERNATIONAL CASH MANAGEMENT TECHNIQUES

While the objectives in using cash management techniques are the same for the international market as for the domestic, the dimensions of complexity are substantially different. The payment systems from one country to another may vary significantly causing concern to the cash manager who is attempting to accelerate collections. To define specific differences between countries in terms of payment and collection customs is beyond the scope of this book. Specific knowledge concerning individual customs of various countries can be acquired from banks and other financial institutions. Conversely, the basic techniques used in international cash management apply from one country to another. It is the *emphasis* that changes from country to country rather than the application.

The basic international techniques discussed in this section, include:

- Lockbox
- Mail transfers
- Wire transfers
- Factoring
- International funds concentration
- Netting
- Delayed payments
- GIRO payment system

ACCELERATING CASH INFLOWS

International Lockbox Utilization

Acceleration of receivables is as vitally important in the international cash management area as it is domestically. Export sales remittances are the principal area of international receivables acceleration. In the domestic environment, the remitter of funds may calculate to pay as late as possible or stretch payment by drawing on remote locations. While this is not generally true internationally, the payment system is significantly different, which causes payment delays. Because settlement must be made internationally, the actual clearing times for international transfers (other than cable) can range between 2 and 10 business days. Consequently, a "value" date is often used in transfers. Under value dating, a remitter's account can be debited a specified number of days in advance before the actual exchange takes place. The objective is to provide a lead time factor to the banks to provide for settlement on the approximate settlement date. The word approximate is used because the bank initiating the transfer is not highly motivated to complete the transfer because it loses funds control. This slower remittance practice is more prevalent in Europe because banks there depend more heavily on float in the absence of compensating balance arrangements. In contrast to the variable clearing times in Europe and Latin America, the domestic cash manager depends on the Federal Reserve schedule, which provides clearance times to corporations. In considering the acceleration of export receivables, the aspects of foreign currency exposure and types of export documents used must be evaluated. These are discussed later in this chapter.

For export receivables invoiced in dollars, the most common lockbox system is one centered in New York. Under this approach, the dollar amounts invoiced below a cable-based economic alternative (about $10,000) would be air mailed to a New York lockbox for deposit. (The lockbox processing services available are defined in Chapter 4). Similarly, dollar lockboxes can be located in other countries and the receipts credited to a dollar account with the foreign bank. Large amounts over $10,000 should be cabled even at the expense of the exporter.

The same principal holds true for remittance of local currency amounts. Establishing a central collection point within the country by using one or more banks reduces the mail float time. An additional consideration is that all receipts must comply with local exchange controls that may be in existence. The use of dollar invoicing in another country, such as France, can be used by collecting dollar receipts at a branch of an international bank in France where credit is granted in the corporate account. At the same time, the corporation has an account with the New York branch of the same bank and can effect a same day transfer to New York of dollars for centralized corporate use. The bank usually makes funds movements even if all funds are not collected because the overall multinational corporate account is analyzed for profitability rather than individual acounts. This approach provides a substantial benefit to the multinational corporation because it permits a vastly improved opportunity to optimize working cash and average results over a large system base if it deals with a multinational multibranch bank.

Mail and Cable Transfers

Many international funds transfers take place by mail. The remitter of funds completes a mail transfer form and submits it to his bank to effect the transfer. The bank converts the transfer amount to another currency if required and may charge an additional payment fee in some cases. The transfer is then mailed directly to the receiving bank or, if a foreign correspondent relationship is not maintained, sent to a correspondent bank to execute the transfer. Since the transfer is mailed from one bank to another, the mail float time occurring between countries can be significant. It is not unusual for transfers made between banks located in two different countries to take between 5 and 10 business days to complete. From a domestic viewpoint, the loss of float as a receiving company is a major consideration. Because of the system of transactional value dating the originating bank may not only enjoy the mail float between itself and its correspondent but also a "back value" day of float, which is sometimes used. Utilization and creation of float is often used because foreign banks do not rely on compensating balances as do their American counterparts. Through cable transfer, the receiving account is credited as soon as the correspondent bank receives the cable, which is usually the same day. Payment by cable can be a very cost effective alternative to mail transfer for intracompany transactions, as well as intercompany payments. If mail transfers are used for intracompany transactions, then the use of the funds is lost to the centralized cash manager until the funds are received. This, of course, varies from the domestic environment where funds could reside for credit in two places until the Federal clearing process was completed. In the international area, banks involved use the mail and clearing float. Cable transfers can also be safer than mail transfer and are considered as a cost effective alternative. Cable transfers usually range from $5 to 10 per transfer. Greater safety can be achieved with cable transfers because cables have no signatures, rather they have a test code associated with the cable that the receiving bank checks. Cable transfers as described do not flow through an international settlement function per se but use correspondent bank relationships to make fund transfers. Because of the growing demand of international cable transactions and growing concern with costs, European banks have joined together to initiate the Society for Worldwide Interchange of Financial Transactions—commonly called SWIFT. The purpose of this group is to establish an international communications network between banks to facilitate the movement of funds-affected transactions. SWIFT does not perform a direct settlement function;* consequently, it is based on correspondent bank relations. It does provide, however, a high-speed, low-cost international communications network that lowers communication costs to less than $1 per transaction. The first phase of SWIFT, a three country communication link, is operational in the United States and was completed in June 1977. The effect of the service available to the international cash manager is to permit lower transmission costs, thereby lowering the economic payback point for international wire transfer. Assuming a 10% money utilization rate, the following table defines break-even dollar amounts for funds transfer.

Days Saved	$2	$3	$5	$10
1	$7,302	$10,953	$18,255	$36,510
2	3,650	5,425	9,126	18,253
3	2,433	3,650	6,083	12,167
4	1,825	2,738	4,563	9,126
5	1,460	2,190	3,650	7,300
7	1,043	1,564	2,607	5,215
10	730	1,095	1,825	3,650

Communication Cost

* Plans for the system include eventual settlement beyond an unspecified initiation period.

Intercompany Transfers

Another international cash management technique used to better control the flow of funds is intercompany transfer of funds. Intercompany transfers arise when a subsidiary in one country buys raw materials or partially assembled products for inclusion in a finished product that is then sold back to the original subsidiary. In making the settlement, firms should generally use cable for transfer because of the value of funds lost if mail transfers are used. The method and level of intercompany pricing can also be used strategically as discussed later in this chapter. In executing transfers between subsidiaries in two different countries, not only is an exchange commission paid but the loss of float is also encountered. In order to increase the efficient use of funds globally, many firms have developed various schemes of netting. Essentially, netting relates to the centralized settlement of accounts within a firm prior to the actual transfer of funds. An alternative to netting and physical transfers exists for the firm dealing with international banks with branches in both subsidiary cities. In this case, an interbranch transfer can be effected with the same day funds value. Often the branch waives any transfer fees because the international account is analyzed on an overall basis and not an individual account basis.

Bilateral Netting

In many situations, multinational firms have subsidiaries that purchase raw materials or partially assembled goods from sister subsidiaries of the same company. In these cases, the settlement of payables due is required. Because supplying subsidiaries often reside in other countries, a foreign exchange transaction is indicated. In a simple two-country exchange, subsidiary A, in country A, may purchase raw materials from subsidiary B, in country B. Subsidiary A may then sell the finished product back to subsidiary B for ultimate sale in country B. Normally, when settling payments between countries, it is necessary for subsidiary A to transfer funds through the mail or cable to subsidiary B in its local currency. The process occurs for subsidiary B to pay subsidiary A for the finished product. Treating sister subsidiaries as normal vendors for international payments results in:

- Exchange conversion expense
- Loss of float for mail transfer
- Cable expenses (if cable is used)
- Clerical time at both subsidiaries.

The alternatives to the full transactional exchange of international payables is the "netting" of intercompany accounts payable. This netting can be bilateral where only two countries are involved or multilateral where more than two countries are involved. In the example described, if subsidiary A owed subsidiary B 100,000 S.F. and B owned A 50,000 S.F., the only net transfer required would be 50,000 S.F. from A to B. In this case the exchange commission cost on 50,000 S.F. is saved by the company. The sharing of savings can be negotiated within the company. The use of simple bilateral netting system as described also provides an additional control element to the international cash manager. Through the control of funds flow between subsidiaries, the cash manager can centrally orchestrate the flow of working capital from one subsidiary to another. In this manner, he may reduce local borrowing and use intercompany sources of funds while providing higher interest rates to the lending subsidiary on its funds. Bilateral netting is simple to use and can be used centrally if the international cash manager desires control over the settlement flow of funds where each subsidiary operates autonomously. Bilateral netting is economical for the two subsidiaries involved: nevertheless, it does not optimize the transfer of funds between several different subsidiaries. To effectively control settlements between several subsidiaries, multilateral netting is often advantageous.

Multilateral Netting

Multilateral netting operates essentially the same as bilateral netting except when multiple subsidiaries are located in different countries. To use a multilateral netting scheme centralized control by the international cash manager is a basic requirement because all payables must be brought together at a common specified time to be netted. Additionally, where multiple currencies are involved, it is necessary to convert payables for the subsidiaries to a common currency base that is usually that of the parent company. In using a multilateral netting scheme the international cash manager removes some of the control over payment from foreign subsidiaries with the objective of saving up to 0.5 or 1% of the total expenses involved in making international exchange. Essential to the effective use of multinational netting is the ability of the international cash manager to assemble all intercompany-related payables from subsidiaries at one time during the month. If payables are billed in various currencies, the cash manager needs to convert the payables to a common currency base. Because intercompany multilateral netting usually takes place only once per month, the payment due dates between subsidiaries are not evenly matched. For example, a 30 day due invoice may end up being paid to a subsidiary in 10 days if the settlement date occurs shortly after the company is invoiced. The opposite situation may also occur where a 30-day term may extend to 40 days. Individual subsidiaries are affected to the extent that payments through multilateral netting varies significantly from the regular customer remittance. To this extent, the subsidiary manager may complain that optimization of working capital is, in fact, inhibited because of the use of multinational netting. Globally, of course, there is no effect on the company. In fact, global optimization can be approached because payments between subsidiaries may be delayed to provide additional working capital to a temporarily cash poor subsidiary by delaying intercompany remittances. To centrally control multinational netting, a worksheet matrix is often developed by the international cash manager. The method of net payment from one subsidiary to another would be based on the cable cost criteria previously discussed. In this manner, the company as a whole reduces currency conversion expenses to a minimum while maximizing funds utilization because only net amounts are transferred. Therefore, there is no "in-transit" float lost on funds, and because of central control, the international cash manager can determine the economically justified transfer mechanism. The individual subsidiaries are still exposed in terms of exchange rate fluctuations because the common settlement date for intercompany transfer in a common currency is advantageous to some and disadvantageous to others. This affects the performance of the local money manager and should be taken into consideration during his performance evaluation. Company-wide there is no effect.

Although multilateral netting has no basic effect on the external position of the countries involved, separate European countries do require a filing with the government. Latin American countries have historically controlled foreign exchange transactions carefully and may pose problems for the company desiring to establish a multilateral netting scheme with Latin American subsidiaries. While foreign exchange regulations should prudently be checked for the countries involved in a netting scheme there will generally be no problem in obtaining official approval where required. Major banks in those countries can be helpful both in obtaining information and approval for the multinational company.

GIRO Systems

Various GIRO systems operable in European and other countries represent significantly different funds receipt and payment mechanisms for the cash manager involved in international receipts and payments. The GIRO system of transfer has been in existence in some European countries since the 1600s.* Under this system, either a corporation or retail customer uses

---

* *The Coming of Credit Transfer: The Developing of Electric GIRO Capability,* by George White, Vice President, Chase Manhattan Bank.

a GIRO bill stub, which has the payees account number encoded on it and authorizes a GIRO processor to make payment from the payer's account. The GIRO processor is often the postal system operating in the country. The use of this type of system for corporate payment and remittance transfer has a significant impact on the control of funds flow for the international cash manager. Through the use of GIRO system for receipt of payment from retail customers, the cash manager can reduce the total clerical resources required to handle receivables. Essential in the use of GIRO systems for low-dollar, high-volume subsidiaries, of course, is daily bank notification of receipts to those accounts so that cash can be put to immediate use. In Eurpoean countries, however, business-to-business payments within a country are often handled through a GIRO system because value dates can be assigned. To this extent, the international cash manager may find that intracountry business receipts may be more predictable. Again, close banking contact is required so that credited funds are included in the daily investment or international capital allocation plans companywide. Payments can also be effected through the GIRO system. Because of value dating and discount practices, where it is receipt of funds, not postmarking, that constitutes the essential receipt criterion. The benefits to multinational corporations of paying by GIRO include: reduced postage cost, reduced cable or mail transfer costs, reduced check expenses, and reduced account reconcilement costs. Additionally, misrouted funds requiring follow-up are eliminated. Use of GIRO systems fit conveniently into the central pooling of funds for multinational companies because the deposit account number of the corporation is stated on the GIRO invoice. This provides the international cash manager with an automatic cash management control technique feature when using GIRO transfer systems.

Multinational Pooling

While concentration accounts provide for central control over receipts, the accumulation of all liquid assets in a central control area of the multinational country constitutes pooling of assets. While multilateral netting effects net intersubsidiary transfers, multinational pooling provides the opportunity to optimize the distribution of liquid assets within the multinational corporation.

There are two basic types of pooling accounts: single country pool accounts and multicountry pool accounts. Under a single country pool account, several subsidiaries within a country forward records of their liquid assets to a central control point for analysis and effective management. It is important that local banking and financial relationships not be disturbed, however, because the subsidiaries need to meet their operational needs. The use of pooling is facilitated when a bank common to all subsidiaries within the country is used since account transfers are easier. Usually, excess funds flow into the central pool account and intercompany loans made from this account. Effective forecasting is the foundation of efficiently operating a multinational asset pool account. Exhibit 11-1 illustrates a single-country pool accounting scheme. Because regulations vary by country (sometimes locally) before pooling accounts are established taxation laws, foreign business, and banking regulations must be examined.

An extension of single-country pooling is multicountry pooling that consolidates liquid assets of several subsidiaries from many different countries with a central collection point. The purpose of multicountry pooling is to provide the multinational company with global optimization of liquid assets by maximizing short-term investment and reducing costs for short-term borrowings. Multicountry pooling is significantly more complex than single country pooling because of the diversity of tax regulatory and currency elements that need to be considered. Each company needs to carefully customize multicountry pools based on the countries and currencies involved.

Factoring

A final cash management technique that is often used in the international area is accounts receivable factoring. Factoring has already been defined; however, as a source of funds to the cash manager it is used more often in Europe than the United States. Factoring can reduce the multicurrency

Exhibit 11.1 Example of single country pool account.

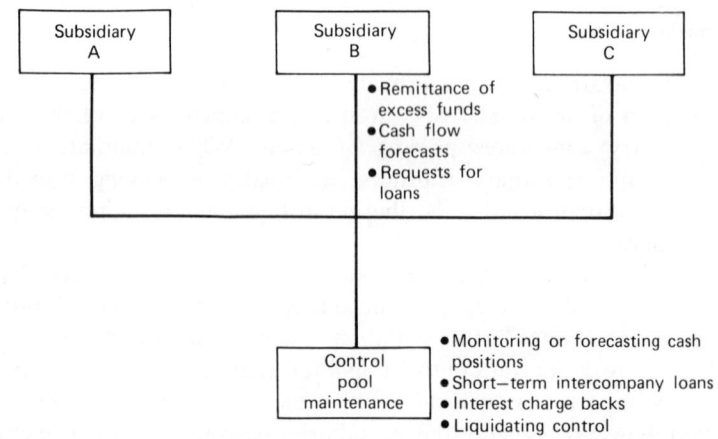

```
  ┌───────────┐      ┌───────────┐       ┌───────────┐
  │ Subsidiary│      │ Subsidiary│       │ Subsidiary│
  │     A     │      │     B     │       │     C     │
  └─────┬─────┘      └─────┬─────┘       └─────┬─────┘
                      • Remittance of
                        excess funds
                      • Cash flow
                        forecasts
                      • Requests for
                        loans
                    ┌──────────────┐  • Monitoring or forecasting cash
                    │   Control    │    positions
                    │    pool      │  • Short—term intercompany loans
                    │ maintenance  │  • Interest charge backs
                    └──────────────┘  • Liquidating control
```

exposure on receivables expecially when short-term working capital is required. The 1 to 2% cost to factor receivables must be offset against borrowing expenses if short-term capital is required.

FUNDS FLOW PROTECTION

The possibility and fear of transaction loss due to change in foreign exchange rates is described in Chapter 10. This section focuses on the transactional risks that exist for the multinational firm in the international market place. The risk of loss in doing business in many currencies far outweighs the potential gains to be experienced in a foreign exchange transaction. Under most situations, the foreign company or subsidiary has an amount of payables or receivables that are denominated in a foreign currency. The type currencies and time span involved have an effect on overall vulnerability of the firm. This aspect of foreign currency exchange exposure is nonexistent with the domestic dealings of a country because all transactions are based on the local currency such as dollars. Consequently, if dollars are devalued as they were in 1971, there is no effect to domestic firms because all receivables and payables are stated in the singular currency. However, in the international market place, the firm may not reasonably expect to have all transactions stated in a singular currency. Although such a policy would simplify the working procedures for the company, it would dramatically reduce the marketability of the firm's goods. Providing transactional invoicing in currencies convenient to the buyer is another service feature of conducting business. The types of transactions that give rise to short- and intermediate-term exposure include:

- Import purchases
- Export sales
- Purchase of services
- Payment of royalties
- Dividend payments
- Capital repayments

In each of these transactional areas, the company is exposed to the effects of devaluation or revaluation. To overcome the basic risks involved, many prudent businesses choose to protect or "hedge" their exposure. Hedging is the purchase, in effect, of insurance that protects the company from changes in exchange rates by assuring a fixed exchange rate at a specified date. The three basic forms of hedging include:

- Forward currency exchange
- Foreign currency swap
- Foreign currency credit swap

Foreign Currency Exchange

Use of forward foreign currency exchange transactions are most often used in export and import transactions to nullify the effect of anticipated currency devaluation. Devaluation occurs when either of the two currencies involved in a transaction change in relation to the other. For example, if the German mark increases in value in relation to the Swiss franc, the Swiss franc in effect has devalued or is now worth less in relation to German marks. For the Swiss firm with a committment to pay an obligation in German marks on a future date for purchase of raw materials, this means that more Swiss francs are necessary thereby increasing the cost of the purchase to the Swiss firm. On the other hand, the receipt of an accounts receivable in German marks and subsequent conversion yields a higher than expected profit from the sale based on the Swiss franc expenses. Because of the inherent business risks associated with devaluation of currencies and their commercial effect, foreign exchange markets evolved. The foreign exchange market provides a forum where currencies are exchanged one for another at exchange rates that are spot or current day price in exchange for future delivery or sale. The normal future market developed is 30 days, 60 days, 90 days, 120 days, 6 months, and 1 year. Not all currencies are traded freely in the foreign exchange market and those that are not, such as rubles, are not widely used in trading because of the exposure risk.

The purpose of a forward exchange contract is to provide for the delivery of a specified amount of foreign currency on a specific date at an agreed upon rate. By using the forward exchange contract, the businessman can avoid the risk of unfavorable exchange rate fluctuations. The forward market can be used to buy or sell a forward foreign currency contract. A firm that might normally purchase a forward contract would be an American importer who knows that payment in Swiss francs is required in 90 days for goods received when the payable is invoiced in Swiss francs. Rather than risking the revaluation of the Swiss franc, which would result in more dollars required to purchase the same number of Swiss francs, the importer can purphase an "insurance" contract (forward delivery) for the required amount of Swiss francs at the stated market rate. This ensures the importer that 90 days from the contract purchase the Swiss francs will be delivered at the agreed price. The cost to the importer for the future contract price varies and depends upon the market expectation for the purchased currency.

While the importer may purchase a contract for forward delivery, the exporter, anticipating a receivable in a foreign currency, such as dollars in 90 days, may elect to sell the dollar receivable forward. In this case, the exporter feels that dollars will devalue in relation to the Swiss francs and so to protect his transactional position the exporter agrees to sell his anticipated receivable. Again, the market determines the future rate and the difference between the spot rate and future rate is the estimate of the market value for the two relative currencies. The key consideration for the company dealing in foreign currencies is to determine the extent of risk involved in forward market transactions.

The price to be paid for a forward currency contract is the commission on the contract, plus or minus, the discount or premium, which is the difference between the spot rate and the future contract price.

To provide a basic guideline for the use of the forward foreign exchange contracts, the following situations may be considered.

As an importer with accounts payable due in the future in foreign currency:

- When future exchange rates on payable currencies are at a discount (lower than spot rates), the market is anticipating a decline in the value of the payable currency in relation to your currency. There is nothing to be gained by a forward purchase in this situation and funds would be expended on the cost of the contract.
- When the future exchange is selling at a premium, this indicates that the market sees an increase in value: consequently, it may be advisable to purchase a forward contract for payment if the difference in the contract is not equal to or greater than the anticipated revaluation.

As an exporter of materials with foreign-based accounts receivable currencies on the books:

- When the forward rate of the receivable currency is at a premium, the market is anticipating an increase in value in relation to the exporter domestic currency. In this situation since the currency to be received is fixed in amount and when converted to the local currency is anticipated to yield a higher number of local currency units little can be gained by selling forward except to protect from a sudden reversal of rates. The exporter may choose to sell forward if the difference between the spot and forward rate is significantly higher than the cost of the contract and safely realize a known profit on the transaction.

- When the forward accounts receivable currency is selling at a discount, the market is anticipating that the value of the currency will be less in relation to the local currency. Where there is a free floating exchange rate, the exporter must decide whether the discount amount is worth the insurance of knowing the actual amount he will receive on that future date.

Regardless of any general rules, the advent of floating exchange rates places significantly more emphasis on the judgement of the international cash manager than ever before. Establishing corporate guidelines assists in the decision making; however, flexibility to the changing monetary environment is required to make optimal decisions.

Foreign Currency Swap

A foreign currency swap takes place when an investor or corporation purchases local currency in the foreign currency market and sells it in the forward market for future specified date and amount. In this manner, the company can be assured of receiving the specified currency in "swap" for the local currency at a known rate on the purchase date. Therefore, the currency is purchased at known current rates rather than waiting until the future date when the foreign currency rate may have changed unfavorably and cause a loss to the company. Sometimes the ability to establish delivery dates that coincide with borrowing needs is difficult. The foreign currency swap is used most often in countries that do not have an extensive forward exchange market.

Credit Swap

Under a credit swap, loans are effected in two currencies at the same time. While this type of funds protection does not constitute a high degree of business, it is useful in countries with tight credit restrictions and weak currencies. In a credit swap, a bank in the host country agrees to loan a specified currency to a corporate subsidiary and assumes the exchange risk when the corporation is usually headquartered outside the host country. The corporation then arranges an interest free loan to the host country's bank in a hard currency through a correspondent bank. The time frame, interest rates charged to the subsidiary, and exchange rates are all negotiated prior to the loan. The hard currency loan made to the cooperating bank is usually higher than that lent to the subsidiary to compensate for exchange rate differentials or added incentives required. Through this type of transaction, the foreign subsidiary can receive a loan in the currency required through a local bank without being exposed to exchange risks. Additionally, the transaction is simple because the local bank granting the loan can specify the use of a cooperating correspondent bank. Using a local bank also increases the work relationship between the local bank and corporate subsidiary, which aids in future business transactions.

The costs involved in currency swaps can be stated as the interest that would have been earned on the funds committed to purchase currency and any discount price for the foreign exchange sold. In the case when a premium is realized, the total opportunity cost is reduced. A credit swap expense is more involved because not only is there the interest expense paid by the subsidiary but also the lost interest in the "correspondent" account because it was deposited for the benefit of the host bank. Additionally, there can be an added expense if the local bank negotiating the swap uses a lower local exchange rate than the current exchange rate. Through this technique, the local bank extracts a higher fee for its services, and the company pays a greater expense.

Exchange Hedging

Size seems to have a practical effect on the extent to which a firm uses various forms of protection in foreign exchange exposure risks.* Smaller firms usually lack the sophisticated knowledge required to effectively use the forward exchange market. Though their total asset size may be limited in foreign currencies, their transactional exposure is often greater. For example, a northern California producer of specialty baking equipment had more than 90% of sales concentrated in western Europe and had not developed a foreign exchange risk program. As a result, an entire month's profit was lost because of shifts in exchange rates. Medium-sized firms, on the other hand, become very sensitive to the need to protect assets and transactions from undesirable fluctuations because larger percentages of the profits often emanate from foreign transactions. The primary consideration for the medium-sized firm is that control be centralized so that some form of overall optimization can be achieved.

Large corporations generally do not partake heavily in international hedging because they have found that overall the cost of foreign exchange is equal to the eventual devaluation. That being the case, there is no stimulus to cover a forward position. Additionally, a multinational corporation dealing with several different currencies can spread its currency exposure risk internally by the acceleration or delay of intercompany payables and receiveables.

* Based on research performed by Robbins and Stobaugh, *Money in the Multinational Enterprise*, p. 131.

In this section, we have reviewed the foreign exchange market that is available to control or limit a corporation's exchange exposure. This covers the risk associated with dealing in multiple currencies. The other primary risk associated in dealing in a multinational environment, especially related to the export of goods, is credit protection to insure low bad debt losses since these have a direct impact on the international cash flow arising for corporate transactions.

EXPORT FUNDS PROTECTION

By its nature, the multinational cash manager finds himself deeply involved in import and export transactions. A discussion of protection of assets would be incomplete without a discussion of the various documents involved in import/export transactions. The objective of the various instruments is to:

- Protect the seller from risk of payment loss
- Protect against devaluation
- Equalize the difference in interest rates between countries

It is not our intention here to deal with an exhaustive survey of import/export multinational transactions since volumes have been written on this subject; however, it is intended to review the basic instruments and provide a review of protections as a basis for the domestic cash manager evolving toward international cash management. The major methods used to effect export/import transactions are:

- Bank drafts
- Commercial letters of credit
- Red clauses
- Production export credits
- Open Account Transactions
- Cash in advance
- Factoring
- Consignments

Bank Drafts

A major advantage to the international cash manager in dealing with a multinational commercial bank is that its extensive correspondent networks can be used as a collection arm of the multinational company. An exporter can use the bank to collect receivables from importers in other countries by presenting drafts or bills of exchange drawn on the importer to the bank for collection. The bank can then collect either directly by presentment to the importer or by dealing through a correspondent bank located in the importer's country. Costs involved in using banks to collect drafts include service charges levied by the bank, cable fees for communication, postal charges, and any import or export fees assigned by the governments involved. Because ownership of export goods does not pass from exporter to importer until legal title documents are in the possession of the importer, the exporter usually draws a time draft on the importer and passes the legal title documents to the collecting bank. This procedure allows the importer to examine the goods prior to final acceptance. When the importer notes acceptance on the face of the draft, it becomes a negotiable instrument known as a "trade acceptance" and as such is discountable for immediate payment. For example, if an importer has noted acceptance of merchandise on the time draft (sometimes called usance draft), the exporter may then discount it with the agent bank even though the draft states payment 60 days in the future. In this manner, the bank serves as collector and provides for immediate short-term working capital for multinational transactions.

Sight drafts, which are payable upon presentment, or time drafts, which are payable on a specific date in the future, have the following protective advantages:

- Drafts are negotiable. Once accepted, they provide a firm financial instrument which is not subject to dispute. If any dispute arises, the recourse normally reverts to the parties involved in the transaction.
- Drafts provide a common basis for understanding the financial terms of the transaction and serve as a terminal point for the acceptance of goods and passing of title.
- Drafts provide a reasonably low cost method of financing for both importer and exporter.

In addition to discounting drafts, the international cash manager may borrow from various banks by using either time or sight drafts as collateral placed against requested loans. While banks provide valuable services in the collection of drafts or providing loans based on draft collateral, banks do not normally assume the exchange risk inherent to a forward payment such as is the case with time drafts. To afford protection, the exporter can insist on payment in a hard currency, buying or selling of forward contracts, or aggreeing with the importer to accept local currency payment if the importer assumes currency exchange risks based on a stipulated exchange rate.

Commercial Letters of Credit

Central to the successful execution of foreign trade is establishing confidence in the buyer's ability to pay and the seller's ability to deliver the specified merchandise. International transactions complicate establishing mutual trust because of the distances and currencies involved. Commercial letters of credit were established to provide a convenient method to establish basic commercial confidence. The following is a definition of a letter of credit: "The letter of credit is a written instrument issued by the buyer's bank, authorizing the seller to draw in accordance with certain terms, and stipulating in legal form that all such bills (drafts) will be honored. It sets forth under what terms and conditions the person in whose favor the letter has been opened may draw drafts against such credit, at the same time guaranteeing the payment or acceptance of such drafts if they comply with the letter's terms."*

It is important to note that the purchase contract for international transactions is between the buyer and the seller. However, the strength of the letter of credit is that it represents a contract between the bank and the seller. Consequently, the bank, not the buyer, stands behind the promise to pay as stipulated in the letter of credit.

Import Letters of Credit

The purpose of the import letter of credit is to assure the seller that when a shipment of goods is made to the buyer in another country that drafts can be drawn against a local bank for payment based on satisfactory documentation. The buyer benefits because cash is not required until the merchandise is shipped. The objective of import letters of credit is to finance transactions and not regulate or monitor the sales contract executed between buyer and seller. To this extent the application made by the buyer to its bank includes:

- Promise of reimbursement to the issuing letter of credit bank for all drafts honored under the credit
- Payment of bank-imposed charges and commissions
- Granting a legal lien to the issuing bank on the documents, the

---

* Henius, Frank, *Dictionary of Foreign Trade*, Prentice-Hall, New York, 1947, second edition, p. 395.

represented merchandise, and the pledging of balances the company may have with the bank
- Understanding that the bank pays on documents that appear valid and acceptable under the letter of credit terms but that may in fact be invalid or forged
- Agreement to sign other documents (e.g., trust receipts) as required by the issuing bank.
- Guarantee that merchandise is insured at all times to the satisfaction of the issuing bank
- Agreement to honor credit arrangement according to applicable foreign and domestic laws

The purpose of these provisions is to protect the issuing bank because it guarantees payment to the seller under a letter of credit not the buyer. Although the issuing bank has a legal lien on merchandise shipped, it may also require security from the buyer prior to issuing the letter of credit if a line of credit has not been issued to the buyer or if the existing line is fully used.

Export Letters of Credit

Export letters of credit are used when American firms are involved in exportation of goods and letters of credit from the buyer required to effect payment on shipments. Most export credits are irrevocable, which provides the bank with instructions to honor drafts provided all specified transactional requirements are satisfied. If the buyer is dissatisfied about an aspect of the transaction not previously specified to the opening bank, the company has no recourse because the bank does honor all drafts presented provided the letter of credit stipulations have been fulfilled. From the viewpoint of any correspondent bank involved in the transaction, it is considered a "correspondent's irrevocable credit" and sometimes called an unconfirmed irrevocable credit. Correspondent banks are often involved in international letter of credit transactions because the seller often presents the irrevocable letter of credit with required documentation to his local bank for collection if the opening or issuing bank does not have a convenient branch. Settlement usually occurs based on correspondent bank balances so the seller has ready access to funds after shipment.

Should the seller be concerned about the integrity of the letter of credit or terms for any reason he can insist upon a confirmed irrevocable letter of credit. The opening bank in a letter of credit issues a document confirming their intention to honor all drafts presented by the seller in accordance with the stipulations in the letter of credit.

Under a revocable letter of credit, the seller is assured that the bank will honor drafts presented but is not assured that the buyer will not alter the relationship by withdrawing the letter of credit. The seller has fewer assurances contracting business under this form; however, it is used where relationships between the companies are excellent and a stable exchange and political environment exists. The essential difference between the revocable and irrevocable letter of credit is that the opening bank explicitly states that it has no obligation to pay drafts even if presented in accordance with instructions. Consequently, because there is no guarantee to pay this form of the letter of credit is infrequently used.

Letters of credit represent the primary international instrument facilitating international trade. To summarize, the major benefits accruing from use of letters of credit include:

- The importer enjoys a stronger bargaining position because the bank backs his promise to pay based on the stipulation in the letter of credit.
- If the exporter requires prepayment and does not deliver goods as required, the bank will not pay on the draft, and the importer can easily recover his funds.
- Financing to the importer using letters of credit is relatively inexpensive. Consequently, the importer enjoys the benefit of lower financing costs compared to alternatives and improved bargaining position.
- The exporter is assured of payment upon successful delivery of goods. Additionally, if the drafts are drawn on his own currency, exchange risks are eliminated. If time drafts are used, future exchange risk can be nullified if the "trade acceptance" is discounted.

Red Clause

A deviation from the normal use of a letter of credit, called a red clause, occurs when the buyer has sufficient confidence in the seller to authorize an assignment of benefits to the maximum specified in the letter of credit. This form of financing is sometimes necessary because of the low-capital position maintained by suppliers.

The red clause originated from China-based fur trading where the seller was often an agent of the buyer. Because of the international nature of the trading and the seller's requirement for immediate cash payment, the negotiating bank was authorized to pay the drafts without all supporting documents. Consequently, the letter-of-credit opening banks endorse on their credits in red ink a clause authorizing the negotiating bank to pay the seller based on drafts presented and a promise to provide the required documents sometime in the future.

Production Export Credits

Once an irrevocable letter of credit has been issued to an exporter, he can approach his local bank with proof of his ability to perform and receive production export credits if capital is needed. After receiving the production export credit based on his ability to perform, the bank provides credit up to the limit of the letter of credit.

Other Import/Export Financing Methods

In addition to the basic approaches discussed, import and export transactions can be effected using techniques more familiar to the domestic cash manager. These techniques include:

- *Open account financing*—This is the carrying of accounts receivable of the importer. Of course, in addition to currency exposure the continued risk of company stability is involved.
- *Cash in advance*—This represents another, though limiting, technique because credit terms often have a significant effect on the level of business experienced in a country.
- *Factoring*—Discussed previously, this method can be used as a strategy for limiting credit and currency exposure, even though it is usually expensive in a "no recourse" agreement.
- *Consignments*—Represents another strategy though physical possession of merchandise resides with the importer and the exporter is dependent upon no more than an unsecured promise to pay. The length of time involved in collection may also be excessive after goods are sold, coupled with currency exposure risks, leaves much to be desired for the international cash manager.

GOVERNMENT INFLUENCES AND INTERNATIONAL CASH MANAGEMENT

In the previous section, we examined basic protections or defensive measures that the international cash manager can take to protect his firm from currency fluctuations and from transactional exposure when dealing in import and export situations. The final major area of challenge to the international cash manager is balancing the funds control of a corporation on a global basis and balancing foreign government actions so that foreign capital is made available to the multinational parent company.

The kalidescopic range of involvements for the international cash manager is ultimately manifested in his functional responsibility to globally optimizing the allocation of funds making both political and tax considerations concerning multiple countries. Foreign governments influence the movement of funds through currency exchange controls imposed because of balance of payment and political considerations. Some governments place restrictions on dividends by placing a percent limitation based on income, asset size, or some other basis. Other controls are imposed affecting the tax status of remittances. For example, charging of management fees by a parent to a foreign subsidiary should be considered an expense to the subsidiary. A technique to reduce this remittance of funds is to limit the amount of management fees allowable as a tax deduction.

Considering the variety of possible restrictions and the various tax implication, the international cash manager has an optimization challenge that becomes geometrically complex based on the number of countries involved. Ideally, the goals of the international cash manager include:

- Minimizing the *overall* global tax liability.
- Exercising a significant degree of financial control over foreign subsidiaries.
- Creating and managing a central pool of multinational cash assets.
- Minimizing foreign exchange risks exposure as related to liquid assets of foreign subsidiaries.

The basic techniques available to the international cash manager for the remittance of funds to the parent company include:

- Dividends
- Royalties
- Management fees
- Principal repayment
- Interest payments
- Transfer pricing
- Intercompany agreements

Dividends

The most common form of moving funds back to the parent company is by dividend issuance. However, many countries where an imbalance exists in the balance of payments picture have limitations on dividend remittances or refuse to allow dividend payments to flow outside the country. It is often advisable for a firm to establish and maintain a strict dividend payment policy for all subsidiaries in case future restrictions are imposed. Past precedent often plays a role in the decision of the host governments. Although dividends are taxed at the normal corporate rate in most parent company countries, this can be a small price to pay to have established access to the foreign affiliate's funds. One awkward factor regarding dividend payment occurs when there is joint ownership with one or more partners. Perception of the goals of the business and definition of working capital requirements can cause significant differences regarding dividend amounts.

Royalties

Royalties are fees paid to a parent company to compensate for technical knowledge, copyrighted techniques, or patented material. The royalty amounts are usually negotiated initially and can be a convenient technique for the remittance of funds. If royalties are significant but based on an easily definable element, such as sales, there can be no question regarding the passing of an annual expense to the parent compant. Since it is an expense it is tax deductible by the subsidiary. Additionally, some flexibility is provided the international cash manager to the extent that as funds are better used locally the royalty payment can be postponed or converted to a capitalized loan for repayment at a later time.

Management Fees

Another convenient form of remittance is the use of management fees. These can take the form of allocation of administrative expenses to foreign subsidiaries or a specific levy based on required management consultation.

While the payment of management fees can be handled similar to royalties, both, in theory, should be handled on an arms length transaction basis from the parent to the subsidiary.

Principal and Interest Repayments

Both forms of repayment are legitimate business expenses that provide a basis for the multinational company to extract funds from a foreign subsidiary. In the event that funds are not required, the loans can be extended with agreements for future payment. In any situation where there exists the threat of devaluation acceleration of the principal, repayment is desirable. Additionally, loan prepayment is also advantageous to convert foreign liquid assets from the foreign subsidiary to American dollars to avoid the effects of currency fluctuation.

Transfer Pricing

While the foregoing techniques are the most extensive capital remittance methods, transfer pricing between affiliated companies offer another opportunity to move funds from one area to another. Although the pricing of goods from one affiliate to another is not, in theory, different from contracting with any other outside customer, its use can be advantageous. The subject by its nature is sensitive, and the extent to which firms increase "intracompany" prices to effect asset movement is unknown. Governments in several areas of the world are concerned about the potential effects of transfer pricing and have imposed strict controls and regulations on transfer pricing policies.

Intercompany Transfers

Though not always legal, a final form of moving funds involves two parent companies agreeing to shift funds in the parent country with a result occurring in a foreign subsidiary country. For example, if two firms have subsidiaries in the same foreign country and one is cash laden but cannot remit funds because of local restrictions and the other firm is in a borrowing position, the two parent companies could develop a mutually advantageous financial arrangement. Company 1 with excess local cash can lend money at a lower than market to company 2 subsidiary. Company 2 parent company would then open an account in the United States for company 1 in the amount of the loan. In this way, company 2 gets the local foreign loan at reasonable rates (in effect lending the money itself), and company 1 gets interest on a foreign loan and a deposit for the amount targeted for remission. When the remittance restrictions are lifted, company 2 pays off company 1's loan through the subsidiary.

The discussion of the various considerations involving international cash managers has been far from exhausted in these two chapters. However, the rudiments of both financing and management of assets in a multinational environment have been discussed. The importance of international cash management has been accelerating over the past few years as multinational corporations begin to realize a high percent of net profit from international business. The trend toward increased development of international cash management techniques are affected, in part, by the proliferation of electronic funds transfer services (EFTS) specifically oriented toward international transactions. The advent of expanded use of EFTS will have a significant and growing impact on domestic, as well as international cash management techniques and services.

BIBLIOGRAPHY

Zenoff, David, and Zwick, Jack, *International Financial Management* Prentice-Hall, Englewood Cliffs, N.J., 1969.

Rodriguez, Rita, and Carter, Eugene, *International Financial Management*, Prentice-Hall, Englewood Cliffs, N.J., 1976.

Robbins, Sidney, and Stobaugh, Robert, *Money in the Multinational Enterprise*, Basic Books, New York, 1973.

Leighton, David, *International Marketing*, McGraw-Hill, New York, 1966.

Wasserman, Max, Prindl, Andreas, and Townsend, Charles, *International Money Management*, International Mangement Associates, 1972.

Shaw, Ernest, *Practical Aspects of Commercial Letters of Credit*, The Irving Trust Company, New York, 1967.

Smith, Edward, *International Banking Services*, Crocker National Bank, International Division.

PART V

EFTS AND CASH MANAGEMENT

CHAPTER 12

EFTS—ASPECTS AND ELEMENTS

INTRODUCTION

Even as cash managers are becoming more adroit at the skills of managing cash flows, there are forces taking shape in the market place that significantly affect the management of cash at the corporate and retail level. The most notable of these forces is electronic funds transfer systems. Because of its potential wide-range impact on the cash management operations of a corporation, a solid foundation of knowledge is necessary in order to determine which aspects of EFTS a corporation should participate in and those which should be avoided.

The purpose of Chapters 12 and 13 is to define EFTS in its varied forms by breaking it down into its composite elements. Second, they also try to evaluate the timing of potential changes, identify transitional guidepost points, and evaluate the probable and projected effects from the implementation of EFTS services as related to cash management. Because elements of EFTS serve both retail-oriented and corporate markets, both are examined so that the interrelationship of both areas may be evaluated for cash management purposes. Because of the historic complexity and vagueness surrounding EFTS, these two chapters follow the general structure presented in Exhibit 12-1. This overview represents the major topical areas that include:

- Definition and elements of EFTS
- Existing and unresolved issues
- Motivating factors influencing change and key events
- Major retail cash management impacts
- Major corporate cash management impacts
- Summary—corporate analysis of the impact

Exhibit 12.1 Contemporary EFTS considerations.

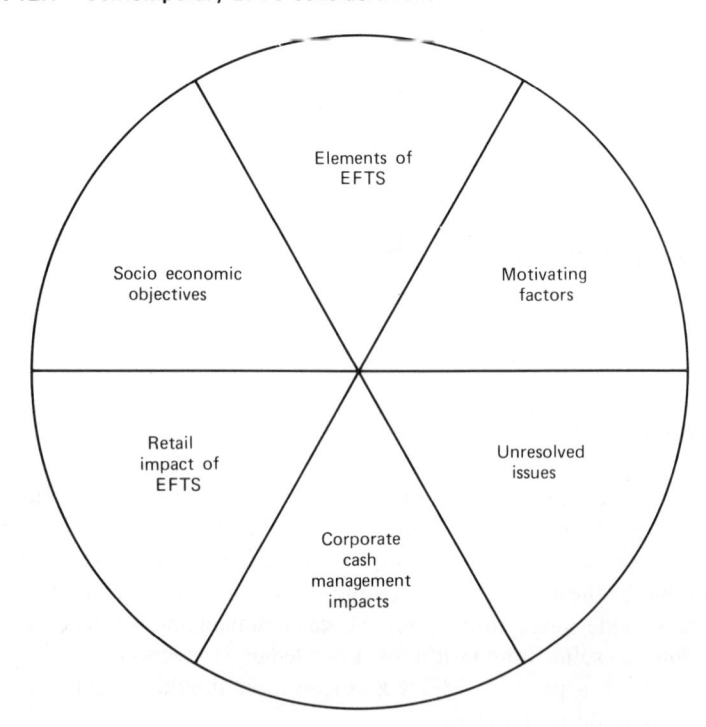

[Circular diagram divided into six sections: Elements of EFTS, Motivating factors, Unresolved issues, Corporate cash management impacts, Retail impact of EFTS, Socio economic objectives]

ELEMENTS OF EFTS

EFTS has sometimes been referred to as a 500-pound marshmallow because of its seeming tendency to change form and expand without lending itself to definitions or containment. Exhibit 12-2 is an overview of how the discussion of EFTS proceeds. As the exhibit describes following definitional areas and discussion of the infrastructures required to suggest EFTS, each element in the major impact areas of retail, government, and corporate involvement are described and defined.

DEFINITION

Electronic funds transfer systems can be defined as any system that replaces paper-based processes with electronic impulses. It is not required that the replacement process be 100%. Consequently, we can rightfully extrapolate

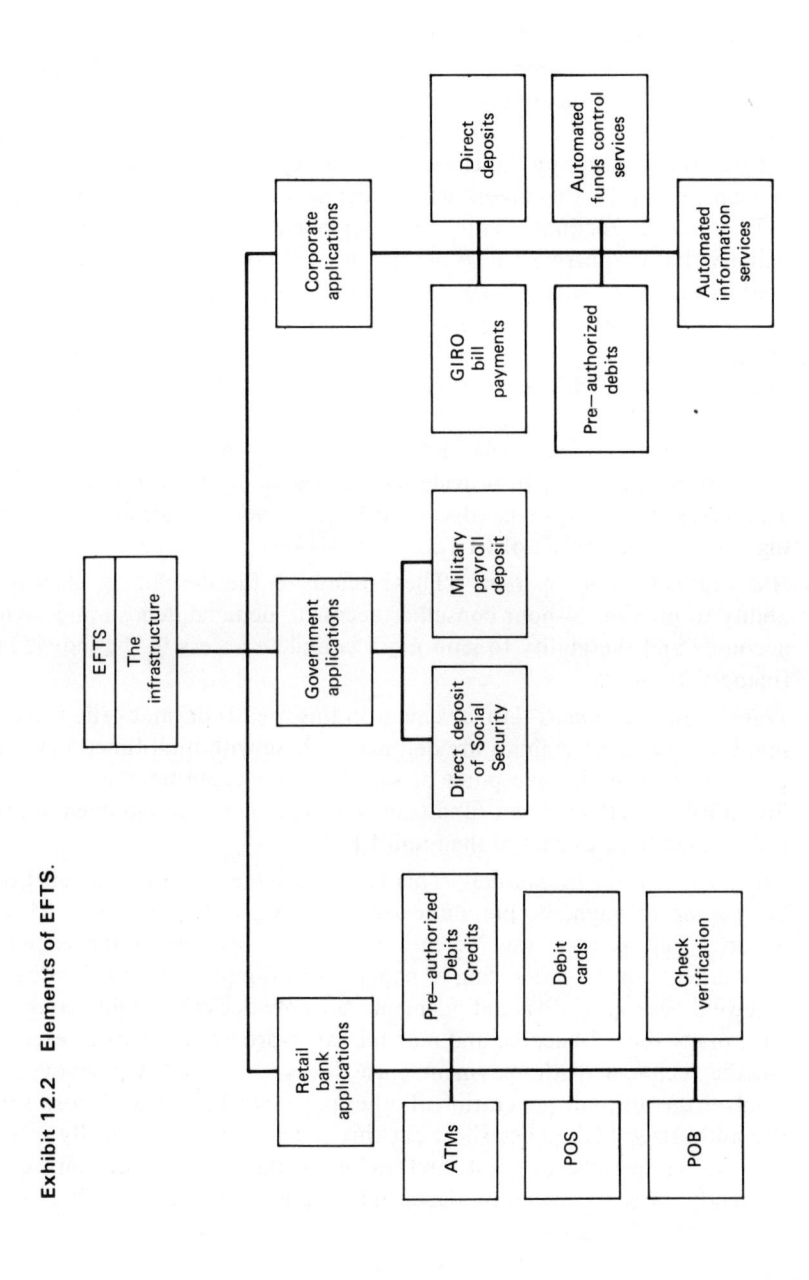

Exhibit 12.2 Elements of EFTS.

that elements of EFTS have existed for years. The growing interest in EFTS has expanded recently because of the increasing availability of electronic's equipment capable of handling multifaceted transactions without any paperwork required. For example, today it is possible to purchase goods with credit cards where the retailer or wholesaler can verify the cardholders credit using the magnetic strip on the back of the card—then enter the purchase amount through the electronic cash register and have that transaction transmitted to the credit cardholder's account and credited to the retailer's bank account. This has increased "synergistic" electronic capability that is spurring EFTS development. In one respect, EFTS can be viewed as an operational change for transaction processors, such as banks, other financial institutions, and credit card service organizations. Involvement in developing systems applications related to EFTS have taken a broad approach but can be generally categorized as:

- *Infrastructure systems*—The infrastructure is defined as the communication systems necessary to provide wide-based electronic transfer of funds. The infrastructure systems (discussed later in more detail) are a developing and essential aspect of EFTS.
- *Automatic banking systems*—These relate to the developing electronic ability to provide 24-hour consumer access to demand deposit and saving accounts and the ability to gain more complete access to the individuals financial resources.
- *Point of sale terminals*—Involvement in this area is dramatically increasing. Point of sale terminals are defined as those with multifunctional purposes. For example, one point of sale terminal could up-date corporate inventory and effect direct fund transfers. The major developmental area is discussed later as part of the retail EFTS.
- *Pre-authorization techniques*—This refers to the elimination of repetitive bill paying through the pre-authorized payment to the recipient. This is an area that is receiving increasing attention because of the expenses associated with the processing of paper. For example, for an individual to receive a payroll or dividend payment, not only does the issuing company have many record-keeping and manual paper-processing steps to execute, but the recipient of the payment must deposit or cash the payment that involves the ultimate generation of other paper work, such as deposit slips. Pre-authorized techniques short cut this process by electronically crediting the recipient's account and debiting the issuers account. Consequently, internal corporate paper handling is eliminated as well as additional external paper generation.

INFRASTRUCTURE

In any development there must be suitable means to reach the end objectives. For EFTS applications, this means the adequate delivery and communication networks required to either move money directly to settlement (e.g., Fed wires) or transmit information that will cause funds to be reallocated (e.g., bank wire). These structures and communication networks are generally referred to as the infrastructure. Exhibit 12-3 illustrates the components of the delivery networks making up the infrastructure as opposed to the individual service element. The major characteristics of delivery networks are:

- Unit networks
- Local switching networks
- Regional networks
- National networks

It is important to note that the infrastructure serves both the providing of information to the corporation and other banks, as well as funds transfer data.

Unit Networks

Unit networks are defined as those autonomously developed for use by a limited number of participants. The unit network could be a check verification facility designed and provided only to those merchants subscribing to the service. A credit card authorization network is an example of a unit network. Increasingly, retail corporations are developing unit networks to check internal credit records prior to credit card sales and are linking many remotely located outlets with a central information network. For example, Montgomery Wards could link all its stores to a unit network for credit verification so that national credit card use would be eased and greater security afforded. This type of unit switching of cash and credit transactional information is under the control of the private corporation and not be generally under common carrier regulatory control.

Local Networks

There are two aspects of local networks. First, they can be viewed as independent terminals linked to a concentrated facility which in turn would

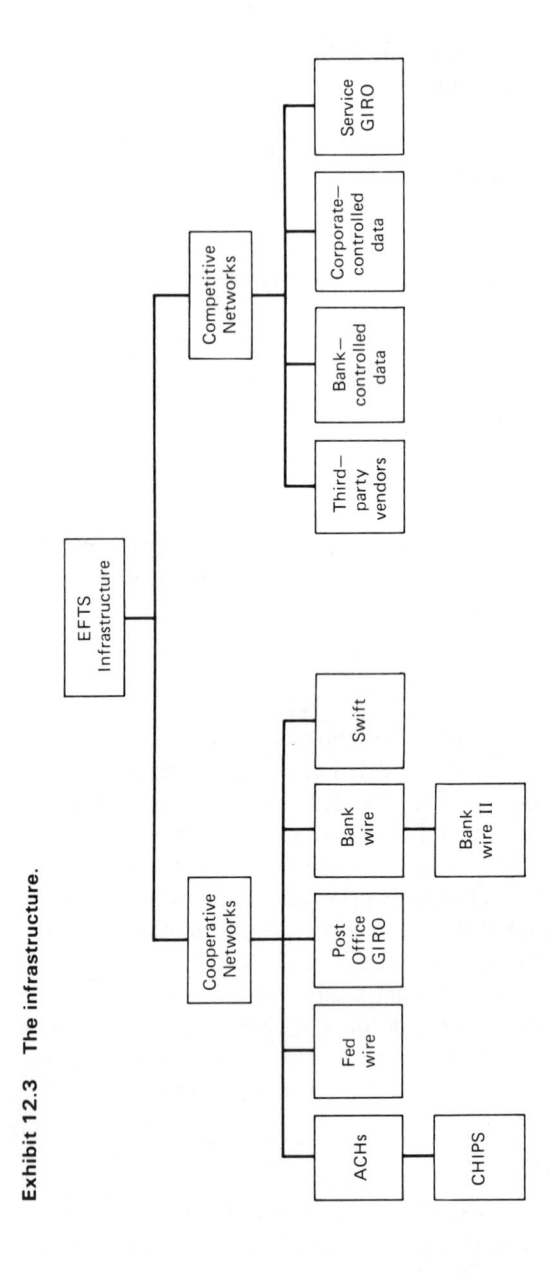

Exhibit 12.3 The infrastructure.

provide access to bank-maintained data bases. Exhibit 12-4 illustrates this approach, which share costs among many users. In this manner, wider use at economical cost may be realized if banks act as "facilities managers" or data base managers. The second extension of local networks is the interface of unit networks described previously in terms of the intergrated local network. This approach intergrates corporate credit data with bank data bases to provide a total credit picture to corporations regardless of banking hours. This type of local networking can be extended to regional networks.

Regional Networks

The purpose of the regional network system is to connect many financial institutions (commercial banks, savings and loans, credit unions, and retail savings banks) to an information system to serve a large city or population-intensive regional area. This type of network offers switching services so

Exhibit 12.4 Local EFTS network.

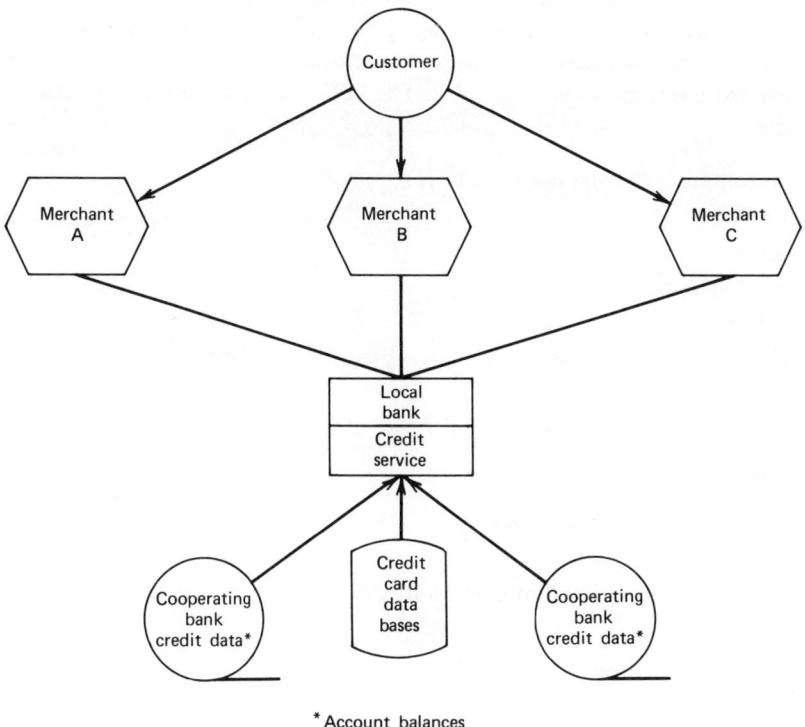

*Account balances
*Credit lines

that messages or inquiries that entered the system would be automatically switched to the correct financial institution for verification.

National Network

Ultimately, national networks will link together all the regional networks. This would accommodate transmission and settlement of all payments nationally in minimal time and with the elimination of associated paperwork. The first step in establishing a national network for funds to electronically clear the system is the national network of automated clearing houses. These clearing houses will provide the mechanism to settle electronic payments locally and nationally and its full development and use will precede any wide implementation of a national electronic data funds network.

COOPERATIVE AND COMPETITIVE SERVICE ELEMENTS

In the current development of EFT infrastructure services, both cooperative and competitive elements are being developed. Distinguishing each set of infrastructure elements illustrates the reasons why service developments, discussed later, are likely to evolve. The cooperative infrastructure elements include:

- Automated clearing houses (ACH)
- Fed wire
- Bank wire
- Bank wire II
- SWIFT
- Clearing House Interbank Payments System (CHIPS)

Included in competitive elements of the infrastructure are:

- GIRO systems
- Data processing vendor services
- Bank-owned systems
- Corporate operational information systems

Automated Clearing Houses (ACH)

Simply stated, the automated clearing house replaces the traditional manual-based check clearing process. Instead of banks exchanging checks and settling accounts, magnetic tape files are processed centrally, and all entries for a particular bank are recorded on one file that is given to that bank for automated processing. Consequently, no physical checks are required to effect payment. Exhibit 12-5 illustrates the procedural flow of the ACH processing. The automated clearing house concept took initial form in 1968 when the Special Committee on Paperless Entries was found

Exhibit 12.5 Operation of automated clearing house system. Reprinted by permission of National Technical Information Service, Department of Commerce, Springfield, Virginia, from "Consequences of EFT", a National Science Foundation Funded Study performed by Arthur D. Little.

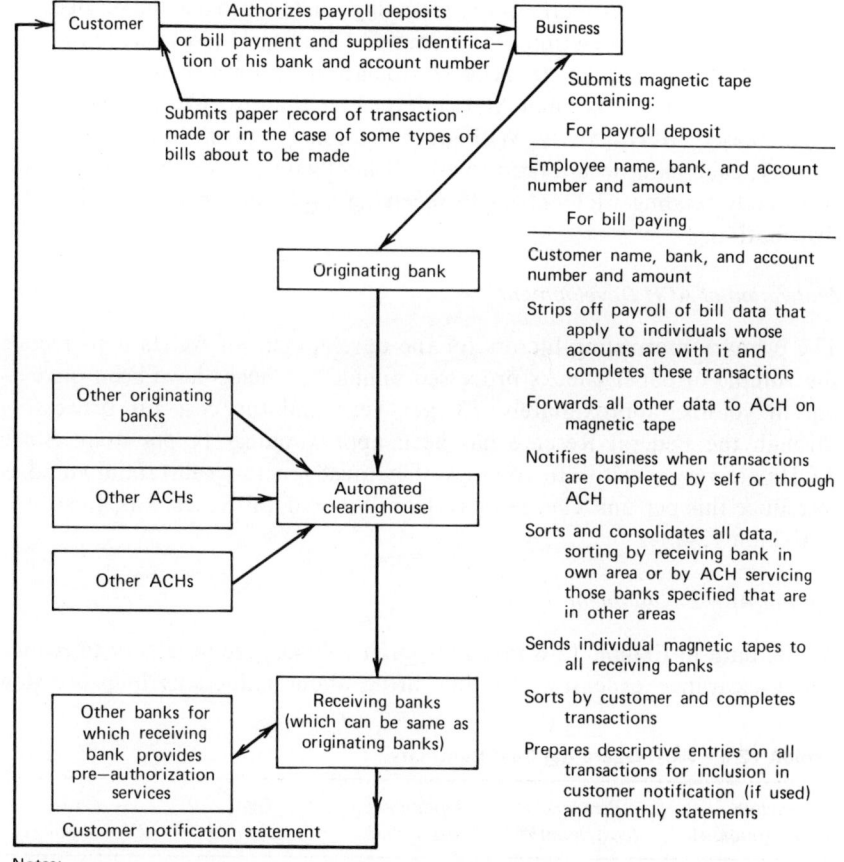

```
                  Authorizes payroll deposits
  ┌──────────┐ ───────────────────────────────→ ┌──────────┐
  │ Customer │  or bill payment and supplies    │ Business │
  │          │  identification of his bank      │          │
  │          │  and account number              │          │
  └──────────┘                                  └──────────┘
```

Submits paper record of transaction made or in the case of some types of bills about to be made

Originating bank

Other originating banks

Other ACHs

Other ACHs

Automated clearinghouse

Other banks for which receiving bank provides pre—authorization services

Receiving banks (which can be same as originating banks)

Customer notification statement

Submits magnetic tape containing:

For payroll deposit

Employee name, bank, and account number and amount

For bill paying

Customer name, bank, and account number and amount

Strips off payroll of bill data that apply to individuals whose accounts are with it and completes these transactions

Forwards all other data to ACH on magnetic tape

Notifies business when transactions are completed by self or through ACH

Sorts and consolidates all data, sorting by receiving bank in own area or by ACH servicing those banks specified that are in other areas

Sends individual magnetic tapes to all receiving banks

Sorts by customer and completes transactions

Prepares descriptive entries on all transactions for inclusion in customer notification (if used) and monthly statements

Notes:

[1] This diagram does not cover the operation of "Bill—Check," which requires a minor modification in the notification/individual approval process.

[2] The diagram does not show the mechanism by which banks receive notice of the fact that a customer has preauthorized deposit of income and/or payment of bills. This mechanism is apt to vary on a local basis and may even be different for different individual institutions. In all cases, however, the banks will have to receive what they regard as adequate record of authorization.

in California (SCOPE). The primary objectives of ACHs is to reduce internal bank item processing costs through use of electronic payment systems. Although there has been a proliferation of ACHs nationally, the current volumes handled do not begin to impact processing costs. As of 1978, 32 operational ACHs nationally processed approximately 5 to 7 million items per month. This represents a maximum of 48 million annual items compared to the approximately 31 billion annual items processed. Of the 5 million items per month currently processed, over 80% are government generated for direct deposit of social security or military payrolls. The ACH's are operated by the Federal Reserve banks in all except Chicago and New York where third-party data processing vendors provide the service.

The National Association of Automated Clearing Houses was found as a result of an American Banking Association recommendation and has actively supported a national ACH interchange that provides the foundation for increased ACH activity. Without the national network of clearing house activity, each bank would need to establish a "window" or electronic means of directly sending EFT entries to receiving banks in other ACH cities for distribution.

Motivation of ACH Development

The primary motivating factors for the development of ACHs is to reduce the volume of paper checks processed annually. Checks have been increasing in volume approximately 7% per year and the cost for processing through the Federal Reserve has been approximately 1¢ per item. Since ACHs are very sensitive to volumes, they must generate substantial volumes to reduce this per unit charge of 1¢ from the Federal Reserve as illustrated in Exhibit 12-6.

Current ACH Environment

As the data in Exhibit 12-6 indicates, high volumes are necessary to reduce direct clearance expenses and thus bring about reductions in processing

Exhibit 12.6 ACH Operating Cost Summary

Transaction (volume/month)	Personnel (cost/month)	Equipment (cost/month)	Total (cost/month)	Cost Transaction (¢)
20,000	1650	500	2150	10.8
152,500	1650	1000	2650	3.3
285,000	1650	1500	3150	1.8
417,500	1650	2000	3650	1.1
550,000	1650	2500	4150	.8

Exhibit 12.7   Item Check-Processing Costs Experienced by a Bank

ON-US Item received through:
• Branch = 13.88¢
• Another bank = 6.21¢
• Federal or city clearing = 4.95¢
	Transit item received through:
	• Branch = 10.6¢
	• Another bank = 2.88¢
	  (not encoded)
	• Another bank = 1.62¢
	  (encoded)

charges from banks to corporations. As operational ACHs expand corporate cash managers can begin to take advantage of lower cost clearance facilities. In January of 1977, there were 28 operational ACHs nationally, with several more in the planning stage. It is interesting to note that the oldest clearing house, which is in California, was as of mid 1976 only processing approximately 152,000 entries monthly, of which 102,000 were government generated. At that level of activity, it costs approximately 3.3¢ per item to process the entries as compared to approximately 1¢ charged by the Federal Reserve. Nationally, there is an increasing trend toward development and implementation of ACHs, even though volumes do not currently approach the breakeven point. This can be explained by:

- *Easy access to the required technology*—This has resulted from the California and Georgia involvements.
- *Low-dollar initial investment*—A shared ACH can be joined for as little as $15,000 with annual operational expenses of $70,000 in a joint effort.
- *The potential for volume handling is large*—The potential payback is large in terms of reducing the paper check-processing expenses for banks. Current per check processing expenses have been estimated to range from 6.21¢ for the simplest process to 13.88¢ per check for complete handling. See Exhibit 12-7.
- The Federal Reserve system is supporting the development of the ACH
- The federal government is encouraging paperless processing through the direct deposit programs for Air Force personnel and social security payments

These are the major factors that are encouraging the development of ACHs nationally. Cash managers are keenly interested in monitoring the ACH development because they alone are a guidepost to *when* the payments system will offer the possibility of faster receipts. Through the use of ACHs and pre-authorized payments, more accurate controls over cash flows are achievable. Additionally, mail and collection float is eliminated through the use of ACHs. Of course, business-to-business payments might be impacted so that outflows of cash as well as inflows may be accelerated. The float problem is the major consideration for corporations today in using ACH entries for payments. However, insurance companies, such as Equitable Life, are currently using available ACHs to establish their own national clearing network so that premium payments may be centralized faster at lower costs. At the same time, they enjoy lower per transaction processing charges from the banks. Additionally, recent reserach has indicated an increasing willingness of corporations to effect business-to-business payments of less than $1000 via EFT. However, many banks are willing to charge lower processing charges to increase volume as a market strategy. Cash managers can look to national ACH developments to be the bellweather of expanded automated receipts and prepare internal strategies prior to market demand to reduce billing and collection costs and reduce float.

Fed Wire

While ACHs represent a new method of funds transfer, the Fed wire represents an established means of moving funds from one bank to another and is an integral part of the EFTS environment. The Federal Reserve wire system is a communication network used to move funds from one Federal Reserve members account to another, as well as to send administrative messages. The settlement of funds takes place daily at the Federal Reserves so funds are immediately available. The Federal Reserve wire system interconnects the 12 Federal Reserve districts through a communication network switch located in Culpepper, Virginia. The Fed wire, as it is called, handles the largest dollar volume of domestic funds transfer. It is estimated that over $31 trillion were transferred in 1975 representing 17 million transactions. The objective of the Fed wire is to reduce float on large dollar transactions while providing a Federal Reserve communication link. For transfers of $1000 or greater, the Fed has not charged for the service, which has created competitive problems for the Bank wire service. Fed wire settlements are effected daily on a net basis between the Federal Reserve Bank's member accounts.

Bank Wire

The Payment and Telecommunications Corporation is a communication utility developed by cooperating banks to provide a media for information exchange essentially through administrative messages. The original bank wire system was operated under contract by Western Union and moved approximately 24,000 messages per day in early 1977. Fund movement transactions occur through this use of correspondent banks' balances. Consequently, bank A will notify via bank wire bank B to transfer bank A funds from their account for credit to a receiving corporate account in bank B. No funds settlement takes place in this service. Approximately 215 banks are members of the bank wire system, which processes an estimated 500,000 messages per month.

Bank Wire II

Because of volume, cost, and quality limitations of the bank wire service, the development of bank wire II was initiated. The objectives of this expanded service is to:

- Provide flexibility to meet increasing transactions volume with constant or decreasing costs
- Provide for expanded administrative message traffic
- Provide for batch communications
- Exploit technical advances recently developed

Compared to the current bank wire system, bank wire II is designed to handle 65,000 messages per day and 50% of these are projected to be funds transfer information. The Bank Wire II system is scheduled to participate more fully in EFT function by:

- Transferring funds to provide immediate availability
- Provide net settlements between members on a daily basis
- Provide for processing future dated (value dated) transactions
- Provide ability for debit transfers

Settlement under Bank Wire II would take place through the Federal Reserve. A major issue to the active use of Bank Wire II is the resolution of pricing by the Federal Reserve. As of January 1978, the Fed does not charge for transfers of $1000 or more and charges $1.50 for transfers of less than $1000 in order to encourage high-dollar transfers. If the Fed prices on a transaction basis for all wires, Bank Wire II may be in a strong competitive position.

Clearing House Interbank Payments System (CHIPS)

CHIPS is designed to handle international interbank money transfers. CHIPS has been operational since 1970 and handles approximately

$12 trillion per year in money transfers. CHIPS is managed as a cooperative by its 69 members and is a clearance and settlement mechanism. CHIPS is operated out of the New York Clearing House with daily funds settlement. CHIPS also provides to its members daily account balance information which is used to manage the banks' positions. As of early 1977, the processing volume for CHIPS was approximately 800,000 to 900,000 items per month. CHIPS will be affected by the implementation of SWIFT, but the extent is not known.

SWIFT

The Society for Worldwide International Financial Transactions is a cooperative bank funds transfer network that provides a network between Europe and North America. Initial membership included 340 banks located in 15 countries. The objectives of SWIFT are to:

- Reduce the complexity of settlement in international transfers involving multiple currencies
- Improve communication and payment mechanisms for international transactions

The SWIFT system operates from switching centers located in Brussels and Amsterdam. There are 14 concentrators for regional collection of data, 12 in Europe and two in North America (Montreal and New York City). The concentrators collect and disburse messages between users. SWIFT is intended primarily for funds transfer, and it is expected that 90% of the volume will relate to fund transfer activity. Although initial operation calls for settlement by correspondent bank balances, eventually it is intended that a complete settlement function will be incorporated. SWIFT became operational in late 1977. It is anticipated that the system will expand to other countries outside Europe and into Australia and Asia. Projected membership could be as high as 859 cooperating member banks. Conceptionally, the SWIFT system could theoretically replace the bank wire system currently operating. The average cost per message over SWIFT is projected to be less than 40¢, which is significantly less than conventional transmissions that average upward of 80¢ per message. SWIFT will have a direct impact on international wire transfer expenses. Consequently, cash managers with international involvement can expect to experience a greater willingness to transfer funds internationally because of lower costs.

Competitive Infrastructure Elements

GIRO Systems

In identifying infrastructure service elements, we would be remiss if the European GIRO system were omitted. Essentially, this system allows a corporate customer to pay the corporation by effecting an electronic payment generated through the Post Office Department or a GIRO receiving station. The customer has control over *when* the payment is executed, consequently float delays may be built in by the customer. Additionally, the control over the use of this system resides with the customer because pre-authorizations are not an integral part of this system. Although this system does not currently exist as a service in the United States, the Post Office has recently commissioned a study to evaluate the possibility and timing of introducing such a system. The primary motivating factor for the Post Office is that over 40% of its prime revenue is derived from consumer-to-business or business-to-consumer payments. With the widespread advent of ACHs and pre-authorized debits and credits, a significant portion of its profit based revenue would be eroded. Corporate cash managers can use this development as a benchmark because it signals a national capability to collect funds faster while substantially reducing internal corporate paper handling expense. GIRO payment mechanisms represent competitive factors because banks and multilocation corporations could offer GIRO processing center services that could receive, process, and forward items to various banks and ACHs for settlement. Pilot GIRO transactions are being initiated out of the New York area. This represents the first attempt at assessing the value of this payment processing mode.

Third-party Infrastructure Suppliers

High-lighting the competitive aspects of infrastructure services is the participation of independent time-sharing companies. These firms (representative: Automatic Data Processing Network Services, General Electric, and National Data Corporation) offer customized and standard data collection facilities for use by banks and corporations. The key contribution of these suppliers is the national communication network offered, plus the ability to use collected data to interface with statistical software packages and the ability to write custom programs for corporate data manipulation. Even though these vendors do not offer any settlement functions, they do compete with information-gathering services developed internally by banks. Participation of third-party vendors in the infrastructure has been expanding. One vendor operates the Chicago ACH and another acts as a store and forwards message switch for wire transfer information. The overall approach is to offer a total service concept that can process receivable, payables and other information.

Bank-owned Services

More limited in scope but still a participant in the competitive EFT areas are information services provided directly by banks. The objective of banks developing these types of services is to both strengthen customer ties and to increase fee revenue while extending use of available computer resources. Because of the cost to develop these services and the technical expertise required, few banks actively offer these services. Corporations are often reluctant to use bank-owned systems because of concerns over data security and bank-established priorities.

Corporate-based Information Services

Corporate-controlled information networks represent the final level of competitive-based infrastructure networks. These unit networks are used to supply to the corporate financial offices information needs, which result in transfer of funds to concentration points or finding of corporate locations.

Summary—Infrastructure

Through a coordinated effort at implementation of EFT-based payment systems, cash managers can:

- Reduce internal costs of paper handling of receipts
- Reduce direct account receivable expenses
- Reduce lockbox expenses
- Increase availability of funds
- Increase accuracy of inputs to cash forecasting

Each of the delivery systems described as well as the EFT elements introduced provides a roadmap marking for the developing of EFT trends. Additionally, it provides the corporate cash manager with adequate time to:

- Develop an overall corporate EFTS strategy
- Define problems and opportunities related to EFTS from a cash management perspective

- Organize marketing efforts required to obtain customer acceptance on pre-authorizations
- Select banks that are capable and knowledgable about EFTS
- Educate other corporate areas about consequences and effect of EFTS on float management and funds control

Although the elements of the infrastructure discussed here provide essential development guidelines to the cash manager, cognizance of the specific applications within EFTS provide the foundation for strategy development.

RETAIL BANKING APPLICATIONS OF EFTS

Discussing the retail applications of EFTS overlaps with the corporate aspects because the corporations' consumer often has primary interaction with the corporation at the retail level. For example, though Montgomery Ward may deal with EFTS centrally, as an issue it is limited to centralized corporate applications. The retail customers of Wards have more direct involvement with the widely dispersed retail EFTS applications employed for point of sale capture. Montgomery Ward, for example, is, through its retail outlet, as much involved with retail-related EFTS transactions as it is from the central office in arranging pre-authorized debits to speed collections. Retail EFTS applications are meaningful in the changing complexion of cash management as corporate applications increase. There are six major application areas associated with Retail EFTS:

- Automated teller machines
- Point of sale terminals
- Place of business terminals
- Pre-authorized transactions
- Debit cards
- Check verification services

Automated Teller Machines (ATM)

The purpose of automated teller machines is to reduce clerical work for the bank and provide 24-hour customer access to their funds. The ATM devices are an important consideration to cash managers because:

- The amount of cash required to service customers in outlets may be reduced if an ATM is installed

- Easy access to funds 24 hours a day via plastic cards can increase a firms potential cash flow and sales
- The ATMs, if installed in a place of business, can actually attract additional traffic

The ATMs are usually free-standing, remote banking service units. These units provide customers with the ability to draw cash or transfer funds from one account to another or to pay loans or bill payment by account debiting. ATMs in their more sophisticated state are called CBCTs or Customer Bank Communication Terminals. ATMs are often attractive to retail outlets such as supermarkets, which traditionally cash large volumes of checks and which suffer significant bad check losses. Currently, there are over 3000 units in operation with half that number on backorder. Many devices stand alone in nature and are not connected directly to a bank data base for on line verification. In the near future, direct data base interfaces help cash managers reduce uncollectable accounts receivable by verifying the customers credit prior to execution of the transaction.

An alternative to the expensive ATMs (about $50,000 each) is a smaller Service Counter Terminal (SCT), which costs $500 and is used by the retailers employee. These devices permit access to bank data bases to verify credit balances and to *directly* transfer funds without paper handling from the retail customer's account to the corporation. Advantages to the cash manager of this type of system include:

- Reduce check handling by employees
- Decrease the amount of cash required for transactions (these funds could be used to generate income)
- Reduce item processing charges levied by banks for checks deposited
- Eliminate collection float on checks cashed

Point of Sale Terminals (POS)

Point of sale terminals are minicomputer-based transaction devices that are multifunctional in nature. Currently they can:

- Up-date multiple accounting records, including inventory stocks
- Provide credit card verification
- Accept and process credit card/debit card or cash transactions
- Provide for immediate "paperless" transfer of funds from customers account to corporations account
- Store data for later analysis and descriptive bill preparation

The point of sale terminals are either unit in nature, that is they operate strictly within the confines of the corporation's structure or locally interfaced with on-line verification files. The potential volume could be as high as 17 billion annually out of a total number of 57 billion transactions. The interaction possible between POS devices and other authorization networks to reduce the risk of credit extension is illustrated in Exhibit 12-8.

However, many corporations are already using First National City Bank's terminal-readable "Citicard" and a similar Master Charge card especially designed for credit authorization. Although neither of these cards directly debit or transfer funds, they do result in a memo debit posting that assures the merchant of reliable information. In summary, the cash manager wants to evaluate POS devices in order to:

- Reduce bad credit extension
- Effect immediate funds transfer where possible
- Reduce paperwork recording expenses

Place of Business Terminal

Place of business terminals are similar to POS terminals, but they do not carry the multiple transaction abilities. Rather they record data in a batch file during the day as transactions are made at the retailers place of business. At the end of the day, information on credit purchases and direct debit, if any, are transcribed on another file that is sent to the credit card-processing organization or bank for processing.

Pre-authorized Debits

An example of a Pre-authorized debit service is where credit card customers of corporations agree to have their checking accounts automatically charged for the minimum payment due each month—the application of pre-authorized debits is generally applied to fixed payment items, such as insurance payments, automobile time payments or monthly mortgage payments. Pre-authorized debits also widely apply to payment of obligations that require payoff each period, such as utility bills (water, gas, etc.). There is a slow but growing use of pre-authorized debits in the retail area to automatically charge the subscriber the minimum amount due each period. This has benefits to the retail cash manager because:

- Delinquencies and their associated expense are reduced
- The timing of receipts can be better estimated
- Lockbox-processing expenses can be reduced

284   EFTS—Aspects and Elements

Exhibit 12.8   Point of sale terminal system. Reprinted by permission of the Practicing Law Institute & L. Richard Fisher from "Changing Patterns of Consumer Credit", 1975 PLI.

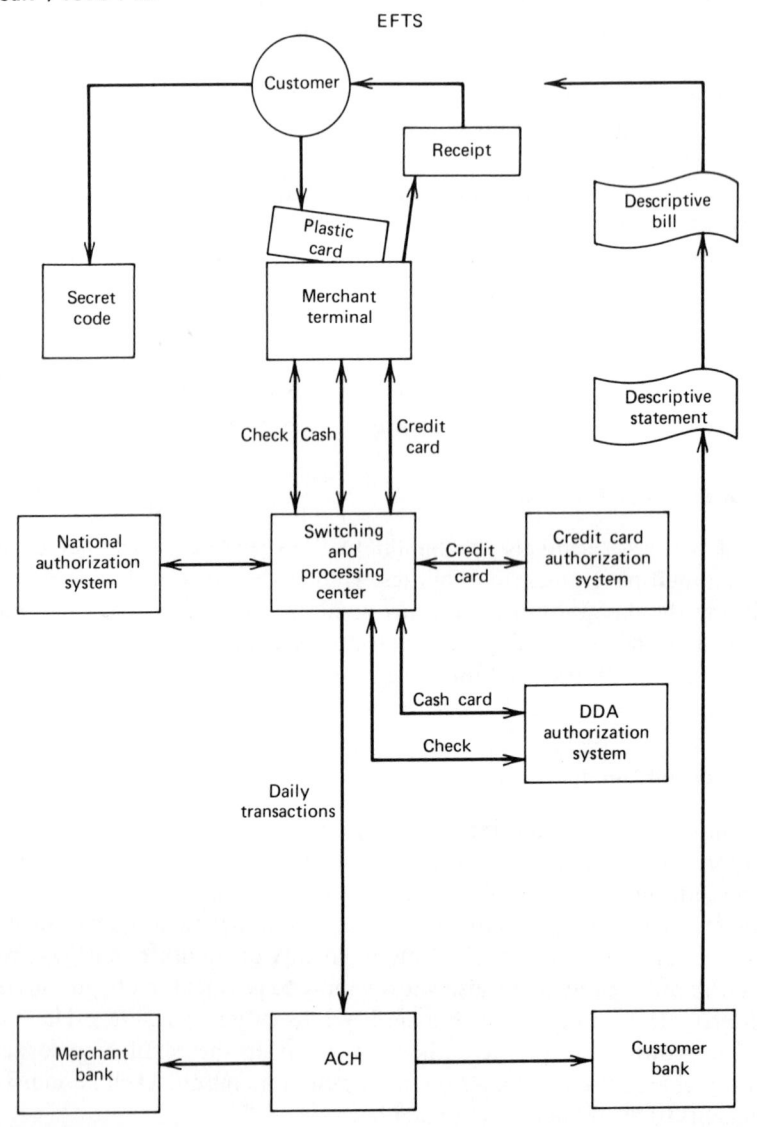

Exhibit 12-9 describes the flow of pre-authorized debit processing for a company. In order to implement the system, it is necessary to obtain authorization from customers and internally generate a magnetic tape with the names and account numbers to be debited. This file is sent to the processing bank, which posts the "ON-US" entries and sends other bank data to the

Exhibit 12.9 Pre-authorized debit. Reprinted by permission of the Practicing Law Institute & L. Richard Fisher from "Changing Patterns of Consumer Credit", 1975 PLI.

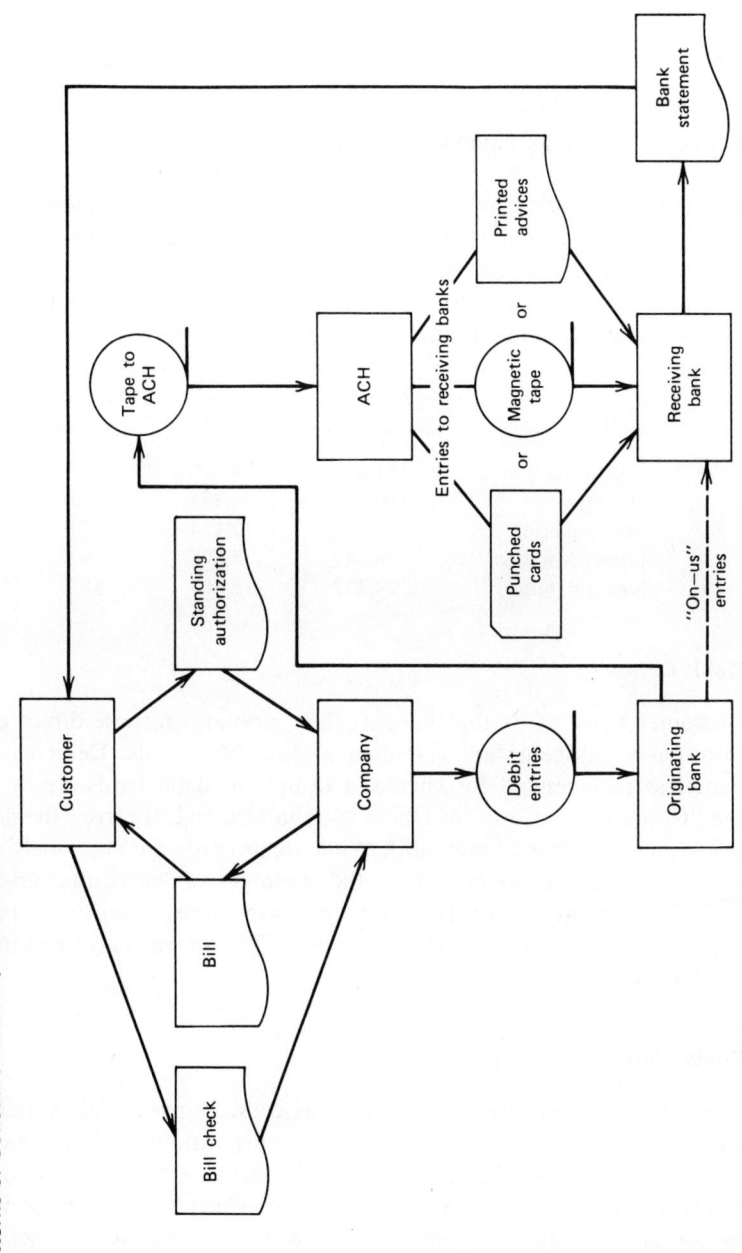

automated clearing house. Currently, several corporations are using pre-authorized debiting; however, there is significant market resistance because of:

- Fear of loss of financial control
- Distrust of computers
- Lack of timing of payment and subsequent loss of float

The major consideration in the implementation of a pre-authorized, corporate-sponsored debit system is not the existing capability but the marketing required. Pre-authorized debits exist in approximately 50% of the currently active ACHs. However, the volume and percent of total volumes is small. For example, the data on some of the highest volume ACH's are:

ACH	Monthly total volume	Total debits	Debits percent
California	151,836	4,400	2.8
Georgia	110,534	34,274	31.0
Mid-America	52,863	12,124	22.9
Upper Midwest	56,645	3,898	6.9
New England	44,477	15,685	35.3

Debit Cards

Customer bank cards that have as their primary purpose direct checkless third-party payments are classified as the debit cards. Debit cards are a paperless replacement for checks. Example of debit cards are "Citicard," the "Convenience Card" of Chase Manhattan, and "Entree" the debit card being issued by BankAmericard. While debit cards are not widely accepted yet, we can expect them to take the same growth curve that credit cards took 10 years ago. To this extent, the cash manager will plan to accept, and, in fact, encourage payment by debit card so funds may be more readily available.

Check Verification

Though check verification has been discussed under POS systems, it is identified separately as a service because corporations have access to these types of automated files from banks. To this extent, corporations need to assess how much they are willing to pay for check verification services and to consider the need to join or develop a check verification service that provides access to all major bank files. This is necessary because individual banks will not be able to provide data about other bank's accounts. Consequently, some switching mechanism will be necessary. Several retail check verification systems interfacing participating member banks are developing the national and regional switching centers necessary. The Western States Bank Card Association is an example of a regional approach to a check verification facility. The major problems encountered by the services currently include:

- Justification to banks via payback and ROI criteria of project value
- Agreement on who would pay for the service—the retail customer or the merchant
- Achievement of adequate geographic subscriptions to justify development of the system

GOVERNMENTAL APPLICATIONS OF EFTS

Governmental involvement in EFT actually arises primarily from payments effected from the Treasury Department through the Federal Reserve Bank. The major reasons for government interest and active fostering of EFTS applications include:

- Crime, including robbery for cash, welfare payments, and social security checks
- Cost to prepare and distribute payroll checks to employees
- Better monetary control over float

The two major application areas of current direct government involvement are the direct deposit of social security payments and direct deposit of military payrolls.

Direct Deposit of Social Security

The Direct Deposit of Social Security program began in 1975 by authorizing banks to receive the physical social security checks directly for the recipient and depositing it to their account. The second phase was implemented on August 31, 1976, when the physical checks were replaced with magnetic tape. Under this method, the Federal Reserve Bank separates payments from the Treasury Department by receiving bank and forwards the tape to the appropriate bank. This application only affects a cash manager to the extent that receipts are generated from retail transactions. If this is the case, debit cards coupled with POS verification would be appropriate considerations.

Direct Deposit of Military Payroll

The second major government-sponsored application is the direct deposit of military personnel payrolls. This is a vanguard service to the extent that this capability will eventually be used by all branches of the services. Due to the current limited applications, there is no direct impact for the corporate cash manager.

The significant point related to government participation in EFTS is not so much the current volumes or activites, but rather the intent of the government towards EFTS and the eventual impact. The government as the largest employer can expect a significant influence on the future of EFTS development. Because of the government's interest in direct deposits, it has become the major influence in the EFTS movement. The extent to which commercial applications will increase in participation has yet to be determined in the market place.

CORPORATE APPLICATION OF EFTS

Corporations are increasingly becoming aware of the transaction processing costs involved in executing the billing and receipt functions. Currently, there is not significant use of corporate EFTS affecting either business-to-business payments or individual-to-business payments, although several specific applications have been identified. The practical use of the various applications outlined here are dependent upon the dollar value of the transaction and the associated benefits lost because of lost float. Corporations today still resist disbursement of high dollar transactions by wire unless specific arrangements have been made with the vendor to mitigate the loss of float.

Generally, Electronic Funds Transfer Services applicable to corporations are formulated within:

- GIRO bill payment applications
- Pre-authorized debits
- Direct deposits
- Automated funds control services
- Automated information services

GIRO Bill Payment

Giro bill payment in the EFTS arena relates to a credit transfer service provided by a network of GIRO payment stations. These stations, as described previously, could be Post Office operated, bank controlled in branch banking states, or privately operated. In considering applications, corporations can be involved through either individual-to-business payments or business-to-business payments.

Individual-to-Business GIRO

Under the EFTS application, the corporation sends a machine-readable bill to the customer. The customer receives the bill and writes on it the amount to be paid. The bill contains as part of the machine-readable line the corporate account to be credited. Since the individual controls the amount paid and the timing, control is retained. Multiple bills can be paid and the timing, control is retained. Multiple bills can be paid either with a singular check or if the individual's account is with the bank operating as the GIRO collection station the account can be directly debited. After indicating the amount to be paid, the individual submits the payment to the GIRO station for execution. The GIRO payment is processed by automated equipment that reads the amount to be credited to the corporation's account number as recorded on the bill. A tape file is created that is used to credit the corporation's account on the same day that the payment is received.

The benefits accruing to the corporation from use of the service include:

- Faster up-dating of accounts receivable files because of tape input resulting from GIRO processing
- Faster funds availability due to the same day crediting of funds received at the GIRO.
- Reduced internal processing costs for lockbox handling and check deposit expenses

Although this concept has been successfully used in Europe, its implementation is slow in the United States because of concerns of customer acceptance and lack of GIRO standards. To be really successful, a GIRO payment system must have significant regional acceptance, and this implies a network of processing centers all using the same standards. Other corporate considerations in moving to GIRO processing include:

- Reduced customer contact
- Loss of control over remittance processing and quality

- Costs related to additional recording keeping required of banks on GIRO stations to maintain physical documents

GIRO bill-payment methods are just starting implementation now as banks, corporations, and vendors are becoming involved in establishing national standards for scan line documents. Beyond standards in the scan line, more efficient processing of low-dollar, high-volume GIRO payments, similar to the automated lockbox system described in Chapter 4, need to be regionally implemented.

Business-to-business GIRO Payment

Another GIRO application is to effect business-to-business payments. Based on the current cash management environment and emphasis placed on disbursement float control, this application basically applies to payments less than $1000 each. Under this service, the corporation generates a tape of credit entries indicating the amount to be credited and the receiving company's bank and account number. This information is submitted to the corporation's paying bank for debiting of the corporation's account and distribution of the electronic entries to the receiving banks via ACHs or direct exchange. The advantages to the corporation include:

- Maintenance of control over disbursement timing
- Elimination of check preparation costs
- Elimination of postage costs
- Reduction of account reconcilement costs
- Elimination of risk of stolen or lost checks

Corporations generally realize that the value of float on payables of less than $1000 is not significant. This service is not generally offered by banks today, and corporations are concerned over inflexible payment dates and loss of available funds sooner than required. The trend is favorable for business-to-business GIRO payments to evolve strongly in the next 3 to 5 years and will precede the individual-to-business payments in general acceptance as the total costs for bill payment increases to the corporation.

PREAUTHORIZED DEBITS

Individual-to-business

Using the preauthorized debit arrangement requires that the customer sign an authorization agreement whereby he agrees to allow the bank to debit his account on established dates for amounts payable to a corporation. The electronic entry produced periodically by the bank replaces the normal check payment function. Banks processing the transactions typically create a tape for distribution to the receiving bank account. These entries are often processed through the established automated clearing houses. The advantages to use this bill paying approach are:

- Elimination of the need for the individual to prepare and send bills
- Reduction of the corporation's delinquent accounts since payment is automatic
- Elimination of the collection float to the corporation
- Elimination of corporate work of issuing and depositing checks

The primary problems with acceptance of this service revolve around customer concerns on how returned items for insufficient funds will be effectively handled and the fact that customers are reluctant to give up control over their payment timing and float.

This type of application is likely to be used for fixed monthly payment obligations, such as insurance payments and utility bills where full payment is required. The concept of level billing where a monthly average payment is made each month and a once a year adjustment is made to balance the account for the year is one of several approaches gaining in acceptance. This approach encourages the use of individual business preauthorized debits.

Business-to-business

Although this is a possible EFTS corporate service, it has no benefits as perceived by the corporation because it would lose control over disbursements and float while increasing the corporation's record-keeping and error control procedure because of increased difficulty in identifying and correcting electronic errors.

Direct Deposits

This EFTS-type has offered since 1974 for payroll deposits and is the most widely accepted corporate-used form of EFTS. Essentially, this involves the corporation's preparing a magnetic tape with the credit entries required. The tape contains the recipient's name, bank, account number, and amount. The corporation-servicing bank receives these entries, credits the accounts domiciled in its bank and forwards the other entries to the appropriate banks, either through an ACH or a direct exchange. Although payroll applications are the most widespread, this service also applies to corporate payment of dividends and pensions.

The benefits of using this service include:

- Provides an inexpensive additional service to employees or shareholders
- Reduction of payment expenses in check preparation, distribution, and direct mail expenses
- Elimination of lost and stolen check problems
- Reduction of reconcilement expenses
- Elimination of need for compensating balances in distant banks to support employee check cashing activity.

There are several tangible benefits to this EFTS; nevertheless, there is still a significant degree of resistance arising from:

- Employee who perceive loss of control over funds received
- Loss of funds sooner than necessary as a result of the direct crediting
- Lack of a national exchange system to the corporations
- Reduced control over late charges
- Continued need to provide earnings statement
- Increased cost to identify and resolve errors

Even though there are perceived problems with this service, the trend is toward expanded corporate use of this service. Greater use of this service will occur as banks begin to more actively market the services. The area of highest corporate application is for salaried and professional workers. Hourly employees can be expected to continue to offer resistance because overtime earnings are often not routinely deposited with regular pay funds.

Automated Funds Control Services

Extensions of EFT corporate services can be characterized as application of increased automation in the remittance processing area and wire transfer area. Both involve the movement of corporate funds through the increased use of electronic methods.

Automated Lockbox Services

As described in Chapter 4, there are several recent developments in the automated lockbox area. Common to any of the available methods is the effective input of data from machine-readable documents using electronic terminals and output of information in machine-readable form, such as magnetic tape. The transmission of the information to the corporations and use of automated lockbox processing results in:

- Improved funds availability, which is a result of later processing cutoff times
- Improved control over the timely updating of corporate account receivable files
- Reduced processing expenses to corporations by receipt of data transmission rather than handling of physical documents

As with other services performed by banks, corporations often cite as concerns this class of receipt processing control, security of the data processed, and the accuracy and reliability provided by the processing bank.

Automated Wire Transfers

An emerging area of EFTS is the automated wire transfer functions. Essentially, a corporate cash manager effects funds transfers from a terminal located in the corporate office. This transfer information is either entered on a data base of a third-party vendor and then accessed by the bank to generate the transfer or is entered directly into the bank's computer-controlled wire transfer system. The benefits realized by the cash manager from utilizing this system include:

- Reduction in the time to make wires, thus increasing transfer flexibility
- Provision of an in office hard copy verification of funds transferred by the bank on a same day basis
- Reduction of bank-caused transfer errors through direct input of instructions

The corporate cash manager can look forward to increased availability of these services, which will make the use of wire transfers—which are increasing—more controllable and less expensive. Many banks offering this service charge reduced wire transfer rates provided the customer directly inputs the data.

Automated Information Services

EFTS relates to both the amount of funds and information related to funds. To this extent, the types of automated EFTS information services are offered today by banks to corporations.

Corporate Bank Direct Interface

This EFTS-related service involves the direct linking of information between corporations and banks. The type of data transmitted would include: GIRO information, lockbox data, direct deposit information, account balance, and detail transaction data. The transmission mode could be via tape or direct computer to computer transmission. The benefits to the corporation of using this service type is faster and more accurate availability of data for internal use. The major corporate concerns about this service centers on the ability of banks to provide these interfaces and potential vulnerability of the data to security breaches.

On-line Information Services

The second major category of competitive EFTS-related information services involves providing terminal access to bank-controlled data. Often on-line information services are provided through third-party vendors. The common services offered in this EFTS category today are deposit and bank balance reporting services. The major benefits of these services include the ability to consolidate multibank information in a central information depositing and that access to other services, such as wire transfers and foreign exchange quotation services are possible. The major corporate problems involved in these service offerings are cost justification to operate the on-line service and difficulties in obtaining the required information from many reporting banks.

SUMMARY

This chapter has presented an overview of EFTS and related applications as applied to cash management. Although EFTS is still developmental in nature, it will have major cash management implications in the next few years. The most important detriment to EFTS from a cash manager's perspective is the loss of float experienced in the payment application. Cash managers can be expected to foster the use of EFTS for receipts of funds to reduce collections float and increase the accuracy of cash flow forecasting. Conversely, cash managers will be slow at implementing processes that deteriorate float control. Cash managers will only be willing to use EFTS services in relation to the cost/benefit analysis that can demonstrate overall profitability. Additionally, cash managers will expect and anticipate lower bank charges for EFT services and look for methods of minimizing the loss of float control through changes in discount practices or alteration in prices. Now that EFTS has been broadly defined in relation to government retail and corporate applications, the next chapter will focus on the outstanding issues and specify how cash managers can use this information to formulate corporate EFTS strategies.

CHAPTER 13

EFTS—IMPACT ON CASH MANAGEMENT

Chapter 13 defines the current scope of electronic funds transfer today and illustrates the diversity of its current development. This chapter discusses the guideposts that indicate to cash managers both the development speed and overall direction of EFTS development. Additionally, the purpose of this chapter is to identify the direct effects of EFTS on corporatate cash management. Since the growth and acceptance of EFTS services significantly change the techniques and methods employed by cash managers (as well as the degrees of direct control over cash flows), this chapter is important because it provides specific event-oriented points of transition in the payments system that signal the timing criteria for corporate cash managers to make changes to their basic mode of operations.

MAJOR ISSUES AFFECTING THE GROWTH OF EFTS

As with all growth processes, there are a myriad of development problems and pain. This is certainly true of EFTS. As with children possessing high potentialties, there is also a greater variety of problems. Because of the broad possibilities associated with EFTS, the range of problems to be resolved is as broad as any national contemporary business problem. The major issues that shape the future of EFTS include the following major areas.

Federal Reserve Involvement

The degree of appropriate involvement of the Federal Reserve has been of concern from the outset in the development of EFTS. The Fed has not taken a specific position on its degree of involvement in the direct development of EFTS services. The Fed has, however, become involved in developing guidelines for handling EFTS-based entries because of its growing importance. Some of those involved in the operations of local ACHs feel the Fed should take on regulatory ACH responsibility. Issues included in the Fed involvement debate are:

- Should the Fed operate the ACH facilities completely?
- Should the Fed charge for ACH services if provided, and how should the charges be assessed?
- Should non-Fed members be included?
- Should the Fed be involved (and to what degree) in the development of switching and processing centers?
- Should the Fed be involved in the operations of the communications systems?

The overshadowing question in the degree of direct Federal Reserve participation essentially rests on how much direct involvement a quasigovernmental agency should have on a centralized national banking communication payment network. The possibility for information manipulation for tax investigation purposes and other governmental sponsored financial audits could be significantly increased resulting in a reduction in individual privacy.

Entry Device Development

This issue is divided into identifying responsibility for establishing industry-wide standards so that broad market utilization can result and identifying the management and control functions for the development of data entry and operational systems. The sharing of automated tellers is a banking example of this problem area. The problem is further magnified when point of sale devices are introduced because of the potential for a wide diversity of operational requests. For example, if I. Magnin's department store required a 14 key input terminal (which required a different coding structure), they could find system-wide incompatibility with other standard type EFTS field equipment and subsequently require special interfaces between retail outlets and bank-provided verification files. Further major issues raised relate to liability for: fraud, errors, or equipment malfunctions. In order to achieve a wide acceptance of EFTS, it may be necessary to limit competition between vendors, such as NCR, IBM, Mosler, and Singer in order to achieve scale economics. If not, it is unclear that small or medium-sized retailers will be able to afford the entry devices or even if national credit and debit cards will have compatible standards.

Network Control and Clearing Operations Control

The expanded and logical use of EFTS service mandates an interconnected national payments system. Beyond that the development of an on-line verification and transfer system is a reasonable extension. The major issues to be resolved regarding network control include:

- Access to the system—which institutions or corporations will have access?
- Restrictions to system utilization-What will the restrictions be in use of the system? What will be the basis for exclusion?
- Charges, both amount and method of allocations, need to be defined so that equitable pricing can be developed for the EFTS services provided by banks and third-party vendors

Of all the areas of current concern the most pressing is ownership and control of access to the developing communication network systems. Currently, the Fed Wire and Bank Wire represent the only two viable domestic electronic funds transfer facilities. However, with the inevitable development of other communication networks the definition of accessability to the developing systems and criteria for utilization become significant if EFTS development is to be saved from endless court battles. For example, credit unions and savings and loans now have direct access to these transfer mechanisms just as they move toward full payment system privileges.

Development of EFTS Standards

Standards development have been a Pandora's box of problems since the inception of data processing. However, with the embryonic growth stage of EFTS, it is still possible to define and enforce (through a National EFTS Standards Committee) a uniform set of standards to cover the range of transaction capabilities and convert these into specifications, define minimal system capabilities for transaction processing, define degree of flexibility that must be resident in the systems and define standards for data field lengths and characteristics. If the myriad of data processing "black box" interfaces are to be avoided in EFTS development, then standards must be established *before* broad acceptance is achieved. The initial step was taken in this direction in April 1976 when the American National Standards Institute decided to establish a committee to define and develop industry standards applicable to scannable documents.

Ownership and Accessability

The ownership issue mentioned previously includes terminals, clearing networks, and payment processes and creates the most controversy of any

EFTS subject. Ownership implies control and accessability to payment systems. For this reason nonbank financial institutions such as credit unions, savings and loans, and national savings banks fear exclusion from a national payment structure especially in light of the diminishing differences in ability between commercial banks and other financial institutions. Conversely, banks view control over accessability to EFTS as a strategic tool in the competition struggle. Further implication of control that concern the cash managers include the extent to which national control over devices or services (national credit cards) will influence the selection decision for terminals and network use. Additionally, if the major credit cards (and eventually debit cards) use separate networks for on-line verification and transaction entry, it is possible that not only two different devices would be required but also costs would be incurred for using two different network systems. Concern over this problem has manifested itself in the form of MINTS which was developed originally as a defensive move on the part of Mutual Savings Bank to prevent their exclusion from clearing networks owned by commercial banks. The same reasoning was applied by a Kansas Credit Union League in 1974 when it purchased a commercial bank to assure that they would have access to EFTS settlement networks.

It is to the cash manager's best interest to foster the development of overall standards even if some competition is subsequently reduced so that scale economics can produce lower implementation costs through interchangeable entry devices and general purpose networks. The result from a cash management perspective will be increased funds availability from quickly installed entry systems to capture and transfer funds electonically.

Cooperation versus Competition

The creation of multiple and separately developed EFTS systems operating with automated clearing houses void of central control illustrates the problem of a complete competitive environment. Under this approach, a national or international electronic clearance system would be slow to develop. Obviously, this would be to the detriment of all involved—both the individual and corportion because electronic payments would be limited to local items.

The resolution of the degree of competition versus cooperation in the designs, development, and operation of EFTS between banks will be crucial to the sustained acceptance of EFTS. An emerging dichotomy distinguishes the delivery systems (infrastructure) from the payment system mechanism and those from the products of the system. Competition should be limited to the product-related areas of EFTS, which can be developed around the technical capability developed through cooperation. This position may be difficult for some to accept, but is only reasonable given the size of R&D

investment required for the delivery systems development. Furthermore, the price of product differentation resulting from competition in all these areas would preclude effective development. There seems to be no reason why electronic banking services, which tend to be generic and not differentiated to any major degree from one bank to another, should alter in approach from noncredit services currently performed. Often in banking it is the marketing of the product and delivery service that differentiates the product rather than the physical features of the product. Although the debate regarding the degree to which banks should cooperate in development of EFTS services is controversial, the author contends that the economics involved suggest that the consumer defined as an individual or corporation will benefit by uniform low cost joint development as opposed to separate banking approaches to EFTS development.

Government Participation

To determine EFTS growth, a major indicator to be monitored by the cash manager is the direct and indirect participation of the government in EFTS programs. *The government is a prime mover in the payments system since it is the country's largest employer and controller of resources.* The Government will impact EFTS development primarily through pre-authorized deposit transactions and its actions as a regulatory agency.

Active interest in the reduction of government costs related to payment of social security and welfare payments was manifested in the direct deposit service initiated by the government in 1975. Even though it began as a card-based systems, it was converted to electronic transfers in August 1976. This was the most definite indication of the governments' planned role as "prime motivator" in the EFTS arena. The program has been enjoying increased acceptance nationally because of socially perceived advantages of the participants, including:

- Elimination of lost or stolen checks
- Greater customer convenience
- Availability of funds even when away from home

Although this is a first step toward active government sponsorship of EFTS, the eventual trend may be toward mandatory payment from the government in this form.

The second major area of government participation is its function as a regulatory body dealing with both the infrastructure aspects and the monetary policy consequences of EFTS. These regulatory areas directly affect cash managers, both for the cost of services supplied to corporations as well as for the basic cost of money.

The regulatory areas include the roles of the Federal Communciations Commission and the Federal Trade Commission, both of which have responsibility for areas where EFTS overlap. The structuring and regulation (control) of the communications network could come under the direct influence of the Federal Communication Commission. Since the infrastructures are so critical to the development and operation of EFTS regionally and nationally, the government has the opportunity to significantly impair, accelerate, or modify the direction of infrastructure development. The Federal Trade Commission may well have much more significant influence over business trading practices with the eventual advent of national EFTS services that reduce or eliminate geographic trading distributions. Policy decision developed in this area can affect the basic business environment of many firms and represents another area for government to significantly affect the development of EFTS.

Government's active participation in EFTS development can be expected because of the major effects it will have on the monetary aspects of the economy. The national payments system affects the volume of money required and hence interest rates—to the extent that float is eliminated the supply of funds conceptually could be reduced. EFTS may well underscore the extent to which the government has been and will be involved in establishing national monetary policies and the effects of the degree of government control exercised in this fiscal policy area.

Attitudes

Another major area affecting the growth of EFTS services are the attitudes of individuals and the business community and their willingness to change historical behavioral patterns to adapt to EFTS-based products. Consumer acceptance of EFTS transactions is the key to the acceleration of EFTS. Currently, the use of and exposure to EFTS techniques is so low that it is difficult to make acceptance assumptions. However, the use profile of checks for current payments provides an indicator of which economic groups educational processes are required. The high and middle economic groups that comprise 60% of the population are the primary users of checks both for receipt of wages and payment of bills. It is these groups that must be re-educated in terms of the replacement of checks with electronic payments if EFTS is to be successful.

The lower economic group comprising approximately 40% of the population still has a need to depend on cash as a necessary medium for bugetary control. Generally, all economic classes are cautious concerning preauthorized bill payments because they have significant concerns in the following areas:

- *Lack of financial control*—Consumers are not comfortable with the lack of payment control when direct payment is authorized.
- *Lack of acceptable records*—Consumers are not sure that the records provided will be acceptable legally or how they would extract information in the banking system if additional back-up data were required.
- *Lack of availability*—Few banks have widely marketed their direct debit or credit capability and few corporations have initiated automated payment services for their customers.
- *Lack of motivation*—This results from a general satisfaction with the current check payment system and notable lack of perceived benefit on the part of the customer.

Overcoming these basic attitude issues will indicate to the cash manager that a direct payment program should be aggressively pursued by his company in order to gain the benefits of EFTS.

The attitudes of business also need to be considered as a factor in the expansion of EFTS based services. The major concern of businesses are:

- The extent to which providing EFTS services will alter the basic customer relationship with the company in a direct debit environment
- The extent to which the company is willing to sacrifice its float in the payment of obligations and how the trade off costs are evaluated

Recent studies have indicated that businesses may never be ready to authorize automatic debit payments for business to business payments over $1000 because of float loss. However, there is a small but growing interest in executing small payments of less than $1000 in a direct debit environment.

Customer-related issues center around how EFTS services are provided by either a financial institution or an independent third-party vendor. The company's major concern is the loss of identification in the customers eyes. To this extent, the services provided for check verification and automatic transfer of funds need to be transparent to the corporation's customers. Maintaining the current customer relationship is one of the central considerations for retail-oriented businesses where a large portion of EFTS is implemented.

The willingness of the corporation to sacrifice disbursement float directly affects the cash manager's decision to use EFTS services. This is and will remain the primary impediment to overcome in use of EFTS services. Through an evaluation process, corporations will need to compare the value of earnings they currently generate from float against:

- Reduced payment preparation expense
- Elimination of corporate check issuance expense
- Elimination of bank reconciliation processing expense
- Reduced postage expenses

For many firms, there are real economic advantages to be gained especially if payments can be structured so that "last day" payment is guaranteed. This last day payment approach eventually results in a general acceptance that payments that are good for discounts are available to the billing company on the last day indicated on the statement rather than the use of a post marked date in a remittance envelope. The acceptance of this last day due and paid approach would go far to eliminate the cash management pastimes of remote disbursement and delayed mailings of company metered payables.

Freedom and Privacy

The last major areas affecting the growth of EFTS are limitations to businesses and individuals freedom of choice through potential accessability to personal or corporate records. Selection of business equipment and systems related to EFTS may well be constrained as a result of conformity to standards. Additionally, both businesses and individuals may be limited in the choice of payments services available as a result of strong government interaction in the development of payment services. This could be carried to final government fiat related to government-originated payments.

Personal privacy of records will be a problem for both businesses and individuals. Since EFTS is widely used, access to most data bases of financial information will be technically possible and feasible for government agencies, such as the IRS. Because of the electronic availability of data and advanced technically based auditing capabilities, many more audits will be possible annually. Resulting from the convenant access to the data, the level examined will be more refined and smaller firms and lower income individuals will increasingly find their financial activities subject to inquiry. Possible extensions of these abilities suggest an environment of increasing direct government control over the actions of corporations and individuals through the use of auditing as a psychological threat.

FORCES MOTIVATING CHANGE

Although there are major issues to be resolved concerning the continued acceptance, development, and implementation of EFTS, there are three primary reasons favoring its expansion:

- Current expenses associated with the payment system
- Limitations of check processing ability
- Elimination of the distinction between financial institutions

The convenient and apparently inexpensive use of checks by both businesses and individuals has been promulgated by banks to their own disservice. Currently, many banks provide free checking accounts to attract funds for both businesses and individuals. The real costs for credit card and check handling has been absorbed by the banking industry generally in order to increase its customer base. However, the level of rising prices has started to make its presence known. Consequently, many banks are eliminating free checking accounts. Exhibit 13-1 illustrates the cost of the current payment system for both cash and checks. Unfortunately most check users do not think of the total economic cost to issue a check. With the 7% annual increase in check volume, it has been projected that not only will cost per check increase but current bank capabilities to physically process checks will be outstripped.

In effect this would mean longer clearance time and a slowdown of the payment system generally. The total payment system costs approximately *$14 billion a year.* The estimated cost per transaction for consumer issued

Exhibit 13.1 Current Business Payment Cost

Business preparation	$0.15
Consumer deposit	0.10
Bank processing	0.18
Other expense	0.02
Total business-based check expense	$0.45

Reprinted with permission of National Technical Information Service, Dept. of Commence, Springfield, Va. From "Consequences of EFT", a funded study of the National Science Foundation performed by Arthur D. Little.

checks is approximately 0.32, whereas credit card transactions cost 0.55. The largest impact on check reduction accruing to the use of EFTS arises from the areas of payment made by:

- Individuals to business
- Business to business
- Business to individuals

Future economic growth projections and the projected inadequacy of the current bank processing and clearance system are the several major factors motivating acceptance of EFTS. If the current payment system does break down because of dramatically increasing volume, then system wide economic consequences result. Politically and economically this would be untenable. To prevent this overloading of current capabilities with vast investment by the banks and Federal Reserve will be necessary in the next few years or automation of the payment system will be a necessity. Economically, the choice is heavily weighted in favor of EFTS automation. However, the timely application of EFTS processing and clearance systems depends on the resolution of the major issues discussed in the previous section.

The last major factor encouraging acceptance of EFTS development is the evolving entry of a broad range of financial institutions to the payments system. The distinction between commercial banks and other financial institutions, such as credit unions, savings and loans, and savings banks, are disappearing as each develops an active interest in participating in the payment system.

The most notable entry to the payment system was executed by the Wilmington Savings Funds Society of Delaware when it introduced checking account services. The negotiable order of withdraw (NOW) account was initiated in June of 1972 by the Consumers Savings Bank of Worcester, Mass., which in effect provided an interest-bearing checking account. Other innovations with similar capability are being used extensively. Credit unions are extensively offering payable-through-draft services called share drafts to their members. Interest is paid on the drawee account until funds are issued. These are just two examples of the multiple new entry to the payment system. The diversity of entries to the payment mechanism suggests that all participants in the payment process are best served with one approach rather than developing many techniques (with their own economic expense) that all have the same objective.

EVOLUTIONARY INDICATORS

As we have seen, there are basic economic reasons motivating the changes that are occurring in the payment system. Cash managers, corporate treasurers, and financial officers being involved in the control of both short- and long-term cash and funds flow scheduling, and control will be significantly affected by changes in the payment system. A primary problem is recognition of the timing of changes that take place so that corporate EFTS progress for individual-to-business payments and business-to-business EFTS transactions can be implemented during a favorable period. In order to schedule the timing of corporate EFTS progress development, financial management needs to be cognizant of major events that indicate conditions conducive to change so that appropriate action may be taken based on strategies indigenous to the company. Basic changes in environment need to evolve in the two major areas of general public acceptance of EFTS payment techniques and legislative and associated regulatory ruling.

Basic enactment of regulatory and legislative measures is necessary to a maturing growth environment so that current ambiguities can be resolved. As regulations and legislation emerges, corporate financial management will be alerted to the stage of development and relate it to corporate EFTS entry plans. While there are many possible areas of legislation, four areas are of bellweather importance and consequently deserve monitoring by corporate financial management:

- Legislation affecting proof of payment
- Safeguards affecting EFTS funds attachment
- Regulatory rulings affecting the status of customer bank communication terminals and authorized bank locations
- Regulatory ruling affecting the scope of authorized activities related to noncommercial banks

Basic to a general use of EFTS services is the elimination of much of our paper-based processing with electronic record keeping as acceptable proof documents. The major legislation statement required in this area is that proof of payment other than presentment of physical checks will be enacted. The type of replacement proof could include:

- Valid receipt by the payee
- Matched debit and credit entries from the ACH processing the entries
- Bank descriptive statement
- Reproduction of checks paid by bank via microfiche

Once a legislative statement in this area occurs, the paper check deconditioning process can begin nationally in earnest. Today consumers and businesses are generally reluctant to forego the handling of a physical check because of the acceptability as proof of payment that has been associated with it by the IRS, vendors, and corporations in the accounting settlement process. Once a legal statement of alternative proofs of payment is disseminated the sacrosanct aurora of security associated with checks will diminish and the convenience of check truncation systems will be spread as descriptive credit card statements are replacing physical return of credit card receipts.

An impediment to a more widespread acceptance of direct deposit of payrolls by employees has been the vulnerability to attachments. The enactment of legislation which prevents the attachment of direct deposits of payroll will signal an improved climate for employers and banks to aggressively pursue the expansion of these programs. Even though this type of legislation will aid in the use of the pre-authorized credits, the general acceptance of this EFTS application needs to be attached with a marketing package that will offer an additional employer benefit package in conjunction with the sponsoring bank. These employee financial service packages will need to be negotiated with the banks by cash managers in negotiating direct deposit services and include:

- Free checking accounts
- Reduced interest rates on various purchase financing
- Check authorization and guarantee cards
- Free debit cards
- Work-site banking facilities through the use of CBCTs

The introduction of customer bank communication terminals has raised significant controversy regarding the abilities provided by banks using them and how they should be regarded. Regulatory definition in this area will affect the whole nature of national banking and will provide the prime indication of future bank expansion. Rulings by the Comptroller of the Currency defining CBCTs as "non" branch status could in effect permit a nationwide network of CBCTs to be issued by any bank. In effect, this would result in a national branching network. A possible consequence is the increased concentration of funds and credit ability in banks initially pursuing national CBCT networks. Corporations can view CBCT rulings as an indicator to gauge the extent to which they need to solidify their major bank relations for future use of banks for:

- Extension of credit

- Provision of network services for check verification and guarantee (a few major banks could centrally access to the majority of accounts)
- Provision of nationally based corporate services
- Provision of nationally based business services

Just as the ruling of CBCT utilization will affect the scope of national banking, so the future rulings of the Federal Home Loan Bank (FHLB) in defining the powers of savings and loans will affect the degree of competition existing between commercial banks and savings and loans. Ruling by the FHLB to permit savings and loans to provide remote service unit capability coupled with expanded credit service capability will significantly reduce the current distinction between financial institutions. Remote service units are in effect branches of savings and loans for providing services. A ruling that permits the use of remote service units for savings and loans, coupled with the ability to make non-real estate-type loans, can indicate to the corporate financial officer the existence of a new source of competitive credit facilities.

Broad regulatory approval nationally for negotiable order of withdrawal accounts will make the formal entry of most financial institutions into the third-party payment structure. While NOW-type accounts exist for several financial institutions under different names (WOW, credit union share drafts), general acceptance by most states signals the first widespread use of interest-bearing checking accounts and foreshadow changes in banking regulations to permit commercial banks to pay interest on demand accounts. However, during any interim period, a significant shift in deposits from commercial banks to other financial institutions will occur. During this period, corporate financial management may find alternate sources of funds for direct borrowing from savings and loans, credit unions, and mutual savings bank at better rates than available at commercial banks.

Monitoring the legislation and regulatory changes that will be occurring will permit corporate financial management to not only take advantage of shifts in the concentration and availability of funds but also take early advantage of EFTS collection opportunities to increase cash flows and consequently reduce working capital requirements. While monitoring the legislative aspects will clarify current philosophical conflicts, the tracking of consumer attitudes in five key areas will signal the timing for aggressive participation in use of EFTS to accelerate collections. The five areas are:

- Signs of general public acceptance of pre-authorized debits
- Utilization pattern of debit cards
- Involvement of supermarkets in EFTS applications

- Acceptance of check truncation services
- Implementation/utilization of a national GIRO system

Of major importance to corporations will be the general public acceptance of pre-authorized debits because it will signal the public's readiness to forego float for the convenience of automatic payment. For the cash manager, this indicates the proper timing to offer a pre-authorized debit program to retail customers. The acceptance of pre-authorized payments system can be monitored by data produced monthly by automated clearing houses. This will provide a measurement mechanism for the corporations to follow the growth of activity. The type of transactions that are initially applicable include:

- Mortgage payments
- Installment payments
- Stock purchase plan deductions
- Pre-authorized check authorizations

As these applications are accepted nationally, corporations should move directly into implementing pre-authorized programs because the public will be ready psychologically to accept new payment approaches.

Another public factor indicating changes in acceptance level attitudes is the implementation and use of debit cards. This development will occur separately by banks as part of the existing credit card structures. The important factor is public willingness to use a debit card transaction in lieu of a check. Even though the use of the debit card will increase the cash flow to the corporation, there is an additional cost to the extent that a verification and guarantee system is required to be assured of the users account status.

Participation of the food supermarket chains will be a critical indicator of public acceptance of EFTS. Because of the large volume of checks cashed by supermarkets and their historic collection problems, which are sometimes 5% of their net profit, the retail supermarket can play a pivitol role in the widespread acceptance of EFTS. Already supermarkets in some areas of the country, such as Georgia, are refusing to cash checks. Instead they are agreeing to the acceptance of debit cards as payment for purchases where they are terminal verified and guaranteed. Recently, a group of four banks in Atlanta agreed to jointly make available demand deposit account files for the purpose of debit card transaction verification for supermarkets. As this joint file development expands nationally, debit cards will become a viable alternative to checks. As debit card use expands, financial corporate management needs to decide when subscription to a verification service is cost justified based on potential losses.

Acceptance by the general public of debit card transactions as previously described will be a leading indicator of public acceptance of significant EFTS development.

A final though significant indication of the need for immediate corporate planning and involvement in EFTS systems development will be the implementation of a national GIRO payments system. Through the GIRO system, the consumer (corporate customers) receive pre-encoded, machine-readable invoices that contain both the customer's bank account number and the company's concentration bank account number. Upon review, the customer signs the full or partial bill payment and forwards it to the processing agent with instructions to credit the corporate account. Payment is made by check or electronically. This system has been successfully operationed in Europe for many years and is just now under full consideration here as part of the EFTS payments mechanism. When the instructions are entered by the receiving agent the funds as defined are transferred from one account to another. Recently, the United States Post Office commissioned a GIRO concept study for a cost of approximately $1 million. The reasoning is that the advent of EFTS will significantly reduce the first class revenue to the Post Office placing it in deeper financial trouble than it currently is experiencing.

The advent of a GIRO system should indicate to the financial management of a company that the time has arrived to re-evaluate its billing process and to foster the use of a GIRO system to accelerate the firm's receivables.

Although there are many other indications of EFTS development, those already discussed represent the most important indicators. Monitoring these developments by corporate financial management, coupled with a defined strategy regarding corporate involvement on EFTS will assure reliable control over corporate EFT development. More with EFTS than any other development area current corporate cash management techniques and practices will be significantly affected as EFTS applications are implemented. As preparation for the changing environment attributed to EFTS applications, a review of probable alterations in current practices is appropriate.

EFTS—EFFECTS ON CASH MANAGEMENT TECHNIQUES

The facets of EFTS services discussed are evolving with ever-increasing developmental acceleration. Because of the intersecting areas of retail and corporate EFTS applications development, the areas will mutually affect each other. As EFTS becomes an accepted reality, the corporate cash manager will discover that cash management techniques used today may be significantly altered. Basic transformation in the cash management function will occur because of EFTS for several major reasons including:

- Effect on float (mail and collection) resulting from EFTS applications
- Increased corporate opportunity for earnings
- Opportunity for cost reduction attributable to EFTS applications
- Other changes in cash management services arising from EFTS

Effects of Float Reduction

The most immediate objections brought to mind whenever EFTS applications are discussed with cash managers is the loss of float control through electronic debiting of accounts. Today many of the cash management techniques that rely on float for their existence will be reduced or eliminated. A number of services will be directly affected.

Concentration Accounts

The current practice of concentrating funds via depository transfer check into a central control account will be significantly reduced as pre-authorized payments are preprocessed so same day crediting of accounts occur, since pre-authorized debits can be distributed to the receiving bank prior to the due date. Consequently, the remittance day funds are immediately settled. It would be redundant to use DTCs in this environment since the purpose of the DTC is to use collection float time on the DTC while the deposits it is to draw against at the remote location are in the collection process. Since deposits are immediately available on the due date, the collection time is eliminated.

Reduction of Remote Disbursement

Perhaps one of the most popular areas to be affected when a mature stage of EFTS is realized is the reduction of remote disbursement. Preprocessing of debit and credit entries for business-to-business payments of less than $1000 and their delivery from the originating bank, through the National Automated Clearing House Association members, will assure national same-day debit and credits. Consequently, the frequency of Federal Reserve cash letter presentments to various banks will be less important. Payments greater than $1000 will continue to be the object of remote disbursement.

Reduction of Disbursement Float Forecasting

The current popularity of disbursement float forecasting by corporations will be dramatically reduced under the expansion of EFTS-based services. Through the corporate use of direct deposit services for payroll, pre-authorized debits for business payments less than $1000, the need to forecast clearings will be reduced. However, large payments (over $1000) will continue to be the object of forecasting. Resistance to corporate disbursement use of EFTS will be strong for several more years, but eventually the economic penalties assessed with continued use of current disbursement manipulation may outweigh earnings occurring from float investment for payments under $1000. The full implementation of corporate EFTS in the final analysis would mean the complete elimination of float. This is impractical to expect especially related to large dollar items. It is likely that the economic penalties assessed against low-dollar items will make EFTS a much more economic alternative.

Increased Earnings Opportunities

Although consideration regarding changes in float manipulation will cause significant behavioral change in the cash management area so also will the potential for increased earnings that will evolve from the careful use of EFT applications. The areas of increased corporate earnings include:

Increased Funds Availability Immediate availability of funds to the cash manager on all EFTS-generated entries will result in more accurate funds flow forecasting and more efficient investment of receipts than is now possible. The area of greatest doubt in cash forecasting is daily receipts. Through EFTS utilization, a high percent of each day's receipts can be known with certainty in advance because of established payment patterns. Consequently, the cash manager can plan in advance what use to make of funds to cover low-dollar disbursements, which will clear with similar certainty. Penalties imposed for being overdrawn because of inaccurate cash forecasts and lost opportunity costs will be reduced. Better control and planning ability arising from EFTS applications will result in better levels of cash optimization.

Use of Automatic Transfer Capabilities. Increased earnings can result to cash managers from expanded use of automatic funds transfer capabilities that will be available in the EFTS evironment. Through this type of service, all balances in one of the few central corporate control accounts except for minimum maintenance balances required (if any) would be transferred to an interest-bearing account. Similarly, any deficits would be automatically transferred from an interest-bearing account to the demand deposit account as required per standing instructions. Although these interest bearing accounts would not earn as much as other available investments, they would assure some base level of return on under utilized funds.

Potential for Cost Reductions

Increased earnings will provide motivations for consideration of EFTS services just as it will provide the potential for cost savings. Reduced corporate expenses related to EFTS use can be realized within the corporation. That is, a reduction in internal effort required to generate a payment or through external cost reductions primarily generated from the banking community and passed on (in some measure) to the corporation.

Reduced Use of Lockbox Services

Lockbox use will eventually be significantly reduced by EFTS preauthorized payments. To the consumer, savings will be reflected in the elimination of postage and check preparation and check-processing charges (about 23¢ in total). Because payments clear on the specified settlement dates electronically, no physical remittance is sent from originator to receiver. And since there is no collection process time required, the need to reduce mail and collection float, the prime reason for lockbox use, is eliminated for these transactions. Consequently, bankers and cash managers alike can look forward to the decline of lockboxes as a major cash management technique as EFTS applications increase in acceptance.

Reduced Credit Losses

An extensive use of check verification and guarantee spreads losses to retail merchants and corporations will be reduced. For some industries this will provide a major motivation to move actively into the use of EFTS verification facilities.

Reduced Check-Processing Charges

Because banks will not physically handle checks, the associated deposit processing charges will be dramatically reduced to the corporation. In addition, corporations that are currently MICR encoding their own checks for deposit to realize a lower processing charge may be able to reduce manpower and machines associated with this process. Banks can also benefit from this process. Because operating expenses will be reduced from reduced physical check processing, it may be possible for banks to enjoy a higher percent of operating profit. Banks will also profit to the extent that peak-and-valley, labor-intensive workload processes will be smoothed, thus reducing overhead. Corporations will enjoy increased funds availability to support noncredit services and loans as a result of EFTS processing.

Reduction in Account Reconcilement Services

As checks are replaced by EFTS entries for business-to-business and business-to-individual payments, the need for account reconcilement services provided by banks will be dramatically reduced. Because a typical corporation can easily issue thousands of checks monthly the use of an automated account reconcilement package is almost mandatory. However, with the advent of EFTS pre-authorized debit transactions, not only will various types of disbursement accounts be eliminated, such as zero balance accounts and remote disbursing, but the number of checks issued will be reduced.

Other Changes in Cash Management Services

Reduction of Draft Use

Drafts will be significantly reduced as a payment mechanism under the development of EFTS services because of the 1-day float, and subsequent control over acceptance or rejection of drafts presented from operating subsidiaries or divisions will be reduced via direct debits for low-dollar items.

Increased Use of Wire Transfer

As funds are available in the specified settlement date, the use of wire transfer will increase to take advantage of excess funds. While the increase in wire transfers is highly probable, the transfer cost per wire transfer will be reduced as use of both the Fed Wire and Bank Wire systems increases. The increase in wire utilization, coupled with direct debit and credit EFTS application, will significantly change the band/corporate cash management relationship.

Increased Unbundling of Bank Services

Perhaps one of the most significant effects of increased use of EFTS service will be the acceleration in the unbundling of bank services. Credit and non-credit services will be made available to corporations on a fee basis because reduced processing expenses will make banks more aware of the need to be profitable in a stand-alone service basis. The overall effect to banks will be lower balances for services performed under EFTS because per transaction costs to corporations will be reduced. Although this may seem unpalatable to banks, it will, in fact, benefit banks if they take advantage of the unique opportunity to reduce operating expenses disproportinate to retail price reductions. This will permit banks to re-establish appropriate profit levels that have been lost in prior years because of disporportionate processing cost increases.

EFTS—ALTERING THE CORPORATE/BANK RELATIONSHIP

Increased use of EFTS services, especially in the areas of pre-authorized payments for business-to-business and business-to-individual low-dollar payments and increased use of wire facilities will result in a significant shift in the corporate/bank relationship. The traditional cash management use of banks has included:

- *Lead banks*—used as a primary source of credit and central relationship
- *Concentration banks*—used to regionally concentrate funds for later use, usually be DTC but sometimes by wire
- *Lock box banks*—centrally located to capture receipts in the shortest time frame from various geographic locations
- *Local deposit banks*—used to deposit funds from operating locations
- *Disbursement banks*—utilized to disburse funds because of increased clearing times resulting from geographic locations

The increased use of EFTS services will have a significant effect on the corporate cash management view of each of these banking relations. EFTS services implemented have an effect on the corporate/bank relationship.

Increase Cash Mobilization

Increased use of wire transfers to mobilize funds will strengthen the relationship of the lead bank with the corporation at the expense of the concentration banks. This occurs because wires will be used to draw funds from the lockbox and local deposit banks as direct payments increase. Since wires will be used, a concentration of funds to a regional cash pool will no longer be necessary.

Individual-to-business EFTS Applications

Individual-to-business EFTS applications will result in a strengthening of the cash managers relationship with the lead corporate bank because greater use of customized data processing and communications will be necessary. This greater sophistication will make corporate bank mobility less flexible.

Business-to-individual Payment Application

Business-to-individual payment application will increase the dependence of the corporation on the lead bank while reducing or eliminating the need for disbursement banks. Since these payment types will be low-dollar transactions, they are vulnerable to an early application. Large dollar transactions, however, will still be separately disbursed to maintain float control. However, the implication is that banks depending on disbursement business will come under increasing pressure as direct business to individual payments are effected electronically.

Business-to-business Receipts

This application area will increase the central role of the lead bank as *the* major concentration bank by eliminating the need for both lockbox banks and concentration banks. This results from the increased use of wire transfer to make business to business payments.

Business-to-business Payments

Using wires or pre-authorized debits will result in a significant reduction in the use of disbursement banks. This implies an increase in lost business to banks focussing on disbursement business as EFTS application in the low- and high-dollar, business-to-business payment area expands.

As electronic services increase in acceptance by business and corporations the cash manager will discover that traditional bank relationships will require re-evaluation because the structure of the corporate cash management system will evolve because of EFTS. As this occurs, the lead bank relationship will increase in importance to the corporations because:

- Increased data communication facilities will be provided by the lead bank
- Increased use of the lead bank as a conduit for current financial data will evolve
- Customized data processing services will be provided by lead banks to service corporate customers.

As a result of an increased reliance on lead bank functions, corporate cash managers will find that not only will the techniques of cash management change but also that the number of significant bank relationships will be reduced for noncredit services. Because a closer corporate/bank working relationship will evolve, the corporation will find that some sacrifice in bank mobility will result. This disadvantage will be offset, however, by the increased ability of lead banks to provide more customized automated services to corporate customers.

SUMMARY AND CONCLUSION

The purpose of this chapter has been to define the factors that are motivating the trend toward EFTS applications. The prime factors include government sponsorship of EFTS applications as well as corporate cost reduction opportunities and accelerated funds availability to corporations. Overall, we have illustrated that public and corporate attitudes are essential in the EFTS development area because without basic acceptance and cooperation between banks, consumers, and corporations there will be no widespread use of EFTS as a replacement for the traditional but costly check-processing methods. Although there are currently several innovative EFTS experiments under way, they are still more pilot projects than production services. The development of EFTS to date can be characterized as being well into the 2% of the "Innovator" stage and the beginning of the 16% early acceptance stage. We have also defined legislative actions that signal significant moves toward an EFTS environment and defined the major effects on cash management resulting from the eventual acceptance of EFTS.

The primary message to be imparted is that corporate financial managers should prepare strategies and plans for the coming widespread use of EFTS so that corporations may plan changes to internal cash management practices and to effect internal system changes to meet the processing requirements of EFTS provided by banks. Recognition of the evolutionary status of EFTS and its effect on the corporate financial structure provides the best defensive and offensive foundation for financial EFTS decisions. Selection of a lead bank relationship becomes more important because of EFTS since greater reliance on use of the lead bank as a conduit of national financial data for the corporation will evolve. Since lead banks mobility will be reduced because of customized services the selection of a lead bank to provide credit and noncredit services becomes a task of increasing importance for the cash manager.

BIBLIOGRAPHY

Bender, Mark G., *EFTS—Elements and Imacts*, Kennikat Press, New York, 1976.

Bankers EFT Handbook, American Bankers Association, 1976.

National Science Foundation–Arthur D. Little, *The Consequence of Electronic Funds Transfer*, June 1975.

INDEX

Accellerating receipts, 39, 40, 49, 63
   international, 239
Account reconcilement services, 24
Accuracy, 164, 179
Adela Investment Company, 230
ARB1, 234
Assets, return on, 13
ATM (Automated Teller Machine), 281, 298
Automated business services, 104
   accounts payable, 107
   accounts receivable, 108
   inventory, 110
   payroll, 105
Automated clearing house, 272, 297
Automated services, trends, 87

Balance reports, 104
Bank drafts, 252
Bank selection, 18
   criteria, 19, 100
Bank services, 100, 280
Bank wire system, 51
Bridge loans, 234

Cable transfers, 248
Cash flow statement, 149
Cash management information services, 49, 102
Cash receipts and disbursements, 152
Centralization, 56
Clearing process, check, 14, 15, 71
Commercial letter of credit, 254
Compensating balances, 13, 27
Compensation, balance, 13
   bank, 8
   fees, 25

Concentration accounts, 53
Concentration banking, 47
Concentration system design, 53
Consulting services, 100
Cost/analysis, full absorption, 33
   incremental, 33
Credit swap, 250
Credit lines, multiple, 22
Currency swap, 250

Debit card, 286
Decomposition model, 171, 181
Depository transfer checks, 48, 67
Devaluation, 222
Direct deposit, 287
Disbursement control techniques, 39, 56
Disbursement services, 59
Discounting, 223
Dividends, 259
Double counting, 24, 30

Earnings allowance, 27, 30
EFT, Standards, 298
Electronic funds transfer service, 265, 268, 269
   infrastructure,
Equity financing, 235
Eurocurrency financing, 236
Exponential smoothing, 175, 202
Export letter of credits, 255, 257
Export protection, 252
Exposure, currency, 222
   transaction, 224
   translation, 224
Expropriation, 220, 222

Factoring, 239

319

Index

Federal Reserve, 30, 275, 296
Federal Reserve Wire System, 276
Float, definition of, 31, 57
 captive systems, 31
 collection, 57
 Federal Reserve, 13
 mail, 57
Forecasting, cash, intermediate term, 12
 long term, 12
 short term, 11
 techniques, 170
 Accounting Approaches, 140
 cash flows, 11
 Cash Flow statements, 149
 Cash receipts disbursements, 152
 Context, 118
 Elements, 131
 environment, 117
 Funds flow statement, 144
 Models, 120, 122, 190
 Needs, 126
 Patterns, data, 121
 perspective, 119
 Qualitative, 118
 Quantitative, 118, 129
 time dimension, 120, 123
 trends, 211
Forecasting models, 190
 Baumel, 191
 Miller ORR, 192
 ORGLER, 198
 SASTY, 191
Foreign Currency Exchange, 248
Funds flow, 141
Funds flow protection, 22
Funds mobilization, 47

Giro, 279
 effects, 310

Hedging, 247

Inport letters of credit, 254
International Bank for Redevelopment, 227
International Basic Economy Corp., 230
International cash management, Giro, 244, 289
 pooling, 245
 techniques, 238
International Development Corp., 227
International Finance Corp., 227
International financing, 225
Inventory services, 190

Linear programming, 194
Line of credit, 20
Link financing, 235
Lockbox evaluation criteria, 54, 63
Lockbox services, developing trends, 87
 envelope, 80, 81
 evaluation, 40, 64, 70
 photocopy, 82
 tape transmission, 83
 uniformity, 68, 69, 84

Management fees, 259
Moving average, 172

Networks, ERT, local, 269
 national, 272
 regional, 271
 unit, 269

ORGLER, 195

Participation loans, 21
Payable through drafts, 61
Payables, centralization of, 56
Place of business terminal, 283
Point of sale terminal, 268, 282
Pooling, 231
Preauthorized checks, 42
 benefits, 44
Preauthorized debits, 45, 283, 290
Private Investment Corporation for Asia, 230
Profitability, service, 34

Quantitative methods, 169, 190

Remote bank disbursements, 62
Royalties, 259

Smoothing technique, 170
Sources and uses of funds, 141
Statistical techniques, 170

Tax payments, 32
Trends, 202

Wire transfer, 23, 51, 65, 67.*
 bank wire, 51
 Fed wire, 51
World Bank, 226

Zero balance accounts, 59